ALI

THE FIGHT AMERICA DIDN'T WANT

ALI

THE FIGHT AMERICA DIDN'T WANT

RUSSELL ROUTLEDGE

AMBERLEY

Author's Note

I found while researching for this book there were various differences in the fighters' records, depending where I looked. For example, Stanford Harris, who fought Jerry Quarry, was sometimes called Stamford Harris. 'Stanford' was listed as being on the short side for a heavyweight, while 'Stamford' was recorded as 6ft 5in! (The confusion seems to have arisen because there was a welterweight of the same name.) Jerry Quarry's and Ali/Clay's boxing records when they were amateurs differ according to source.

While describing some events in this story, I have had on occasion to use my imagination based on what I could gather from the factual reports of the time and for this I beg the reader's indulgence.

First published 2018

Amberley Publishing
The Hill, Stroud
Gloucestershire, GL5 4EP

www.amberley-books.com

Copyright © Russell Routledge, 2018

The right of Russell Routledge to be identified as the Author of this work has been asserted in accordance with the Copyrights, Designs and Patents Act 1988.

ISBN 978 1 4456 7450 6 (paperback)
ISBN 978 1 4456 7451 3 (ebook)

British Library Cataloguing in Publication Data.
A catalogue record for this book is available from the British Library.

Typesetting and Origination by Amberley Publishing
Printed in the UK.

CONTENTS

INTRODUCTION

There have probably been more words penned about Muhammad Ali than any other sporting person in history – and the books still keep coming. Most of them are sitting on my bookshelves at home. Many authors of course recount stories of his former career as a boxer, some about his stand against the Vietnam War. Many remind us of his remarkable character and personality outside of the ring.

The iconic boxer was and will always be a compelling subject. His fights with the boxing and political elite are legendary and his legacy I feel will be one of great inspiration and belief in oneself. Many of the boxing fans I talk to today weren't even born during Ali's career, but some still take more than a passing interest in the ex-champion's life. I find it especially enjoyable when some fans from the younger generation tell me they would have 'loved to have met Muhammad Ali – the greatest!'

Nowadays, if that new generation of fans wants to watch the majority of his fights, they can be viewed on YouTube. His bouts – especially with Liston, Foreman and Frazier – have all been well documented. However, some of his lesser-known bouts are confined to one or two paragraphs in books. This is insufficient to grasp the sometimes historic importance of certain fights, or to convey the turbulent times which surrounded them.

The best example of this is when Ali first returned to boxing in 1970 and fought top contender Jerry Quarry. For some reason, in historical terms, this bout is recorded as a mere footnote. In reality, at that point in time, the bout was arguably the most highly anticipated big fight involving a returning champion since the 'Great White Hope' Jim Jeffries fought Jack Johnson way back in 1910.

The reason Ali's first return fight only receives a limited mention is perhaps because he was a (relatively) easy winner. Or maybe it was because his biggest challenges were just around the corner – his fight against undefeated Smokin' Joe Frazier and the outcome of his battle with the Supreme Court, both happening in 1971. Later, there was so much happening in Ali's supercharged life that his return bout after a three-and-a-half-year hiatus only served as an introduction to the title-fights that followed.

I have searched through my extensive selection of books on Ali and at most, authors dedicate a chapter or two to Ali's comeback fight. Yes, the first Quarry fight can be viewed, but the battle alone doesn't reveal the highly controversial events surrounding it. Some accounts concentrate on the day before and the day after the bout, while some talk about the fight but only give a short account of the build-up and events afterwards. Movies detailing the life of the former champion fail to give this event the recognition it deserves. (One of the main characters in this story complained in a 2005 interview that one of the major Ali biopics only gave this bout a cursory mention.) There are snippets of information everywhere about the fight and events surrounding it, but no full retrospective account. So, here it is.

I also hope to give one man the credit he deserves – the accounts I have researched seem to mention him only briefly.

That's the man standing opposite Ali in the ring on the night of 26 October 1970 – Jerry Quarry.

Even leaving out the importance of the fight as the first for the ex-champion after his exiled years, the drama, characters and shenanigans outside of the ring make this an extraordinary story. This fight, which happened almost by accident, was hosted in the unlikeliest of places: Atlanta, Georgia, a city burnt to the ground in the American Civil War and the site of deadly race riots in the early part of the 20th century, but by 1970 the epicentre of the New South and one that had evolved as regards the balance of political power.

Even before Jerry Quarry set foot in Atlanta, many newshounds and fans around the globe had him cast as a modern-day 'Great White Hope'. There were also comparisons made between Ali and another once exiled champion, but one from the turn of the century: the first black heavyweight champion, Jack Johnson.

In 1970, the Ali v Quarry fight was an international event and the press around the globe went to town. For Ali's comeback, promoters brought all the way to Georgia a fighter regarded by many commentators as the hardest-hitting white fighter since Rocky Marciano. Jerry Quarry was the real deal, and just prior to his arrival in Atlanta the talented fighter from California was rated number one among the world's elite heavyweight contenders by *The Ring* magazine. In addition to his number one status, he had been voted the world's favourite active fighter by readers of *Boxing Illustrated* for the second year running (1968 and 1969).

Jerry Quarry was riding high in the boxing world. He had previously made comments to the press about wanting to drop the 'white hope' tag, but in taking on the hugely controversial former black king of the ring, Muhammad Ali, the similarities with Jack Johnson and his fights with Great White Hopes Jess Willard and James J. Jeffries ensured that wasn't going to happen.

When Ali returned to boxing, he was still years away from the adulation he would eventually attract. Then the fighter evoked intense feelings of love and hate, which ran through the veins of people the world over, especially in America. This was mainly because of his allegiance to the Nation of Islam and his refusal to take part in or support the war that was still raging in Vietnam. His publicly espoused views, combined with his character and personality, made him the most controversial athlete on the planet.

The fight was headlined with slogans such as 'The fight nobody else wanted', 'The Return of the champ' and 'The Battle of Atlanta' (the original battle of Atlanta having taken place from 22 July 1864 to 2 September 1864, with over 9000 casualties). A hundred years later, in October 1970, another bloody battle took place in Downtown Atlanta – just on the intersection of Courtland Street and Gilmer Street in an old arena called the Atlanta Municipal Auditorium.

The fight attracted mainly African-Americans, who turned up to see the ring rebirth of 'their' champion. At the time, Ali's night in Atlanta was called by some a 'black awakening'. Many who turned up came from the entertainment world, and some were hugely rich and successful. Their wealth was openly on display as they preened in the international spotlight, draped in expensive furs and jewels. It was a way of saying that Ali, and everything he represented, represented them too – black, beautiful, bold and the best in the business. It was certainly a night of 'soul-power' and soul at its most colourful.

However, this jamboree in Atlanta also attracted some of 'the best' from the underbelly of American society; it wasn't only the rich and famous that turned up, but also crooks, racketeers and gangsters. Big-time boxing always had a reputation for attracting both the famous and infamous in society. They said Sonny Liston once had links to the mob, and even the most famous gangster of them all, Al Capone, was regularly spotted ringside at the big fights, especially the ones involving his sporting hero, the 'Manassa Mauler' Jack Dempsey. At these events, film stars of the day settled into their expensive ringside seats alongside the gangsters.

The fight itself was the climax of a big sporting weekend in Atlanta, and for a few days the cash poured in. The bucketfuls of moolah in town presented a prize opportunity for some villains to win big themselves. All they needed was a plan, and when that plan came to fruition it ended up with some of those bejewelled spectators who sat in the $100 ringside seats being victims of armed robbery. After all the money and diamonds were bagged and carried off into the night, one detective who worked on the case called it possibly 'the biggest armed robbery in Atlanta's history up to that point'.

The year 1970 meant 'flower power', black power and peace protests. It was also a time of great disillusionment and anger, and the start of great changes, not just in the social and political world but also in the world of heavyweight boxing. The former champ would return to more than a reshuffled division. It would be one with some new additions – a division some experts said was the strongest in a while. At the beginning of 1970, the heavyweight boxing ratings now included 1968 Olympic heavyweight champion George Foreman, and knockout artist and undefeated ex-marine Mac Foster. Another new face on the scene was Leotis Martin, who caused a huge upset by knocking out the 'bear', Sonny Liston, in a pre-Christmas brawl in 1969. Teak-tough brawler Oscar Bonavena was still riding high in the ratings, with former 1964 Olympic Heavyweight champ Smokin' Joe Frazier recognized by the New York State Athletic Commission as world pro champ. Ali's former sparring partner, Jimmy Ellis, was WBA Heavyweight Champion.

The sandy-haired Californian slugger Jerry Quarry, who started his pro career back in 1965, also added glamour and power to the division. Many thought Jerry was a sure bet to be a future champion, despite losing previous title shots to Jimmy Ellis (1968) and Joe Frazier (1969) during Ali's enforced exile.

In early 1970, the heavyweight division still included some of Ali's old opponents, including Sonny Liston, Henry Cooper and George Chuvalo. Cooper was reaching the twilight of his career, with Liston just hanging in there with plans for a 1970 comeback, while George Chuvalo, who also had a controversial win over Quarry, was mooted to take on undefeated heavyweight sensation George Foreman later that year.

Other new and young heavyweight hopefuls on the horizon were lining up and the one that showed the most promise in the UK was a then 19-year-old blonde Adonis called Joe Bugner (he would turn 20 on 13 March of that year).

However, at the beginning of 1970, although Ali had been inactive for years, his name was still printed in the respected *Ring* magazine above all others as the heavyweight champion. The 'bible of boxing' would stand by the inactive boxer until the law courts gave a final verdict on his fate, or he permanently retired. So, for many, Ali was still champ, but a champion without an opponent as he was not allowed to fight.

There was and still is, nothing crazier than boxing politics and at the beginning of 1970, Frazier, Ellis and Ali were recognized by various organizations as world heavyweight boxing champion. So let's go back to those crazy times and follow the turbulent events, which led all the way to that wild, celebratory and for some, dangerous night of Ali's return to boxing in Atlanta, Georgia.

FALSE STARTS AND A 'FAKE' FIGHT

The date was announced in early December 1969 and the long-awaited ring return of Muhammad Ali was expected to take place on 10 January 1970 in Oklahoma. A charity exhibition bout involving Ali was meant to take place inside a 4,000-seat rodeo arena on the Gene Hopkins Maverick ranch just outside of Tulsa. It didn't take long before the proposed promotion hit problems. Health officials said the site was not suitable and it was cancelled. Undeterred, promoter Hank Moore proposed a new venue and date. This time, Ali's exhibition was rescheduled for 12 January 1970, in a 12,000-seat outdoor marquee, which would be temporarily erected in the small town of Boley. It would be pretty cold for a marquee event to take place at that time of year, but it was still hoped the exhibition would proceed as it would not only see the return of Ali to the boxing ring, but also see many underprivileged children benefitting from the event revenues.

The small town of Boley may seem an unlikely setting for Ali's first ring return since his last bout in 1967, but Oklahoma was without a boxing commission, so organizers didn't have to receive a state commission's authority to go ahead. The press were informed Ali would be facing fringe heavyweight contender Billy Joiner, from Cincinnati, Ohio, in an exhibition bout. The proposed 'dancing partner' for Ali's charity bout was no stranger to him, as Ali had already fought and beat him twice, but that was back in 1960, when both Ali, then known as Cassius Clay, and Joiner were amateurs. Their first bout took place in the semifinals of the 1960 AAU light-heavyweight championships in Toledo. Joiner's second loss to Ali/Clay happened only one month before he went off to the 1960 Rome Olympics. That amateur contest took place at an open air show in the Parkway arena in Joiner's home city, Cincinnati.

Joiner, a talented boxer, won both the Golden Gloves and AAU light-heavyweight championships in 1962. He also beat Ali/Clay's brother, Rudy/Rahaman by a points decision in the second round of the 1960 Golden Gloves light-heavyweight competition. (This was the same competition that Ali/Clay took part in, but in the heavyweight class.) Cassius Clay/Ali won the 1960 Golden Gloves Heavyweight title and the 1960 AAU light-heavyweight title and in 1959, he had won both the AAU and Golden Gloves light-heavyweight titles.

By 1970, Billy Joiner was into his eighth year as a pro. He made his winning debut inside Madison Square Garden the same year he won those National amateur championships in 1962. His professional career then consisted of 19 professional fights, which included two meetings with Sonny Liston during 1968 and 1969, both of which he lost. He had also lost his last paid fight against Zora Folley on points in November 1969; but for the Boley charity event, none of that really mattered, as getting Ali back into his profession was the priority, so the exhibition bout was definitely on. Then it was definitely off, just like all other previous attempts of getting the former champion back into the ring.

Ali certainly wasn't popular with many of the US war veterans. Only days before the proposed marquee exhibition bout was to take place, promoter Hank Moore cancelled the event. Even though there was no official reason given, most knew that any promoter who dared put on an Ali fight/exhibition would come under immense pressure from war vets, who wielded a great deal of influence. It seemed in Oklahoma, some didn't take kindly to a man that refused the military draft 'fighting' in their home state. War veteran groups in Tulsa reportedly represented over 25,000 residents. So once again, all plans and hopes of an Ali return came to a sudden stop.

Surprisingly though, a few days later, Ali said that it was he himself who opted out of the promotion. At a press conference back in New York, Ali said that he wasn't happy with conditions surrounding the bout, as it was too cold, with the bout going on outdoors in a marquee. He also declared the venue didn't befit his status as a former world champion. Anyway, whatever the reason, the bout didn't go ahead.

Just days after that latest cancellation, Ali was surprisingly seen on British TV, still looking happy and relaxed, but seemingly on this occasion reluctant to talk about his ring future. This time his image and unmistakable voice came by way of a satellite link-up from Cleveland, Ohio, on 14 (or the 15th, the records are contradictory) January 1970. Ali came on TV to pay tribute to his old foe, Henry Cooper, who was the subject of a 'This is Your Life' programme on ITV. Britain's Henry Cooper, who the previous year had been awarded an OBE, was presented with the famous red book by ex-amateur boxer turned boxing commentator and TV show host, Eamonn Andrews. It just so happened Ali was in Ohio that day as part of a nationwide promotional tour to advertise something that would not only bring him back onto British TV screens one week later, but also into cinemas throughout America, Canada and other parts of the world.

Although there was great difficulty organizing a real fight for Ali, nothing stood in the way of a computer coming up with a 'fight' for him. And the computer would allow fight fans around the globe to see the impossible – Ali trading punches with another former undefeated heavyweight champion, but one from a bygone era. His name was Rocky Marciano, the 'Brockton Blockbuster', who hadn't been seen in a boxing ring since he punched Archie Moore into brutal defeat way back in 1955.

A couple of days after his UK TV appearance and one day before his 28th birthday, on Friday, 16 January 1970, Ali promoted the same 'impossible fight' in a Chicago press conference and also announced that he would never box again and he was now a retired champion. Ali sounded convincing, but fans had heard the word retirement from him at various other times during his exile years and when the possibility of a real or exhibition fight came along, his retirement plans seemed to get temporarily shelved. Only a short while before his Ohio-UK satellite TV link up, while at another promotion for the 'computer fight', but in Boston, Mass, Ali said that 'the *real* champ' (himself) must return to boxing as the game was dying and 'paper-homemade champions' were turning the game into a dull sport. (*The Bridgeport Post*. Bridgeport, Connecticut 14/01/70.)

Ali also informed those at the same press conference that he could beat champion Joe Frazier that very night, without any training at all, using only his natural speed and ability. It seemed Ali's desire to resume fighting depended on his mood on a given day, as each statement seemed to contradict the next. In reality though, it didn't make any difference as boxing commissions and pressure groups foiled every behind-the-scenes attempt that was being made.

So it appeared the only way fans would ever see Ali in action again was to buy a $5 cinema ticket for the 20 January computerized bout between him and Rocky Marciano. The 'fight'

Ali promoted certainly generated worldwide interest and heated debates among boxing fans. It all came about through a Miami radio producer/promoter called Murry Woroner.

In the fall of 1969, Murry had been another who tried but failed to organize a *real* fight for Ali. (His attempt took place soon after the filming/production of scenes of the Ali v Marciano 'Superbout'.)

He had been hopeful of putting on an Ali v Joe Frazier bout in Miami, some time in early 1970. His 'unique plan' was for both fighters to face each other in a TV studio, with only a limited audience paying a then whopping $2,000 a seat to watch it. The fight would be screened around the world by satellite, bringing in millions of dollars in revenue.

Unfortunately for Murry, around the same time in 1969, rival promoters wanted the Ali v Frazier fight to go ahead at the 48,000-seater Tampa stadium, in Tampa, Florida, in February 1970. That sounded promising too, as the state governor, Claude Kirk, welcomed the fight and despite Woroner's objections, the fighter's management favoured the Tampa promotion.

All sounded well and good until threats of massive protests arrived. Tampa Mayor, Dick Greco, said the calls of protest ran into thousands, while the American Legion claimed 80,000 veterans from 90 organizations threatened to boycott the fight. Soon after, promoter Ron Gorton withdrew his application for the event.

Then, there were plans to shift the promotion to the Orlando Sports Stadium in Orlando, but that also failed to materialize. Additionally, according to a report in *The Age* (Melbourne, Australia 17 December, 1969) around the same time in 1969 yet another promoter made a proposal to stage an Ali v Frazier fight, but on the other side of the world. His hope was to organize the fight in the same city where 61 years previously, Jack Johnson won the world heavyweight, when he beat Tommy Burns back in

1908 – Sydney, Australia. That proved a non-starter as Ali's bail conditions confined him to the United Sates.

So in the short term at least, it seemed Murry came out the winner in the ongoing battle of the promoters, as he still got to promote/produce an Ali 'fight' – albeit, a computer fight, involving the defrocked champion and the champ from the 1950s, Rocky Marciano. But even that one came about after a $1million lawsuit in 1968 launched by Ali.

It all began one year earlier in 1967, when Murry Woroner came up with an imaginative radio series of weekly boxing programmes. The radio slot featured the sound of impossible fights that involved past heavyweight champions fighting each other. The series was called 'The All-Time Heavyweight Tournament and Championship' and listeners got to hear an excitable running commentary from sportscaster Guy Le Bow. The last programme in the series revealed which champion was crowned the all-time greatest heavyweight. The boxers included in the series came from different eras, so some were either drawing their pensions or had even been long deceased. Heck, Jack Johnson was one of the fighters in the tournament, but he was born in 1878 and died in 1946. If he had still been alive, Jack would have then been 89 years old by the time the radio fights were broadcast in 1967.

To make the impossible seem possible, Woroner used a computer to assimilate various pieces of information on the former champions that had been gathered from boxing experts around the country and an NCR 315 computer would apparently digest the data and evaluate the strengths and weaknesses of each fighter in his prime and eventually spew out how a 'fight' could turn out. The radio series was extremely popular, with 16½ million listeners tuning in to hear Rocky Marciano become the all-time champion of all champions after 'knocking out' Jack Dempsey in 2 minutes 28 seconds of the 13th round.

The computer had already knocked Muhammad Ali out in the quarter-finals after he was 'out-boxed' and lost a points decision to former heavyweight champion, 'Great White Hope', James J. Jeffries, who had died fourteen years earlier. The 'points loss' upset Ali so much that he sued Woroner for defamation of character.

The lawsuit was eventually settled, after Ali agreed to take part in another "fight', with the champion of champions, Rocky Marciano; but this time the simulated contest would be captured and shown on motion picture, not by radio. Ali reportedly received $9,500 and a percentage of ancillary rights for taking part, while Marciano was rumoured to have had a different arrangement.

So with the help of the NCR (National Cash Register) 315 computer and a marketing and media campaign, Woroner again set out to make the impossible seem possible. All that was needed was for the then 44-year-old Mariano to lose 50lbs of blubber, don a toupee to conceal his thinning mop and climb through the ropes to act out various fight sequences with the then 26-year-old Muhammad Ali. The computer would do the rest. For four days in December 1968 Ali and Marciano took part in a photo-shoot, where stills would be used in a process Woroner called 'photo-mation', along with seven hours of filmed rehearsals in a darkened film studio in Studio City, Florida.

The electronic 'champ v champ' idea was introduced to the press at the Fontainebleau Hotel in Miami on Friday 27 December 1968. Woroner said his computer could not only settle arguments about fighters from different eras competing against each other, but could even be used in other sports. He said the 'dream fight' would take about a year to bring to the cinemas. The final scenes took a further two days in early August 1969 – Ali was then 27 years old and Marciano 45. The two former undefeated heavyweight champions, Marciano, with 49 straight wins and 43 knockouts and Ali with 29 straight wins with 23 knockouts, were filmed throwing 'every fake punch in the book' for a total of 75 one-minute rounds. Woroner's computer would then produce an 'electronic winner'.

As part of the marketing campaign, the press were shown a few highlights of the bout, which showed both fighters being floored and Marciano suffering a cut. Two knockouts, two technical knockouts and two decisions were staged, with theatrical blood used to add realism to the battle. The sound of leather belting against flesh also came by way of a sound engineer and commentary once again was by Woroner and Guy Le Bow.

The result would come by way of the programmed NCR 315 computer and the man acting as 'referee' would be under the guidance of the computer's probability printouts. This was in spite of the 'referee' having more than a slight connection to one of the 'combatants', Muhammad Ali. The third man chosen to be in ring was Chris Dundee, who was not only a former promoter of many of Ali's earlier bouts and the owner of the gym Ali had once used in Miami, he was also the brother of Ali's one-time trainer, Angelo Dundee.

Back in 1964, superbout referee Chris had one of his greatest parties ever on 25 February, when on his 57th birthday, he co-promoted one of the biggest boxing upsets of all-time – Sonny Liston's encounter with a young fellow by the name of Cassius Clay. Now, six years later he found himself part of Woroner's dream bout, with his kid brother, Angelo, acting/starring as Ali's corner man. Mel Ziegler, had the same role in Marciano's corner.

The electronic fight received plenty of attention, as the promotional build-up in newspapers was just as big, or even bigger, than for many *real* world title fights.

Hundreds of cinemas in the US and Canada hosted the fight. Closed-circuit TV screenings were also be piped to sixteen Latin

American countries and around Europe. The screening of the fight was promoted as a once-only showing, so fight fans were keen to hand over their $5 not to miss Marciano v Ali.

The sealed and guarded copies of the completed film were planned to arrive at each cinema outlet no earlier than one hour before the planned showing time, with the worldwide distribution carried out by Trans-International Films. The secrecy and security was of course designed to ensure no one could find out the result until they were sat in their $5 cinema seat – and that included Ali himself, with the presentation going out at 10 p.m. Eastern time in the US on Tuesday, 20 January 1970. Sadly for Marciano, he wouldn't ever get to know the computer's verdict as he was killed in a light plane crash only three weeks after the final filmed sequences on August 31 1969.

Ali turned up at a local film theatre in Philly along with a few friends on the evening of 20 January and sat in the audience with about 500 others, intrigued to find out how he electronically performed against the legendary 'Rock'. Some people believed they were seeing a real fight. Twenty other countries were eager to see it, but somewhat surprisingly, initially, the UK was not one of them.

In November 1969, British boxing writer John Jarrett had visited Murry Woroner's Florida studio while on a privileged invitation to meet up with Jimmy Ellis and fellow fighters at Chris Dundee's 5th Street Gym in Miami. Woroner was more than keen to show Brit John some filmed scenes from his Ali v Marciano masterpiece and the realism of the 'fight' highly impressed Mr Jarrett. However, Woroner was also keen to show John a letter that he said came from the purchasing department of the BBC. The letter stated that the Ali v Marciano film would not be part of their January 1970 schedule. When John returned to the UK, he wrote about his experiences back in Miami and told how the 'Superbout' was attracting world-wide attention.

In one popular boxing magazine, the phone number was printed of Murry Woroner's office for any interested parties to give him a call.

Telephoning Miami from England was an expensive business in 1969 and it isn't known if the BBC made that transatlantic call, but what is known is that in January 1970, the Ali v Marciano 'fight' would be shown after all on BBC TV at a reported cost of $25,000. It was then hyped to potential viewers as the most 'sensational fight of our electronic age'.

It appeared a good decision too, as 11 million people tuned in to watch it. Unfortunately, though, viewers in the UK didn't actually get to see it until a few hours after the US screening on the evening of 21 January 1970.

To put the Ali v Marciano event in perspective, according to figures supplied to *Boxing News* at the time, when the *real* fight between Henry Cooper and Jack Bodell took place for the British and Empire boxing titles in March of that year, the 15-round bout drew 8½ million TV viewers – 2½ million fewer than the electronic 'fight', despite BBC radio listeners being informed of the result shortly after the US screening. Even with some in the UK being aware of the result, most boxing fans and those linked to the fight game still didn't want to miss seeing it and were eager to get access to a TV set that night to see something that was thought of as an electronic miracle.

It just so happened that the prestigious annual boxing writers dinner was held at the Cafe Royal in London on the same night as the Ali v Marciano UK screening. Colour television monitors, apparently courtesy of the BBC, had been set up around the venue, so that the 260 guests could watch.

Additional to the 'Superbout' that evening was an award presentation from UK boxing writers to the 'best young Brit boxer' of 1969, Joe Bugner, who began his pro career in 1967. During 1969, young Joe had taken part in 11 pro bouts, winning

10 and losing 1, with his sole loss coming against a fighter called Dick Hall in August. Joe began his 1970 season with a good win. On the evening before collecting his 'best young boxer' trophy, on 20 January 1970 at the Royal Albert Hall young Joe beat the tough and skilful Johnny Prescott on points. That win took the promising fighter's overall pro tally up to 24 fights, 22 wins with only 2 losses. (Bugner's first loss was in his first bout.) Bugner would be meeting up with Muhammad Ali in the US later that year, having already met Marciano in May of 1969 when the 'Rock' made a visit to London. Joe, born in Szeged, Hungary, but raised in England, sat alongside the other guests and with eyes pinned, watched the technological 'champ v champ' scrap.

And what did Joe and everyone else see that night? Well, they saw an avalanche of pulled punches exchanged by both fighters, with gushes of fake 'blood' running down the face of Marciano during much of the 'bout'. Even though there was no audience, the sound of a cheering crowd was still heard, as was the sound of punches landing on flesh. When the leather landed, the 'shots' looked real enough, but sounded less like a genuine punching thud and more like metal trash can lids being tapped by a wooden bat.

As each round ended, a computer-style printout was displayed on the screen that informed viewers how the computer adjudged the progress of the fight. After 12 rounds, Marciano had been 'floored' in the 8th, while dancing master Ali suffered 'knockdowns' in the 10th and 12th, but the computer still had both fighters even (114–114) going into the 13th round.

The performance eventually came to a climax 57 seconds into that round when the 'Rock' slung a swiping left hook that crashed to the side of Ali's head, knocking him along the ropes and then onto the canvas, where he was counted out by 'referee' and good pal Chris Dundee.

The number thirteen was certainly lucky for one and unlucky for others, as this was also the same round the computer made

Jack Dempsey a loser to the 'Rock' in the radio tournament. It was also the same round the 'Rock' demolished Jersey Joe Walcott, in a real fight, back in 1952, when he first won the heavyweight title. (The Marciano v Walcott real fight ended 14 seconds earlier than the Ali 'bout' in the same round.) Bugner found the result hard to believe and was later quoted in *Boxing News* (June 1970) saying that the computer must have had an electrical fault.

Back in America, Ali wasn't too happy about the result or the computer either, saying publicly that the machine must have been made in Alabama! Not long after, he described the whole thing as a 'Hollywood fake'. It seemed Woroner also wasn't happy, when he insisted that it was the computer that came up with the result and threatened Ali with a lawsuit for implying he was a fraud.

I still have vague memories of watching parts of that Ali v Marciano 'bout' on television. I was twelve years old at the time and my attention span was brief at best, but I do remember glancing at the screen at two boxers my grandfather said were the best ever. I am sure everyone in our home that night, including my grandfather, thought we all were watching some kind of miracle made possible by modern technology. (Today, it would be the same as fans getting to see a screened version of Mike Tyson fighting Tyson Fury. I am sure if such a meeting was made believable, it would generate much interest.)

It wasn't until fourteen years after the 'Superbout' creation that I found myself sitting alongside Ali himself, on his couch in his impressive white-pillared colonial style mansion home in LA, that I finally got to ask him about that mysterious 'electronic battle'. And unsurprisingly, his opinion on the 'fight' hadn't changed since 1970, when he just said the 'thing was all make-believe'. However, for fans around the globe, it didn't really matter, as the 'Super-fight' was 'super-intriguing' and an extremely entertaining event at the time.

One other positive that came out of the 1970 computer fight, apart from the $2.5 million it had reportedly grossed worldwide, is that the international spotlight centred on the now inactive former champion. Seeing Ali 'in action' once again, albeit in a darkened film studio and losing, still attracted a huge amount of worldwide attention, which helped keep him in the minds of boxing fans. This was aided by the firm stance of the 'Bible of Boxing', *The Ring* magazine, editor Nat Fleischer, who adamantly, some say controversially, continued rating Ali as World Heavyweight Champion, despite him being inactive for 34 months.

Fleischer believed a champion should only lose his title in the ring and until either Ali formally retired from the sport or the final result of the numerous court appeals on Ali's ring future was known, Ali would remain on top of the *Ring's* list of international heavyweight boxers.

2

ALI RETIRES (FOR THE FIRST TIME)

At the beginning of 1970, the on-off hopes of matching Ali with Frazier, or Ali with anyone else for that matter, only added to the continuing confusion of the world heavyweight championship. While Ali was recognized by *The Ring* magazine as champ, Frazier was titled world champ by the NYSAC and Jimmy Ellis started the year off as the remaining WBA champion.

According to a 1970 *Ring* magazine article, Jimmy Ellis first took up the sport of boxing after watching his friend Donnie Hall lose to Cassius Clay on a local TV show in Louisville called 'Tomorrow's Champions' (*Ring*, April–May 1970). Now, even though he had reached the pinnacle of being WBA champ, he had also been inactive himself for 16 months. It was no fault of his that he hadn't fought since way back in September 1968, after outscoring Floyd Patterson in his first defence of his title. Proposed bouts against Britain's Henry Cooper and Greg Peralta disappointingly fell through.

The New York State Athletic Commission (NYSAC) world champ, Joe Frazier, had his own problems, with Ali supporters picketing outside some of his world title fights, their placards reading 'Ali is the real champ'. The WBC refused to recognize either Frazier or Ellis as world title holders and had already declared their version of the world heavyweight title vacant as of March 1969. One can only imagine that it must have been frustrating for Joe and Jimmy, as the inactive Ali still consumed much of the attention from the press and fans alike.

Apart from the computer event distracting attention away from the other boxing champs, Ali was also a well-known figure to the young in America, as he was seen regularly conversing with them during his lecturing tours around colleges. It wouldn't take long before Ali turned his rehearsed speeches into sometimes heated debates. The entertaining and sometimes controversial and raucous banter would usually end with him 'winning the students over', when he would ask those present who they thought the real heavyweight champion was or should be – him, Frazier or Ellis? Invariably, anti-war hero Ali would hear *'Ah-Lee!'* screamed back at him.

If Ellis or Frazier switched the TV on, they wouldn't be surprised to see Ali on screen, endorsing products or popping up on chat shows, such as Joe Namath, David Frost, Mike Douglas and Ed Sullivan, or him disguising his voice on the popular *What's My Line* program in the US. A similar thing happened on most streets Ali walked down. On the way to the taping of the *What's My Line* show in 1969, Ali decided to make his way to the studio on foot from Toots Shor's restaurant in New York. On the way there, he was swamped by fans and passers-by, all wanting autographs, or asking him when, or if, he was going to fight again.

Ali was usually up for giving a good quote to the press. When his WBC title was declared vacant in 1969 for example, he said taking his title on paper was the only way he could be defeated, as he was the best fighter on planet earth and when America went to the moon (this was four months before astronauts landed there) if astronauts found anyone at home, he could beat them too!

By February 1970, much of the confusion and some of the banter about who was the *real* champion ended. Shortly after a proposed title defence of Jimmy Ellis's WBA crown against Argentinian Gregorio Peralta, set for December 1969, was cancelled and with Ali fighting Frazier only happening in people's minds, an Ellis v Frazier bout was quickly agreed and arranged. At this point Ali announced his retirement, so the fight to settle many of the arguments in world heavyweight boxing was set for 16 February 1970.

Ellis, who according to a report in *The Louisville Courier* had already lost one and then won one against Ali/Clay when they were both amateurs, had also fought on the undercard a few times of Ali's title bouts during the 1960s. The last was when Ali successfully defended his title against Zora Folley in Madison Square Garden in 1967. On the same bill, Ellis stopped Johnny Persol in 2:44 of the first round.

Jimmy had also been regularly employed as Ali's chief sparring partner during his championship years. Now, he found himself in a role reversal as Ali was sometimes spotted back in Chris Dundee's 5th Street Gym in Miami, where he helped his old pal prepare for his on-off fights during 1968–1969. Shortly before the Frazier v Ellis bout, the 'retired' Ali even offered his championship belt to the winner of the fight, but according to a report in *The Sheboygan Press*, Wisconsin (12 February 1970) he changed his mind after reading newspaper reports that Jimmy and Joe wouldn't accept it and that the boxing authorities weren't going to allow him into the ring to hand his belt over anyway. After that, Ali said he planned to donate his cherished championship belt to his old high school in Louisville Kentucky.

Preceding the title fight, which would also include the vacant WBC title, as well as the WBA and NYSAC titles, the retired Ali dismissed the legitimacy of the bout, calling the encounter a fight between his sparring partner (Ellis) and an amateur (Frazier) and declared that the people on the streets would still recognize him as the *real* champion.

The title fight, which produced an undisputed champion, ended after Frazier quickly smashed through Ellis's defences by employing ferocious power along with a wicked left hook, which eventually left Ellis battered and bruised and him failing to answer the bell for the start of the 5th.

It just so happened that on the same bill a young George Foreman, who began fighting for pay on the undercard of Frazier's previous title fight against Jerry Quarry in 1969, took part in his sixteenth pro bout and it had been his toughest encounter so far. He hammered out a hard, but impressive 10-round unanimous points decision win against Ellis's cancelled opponent, Argentinian Gregorio Peralta.

After the main event, Ellis wouldn't put the gloves on for pay again for another nine months and Frazier, even though now official king of the heavyweights, also demanded an extended rest and it came by way of a singing stint with his musical group, appropriately called, 'The Knockouts' in Las Vegas. Ali, already sidelined and now retired, said the computer fight was the last his worldwide fans would see of him inside a boxing ring, real or virtual.

And yet, despite Ali's retirement and his future possibly including a five-year stint in jail, he still seemed more than keen to have a 'showdown' fight with Joe Frazier. People behind the scenes battled on trying to get him a licence to fight but in vain; the longer his inactivity stretched, the more unlikely it was for him to return anywhere near his previous fighting form. It was thought if a breakthrough on getting him licensed in 1970 failed and he went into 1971 before the possibility of resuming competitive fighting, it would probably be too late for him to return successfully. By January 1971, Ali would be 29 years old and would be entering his fourth year of inactivity. To come back after that amount of time on the sidelines and face a younger, active and devastating punching champion like Joe Frazier was thought by many both unrealistic and unwise.

The rivalry between Ali and Frazier was very real. The two now both resided in Philadelphia – the city of 'brotherly love'. Both fighters felt confident they would be winners if they were ever paired off inside a boxing ring and living almost next door to each other only intensified the needle between the two.

Many believed the seeds of bitterness was first sown back in 1969 after Joe had previously spoken up for Ali to various boxing authorities about him having his boxing licence returned. Eventually, Joe felt Ali didn't appreciate his efforts. Then, one day in 1969, when Joe listened to Ali's lips rattle on a local radio show demeaning his fighting talents, Joe didn't take too kindly to Ali's verbals. During that radio programme, Ali even challenged Frazier to a fight at the Police Athletic League gym that Joe used on 22nd Street and Columbia Avenue in the north of the city. Ali's radio challenge may have started off as a publicity stunt to keep his name linked with the then NYSAC champion, but his words cut deep and turned Smokin' Joe, into steamin' Joe.

To say Joe wanted to hang a permanent 'closed sign' on Ali's Louisville lips was an understatement. The 'Smoke' was fuming and eager to confront the guy he thought had gone too far with his mouth.

It all kicked off on 23 September 1969, when Ali made his way to the gym Joe used. Along the way, a horde of others joined him, who believed they were going to see the 'battle of the century' for free. Once there, everyone attempted to squeeze inside, as they didn't want to be the ones that missed the action. Of course, it wasn't long before pandemonium erupted and police sergeant Vince Furlong who was in charge of the gym at that time demanded both take their fight and all the commotion they had brought along with them outside.

Ali, in 'Pied Piper' fashion, made his way out of the building and from his Cadillac, mic in hand, invited everyone to make their way to Fairmount Park, where he was going to 'punch it out' with Joe. As Ali drove to the park, a small army (reported to be over 10,000) of wildly excited fans and passers-by joined him. Traffic came to a standstill.

Joe was deterred from following him by his trainer, Yank Durham, who said they could and would fight each other if Ali regained his licence. 'Then Joe would shut his big mouth for good.' So Ali and Joe didn't fight in the park, but after that point, many said there was always an atmosphere when they ever came face-to-face. This was seen only one day later after the ballyhoo in the park, during a taping of the Mike Douglas TV chat show on 24 September. When both fighters came together the needle was apparent and it wasn't just confined to the TV studio. According to a report in the *Beckley Post Herald,* West Virginia, there was a physical confrontation after they both left the studios. What reportedly took place was a lot of grabbing and scuffling, with the 'Smoke' slipping out of his expensive jacket, looking for a face-off, until both were eventually separated and restrained. Ali, in front of a bunch of wide-eyed bystanders, made a show of trying to break through a barricade of minders to pop the champ on the nose. The then retired and former champion always thrived in those types of situations, especially when there was a large crowd present, but Joe ignored the tongue lashings and the theatrics as best he could, hoping to silence the 'Ali Rap' in the way Yank Durham suggested, inside a boxing ring.

Despite all this, by the time of the Ellis v Frazier fight in February 1970, a fight between Joe and Ali only remained a pipe-dream and the two fighters somehow reached a temporary truce, as any theatrics/challenges or predictions were pointless; most believed Ali was serious about his retirement. In the UK, *Boxing*

News headlined one of their February 1970 articles about the former champion bidding a farewell to fight game.

Ali's short-term future seemed to be that of a business man/college lecturer, who sometimes showed up doing TV commercials and occasional interviews. He still had a wife and child to support, and his long term future still pointed towards a possible jail term. In March 1969 he was suspended for one year by the Nation of Islam (N.O.I.) because he upset the leader, Elijah Muhammad, with comments he made on TV about how he needed to return to fighting to pay his bills. The former champion, who just happened to be in Atlanta not long after the N.O.I. ban, had given a lecture at Georgia Tech University on Friday 4 April 1969, and while there, he said he would never climb in a boxing ring again and vowed to give up all talk of a ring comeback.

Now a year later, Ali really was retired and publicly at least he seemed to accept his fighting days were in the past. Even *The Ring* replaced his name with Joe's as heavyweight champ. (Some sources claim that *The Ring* magazine continued to recognize Ali as champion until he eventually fought Joe Frazier in 1971, but from the May 1970 edition, Frazier was recognized as champion and Ali was dropped from the ratings altogether.)

It was now three years since Ali was in a real fight and it wasn't just the courts and boxing commissions that were against him ever being a prize-fighting champion again, but boxing history itself. Up to that point, only one world heavyweight champion regained his title, and that was Floyd Patterson, but he regained the title only 12 months after losing it. Old-time boxers had a saying – 'they never come back' – meaning heavyweight boxing champions, once they retire, can never regain their previous form and regain their former ring glories or titles. Some say Floyd proved that old saying wrong, but he never actually retired, as Ali now was. Even though Ali hadn't lost his title in the ring, the lost time made it unlikely he would ever get the chance to disprove that old fighters' saying.

After watching a screening of the Frazier v Ellis bout, Ali returned to his Philadelphia home, which he had purchased after moving from Chicago. He said the change of house and State was to be near New York for business reasons. He reportedly bought the house for $92,000 in the middle class section of Philadelphia called Overbrook. Reports suggest he made the purchase only one week before the Marciano computer fight.

Although Ali was inactive in the ring, his business interests 1968–1970 meant he could pay the bills. He had already signed a $900,000 contract to put his name to a Champburger restaurant chain, which had its grand opening on 28 December 1968 and he also signed a lucrative $200,000 deal with publishers Random House for a future autobiography. The money Ali earned at that time may have sounded great but it was sorely needed as the lawyer fees for his lingering court case helped evaporate most of the moulah that came through the door.

Apart from spending a great deal of time touring the country doing those college lectures, he also appeared in a Broadway musical called *Buck White*. The play was about a black leader saw the former champ don an Afro wig and sing six songs, with names such as 'Black balloons', 'Mighty Whitey' and 'We Came in Chains'. The show opened on 2 December 1969 and ran until 6 December. The show wasn't a huge success, but surprisingly the champ exhibited a 'mean beat'.

Besides the Broadway musical in 1969 and the Rocky Marciano event the following year Ali also took part in a documentary-movie in 1970. The film was called *AKA Cassius Clay* and featured former managers of past champs, Jose Torres (light heavyweight) and Floyd Patterson (heavyweight) and one-day trainer of a future champ, Mike Tyson, Cus D' Amato. Former hand ball champion Jim Jacobs, who would also one day assist in managing the career of Tyson, directed the movie, which included, among many other things, a debate between Ali and D' Amato on how he (Ali) would 'handle' past heavyweight boxing champions. According to Ali, he was the 'Greatest' and every former champion would only have come a poor and sore second. Cus on the other hand, gave his own reasons why he thought the 'Brown Bomber', Joe Louis, would justify his own observation that 'he can run, but he can't hide' (reportedly said of NBA world light-heavyweight champion and Louis's opponent twice, Billy Conn) and eventually catch up with Ali and flatten him.

Just prior to the Frazier v Ellis bout in February 1970, in the UK, the name of Muhammad Ali and his plight in the US was still causing interest and sometimes protest. Boxer Paddy Monaghan was one who believed a great injustice had been done to the champion. He made his and other people's feelings felt after he collected a petition of 22,224 signatures from British fans in support of Ali and against the WBA and NYSAC. Paddy sent off by mail his collected names and addresses to the headquarters of the WBA. On the day of the Ellis v Frazier fight, Paddy held a one-man protest outside of the offices of the British Boxing Board of Control, then situated in Ramillies Buildings on Hill's Place in central London.

He believed the Ellis v Frazier fight shouldn't be recognized as a world title fight, as Ali was still the real champion.

Even the white satin 'Ampro' boxing shorts that Ali had worn in his bout with Henry Cooper four years previously attracted press attention in the UK. This came about after community leader and civil rights activist Michael X, who was born Michael de Freitas, but also known as Michael Abdul Malik, somehow persuaded Ali to visit his 'Free School' on Holloway Road in London at the time of the Cooper bout in 1966. Ali turned up at what Michael X called 'The Black House' and he eventually found himself possessing the blood-stained boxing shorts he wore in his championship encounter with Cooper.

Malcolm X himself had already formed a friendship with Michael X during a previous visit to the UK. Malcolm was soon to be assassinated back in the States on 21 February, 1965. Fast forward to February 1970 and Michael X was photographed holding onto Ali's shorts alongside John Lennon and Yoko Ono, who held a plastic bag containing their recently cut mops. The hair of the two singing stars and shorts of the now former world boxing champ certainly caused quite a stir. The hair and shorts were later said to be sold to raise funds for Michael X's 'Free School'.

Ali garnered publicity effortlessly, but his college tours in the US eventually had the effect of making him more popular at the grassroots level, especially among the young in many universities and colleges throughout America. The longer the unpopular war in Vietnam went on, the more popular Ali became with those students who witnessed TV images every day of the killings in the far-off war.

3

QUARRY AND THE WAR PROTESTORS KEEP BUSY

Ring inactivity wasn't a problem for Jerry Quarry. In 1970, he was on a comeback after suffering a controversial KO defeat to Canadian George Chuvalo. Their bruising encounter took place in a 1969 pre-Christmas tear-up on 12 December 1969 in Madison Square Garden.

In that fight, at the beginning of the 7th round, it looked like Jerry was on his way to victory as he was leading on two of the three scorecards and Chuvalo's right eye had been busted up and was severely swollen. Then, in the closing seconds of the round, Jerry was floored by a left hook. Although he pulled himself up off the canvas, Quarry then squatted back down, presumably to take more rest time. However, referee Zach Clayton counted him out, while Quarry looked like he was in a position to jump up and resume fighting. Pandemonium erupted as Jerry claimed he hadn't heard the count and wanted to continue and it was little wonder as the count came only a few seconds before the end of the round.

By February 1970, Jerry, known as the 'Bellflower Belter' was to be found in, of all places, Ali's former 'fight factory' in Miami Beach, Chris Dundee's 5th Street gym on the corner of

Washington Avenue. He was there training for a fight against fringe contender, Rufus Brassell, from Lima, Ohio, with their bout set for the Miami Beach Auditorium on 3 March 1970.

By the time of their fight, Jerry Quarry was a big name in boxing and many fans and stars turned up just to watch his sparring sessions. Legend has it, Quarry and his kid brother, Mike, a fellow pro-slugger, would have many a brutal sparring session together. Although Jerry's brother was a light-heavyweight, he was an extremely talented one, who would fight for the world title two years later in 1972.

Jerry's 1970 comeback fight against Angelo Dundee-trained pugilist Brassell was both short and wildly exciting. According to the fight report in *The Miami News*, Jerry out-punched Brassell in the first round, but seconds before the bell, Brassell clipped his opponent, causing Jerry to drop his hands. When the bell rang to end the round, Brassell kept punching and one neat right hand dropped Jerry. Fortunately for Quarry, the knockdown wasn't ruled official, as it came after the round ended. At the start of the second, a seemingly enraged Jerry went out to crush Brassell, but he was already bleeding from a cut near his left eye and blood oozed from inside his mouth. 78 seconds into the round, Quarry connected with a crunching left hook, which sent Brassell down for the full count. Smelling salts were called for to bring Brassell round.

Quarry's regular ring work continued without much reprieve, and only a couple of weeks later, on 19 March, he was back in the ring, this time against George 'Scrap Iron' Johnson, a fighter that he had already scored a stoppage win over in 1966. The return was billed as a 'grudge fight' and took place in the same venue as their last meeting, the Olympic Auditorium in Los Angeles.

'Scrap-Iron's' previous professional fight was a 7th round stoppage loss against Sonny Liston in May of 1969. He had also shared the ring with Joe Frazier and surprisingly, 'Scrap Iron' fared much better against Joe than with Sonny, as he managed to last the whole way with the 'Smoke'. In the Quarry v Johnson second fight, Jerry emulated Frazier and smashed out a points decision win, but according to the fight report in *The Times Record* Jerry's win came with some eye damage that required minor stitching, along with a reported $10,000 purse.

The victory over Johnson eventually moved the 'come-back kid' into a spring bout with Mr 'Knockout' Mac Foster, who was a former marine and undefeated at the time. 'Mighty Mac' was also rated number one heavyweight contender in the world by *The Ring* and was talked up as being a future opponent in a big money fight with champion Joe Frazier. Foster's fight record stood at an impressive 24 fights, 24 wins and all those wins came by knockout. The bout with Quarry was planned to take place on 17 June at Madison Square Garden.

In the same month as the proposed New York fight, Brit manager Andy Smith planned on taking his young protégé, Joe Bugner, who had just turned 20 years old in March, for additional boxing tutelage in the States. At the time, *Boxing News* reported that Joe was extremely excited about the visit, which would begin in June and last a few weeks. The Transatlantic educational sparring tour, which reportedly cost about $15,000 (*Boxing Illustrated*) would include visiting boxing gyms in the same city of the Foster v Quarry bout, New York, as well as gyms in Los Angeles. Newark and Miami.

However, before Joe crossed the pond he had to get past his next ring opponent, who just happened to be a former opponent of Muhammad Ali, back in the days when Ali was champion, Brian London. The Bugner v London bout was set for 12 May 1970 at the Empire Pool, Wembley.

While the sport of boxing carried on without the magnetic presence of Muhammad Ali, wherever the ex-champ went outside of the ring, he still attracted media attention and huge crowds.

In April in New York, his presence brought traffic to a standstill again, this time while filming a commercial on the streets for an aftershave. At about this time, fellow Philadelphia resident and officially recognized champion, Joe Frazier, ended up having something in common with his ex-rival, Muhammad Ali. The champion would join the retired title holder in being sidelined from boxing by virtue of a broken ankle he suffered while performing on stage during his singing stint in Las Vegas. When Frazier returned to Philly from Vegas, his ankle was in a cast and it wasn't likely to be removed until June – so at that point, while both Ali and Frazier pondered their fighting futures outside of the ring, events were turning in such a way that could increase the chances of them one day meeting inside it.

This came about through the increasing disenchantment of the American public with the US role in the Vietnam War. By the time of Ali's draft refusal in 1967, support was fading.

In January 1969, new US President Richard Nixon claimed he had a plan to end US involvement in the war, and would put an end to the draft. His pledge sounded promising; a Commission report in February 1970 said US military strength could be maintained by volunteers – but the draft and the war continued.

The media coverage of the conflict had a massive impact on the American public, with television especially proving to be the most powerful medium. Millions of Americans tuned in each day to see images and hear stories that shook their previously held convictions about the domino effect, the Red Menace – and American military invincibility. Anti war protests increased, led by the younger generation, unsurprising as the average age of a US infantryman who fought in Vietnam was twenty-two.

On 20 April 1970 Nixon went on TV to reassure the public when he said 150,000 troops would be withdrawn over time from Vietnam (depending on the success of a strategy he introduced in 1969 called 'Vietnamization', which increased the South

Vietnamese involvement). Then, only a few days later he went back on TV and admitted to authorizing attacks into Cambodia. For many, his words of 'de-escalation', sounded more like the opposite; the strikes had actually expanded the war and the Cambodian invasion/incursion triggered massive student protests across America.

One was at Kent State University in Ohio on May 4; the 2,000 students on the campus grounds heard the crackling sound of gunfire and it came from the Ohio State National Guard. In 13 seconds, 67 rounds were fired, four students lay dead and nine others were wounded. It goes without saying that support for the war hit a low and millions of students in universities across America,protested or went on strike. However, the strength of feeling for as well as against government decisions and actions in Vietnam still ran deep. Four days later in New York City, over 1,000 anti-war protesters took part in a march along the streets of Manhattan and were attacked by 200 construction workers. The resulting melee led to 70 people being injured and the incident became known as the 'hard hat riot'. And the anti-war protests were not confined to America. On the same day as the hard hat riot, in Australia over 100,000 people took part in a protest march in Melbourne. The next day back in the States, thousands held another protest in Washington, which was followed a week later by yet more protests at Jackson State College in Mississippi where another two people were killed and twelve others injured on May 15. The news agencies stoked feelings by the images they portrayed, as their cameras pointed towards the thick of the action and recorded images of casualties both in Vietnam and among the home protesters.

Over time, both the protests and protesters increased, with some looking to a man that was becoming one of the symbols of the anti-war movement – Muhammad Ali. Possibly unbeknownst to him, the tide of feeling had turned in his favour. Ali probably still believed a prison term was going to be the outcome of his ongoing legal case, but he could not have been oblivious to the growing anger about America's involvement in that far-off war. That's not to say that the hate mail and anti Ali feelings dried up. Even though he had more than his share of idolaters, at the same time, there were still plenty of people out there who despised him for his draft refusal and links to the Nation of Islam. Newspaper offices and the various boxing magazines throughout the world still received a steady flow of letters fulminating against a man many people believed had turned his back on a nation that had been good to him. Ali was riding a wave that was heading in the opposite direction to war and he was only getting off wherever that wave came to a stop – either with jail or vindication.

Richard Nixon's administration would eventually end America's direct military involvement in the war and also end the draft, but it wouldn't happen until 1973, which would be during Nixon's second term in office. The end of the war in Vietnam didn't take place until April 1975, when North Vietnamese troops took over Saigon.

4

MAC 'THE KNIFE' FOSTER; BUGNER TAKES A TRIP

Back in the UK, only one week after the protests and shootings at Kent University, young boxer Joe Bugner fought Brian London. Brian was from Blackpool in the north west of England and had been a pro fighter since 1955. He had challenged twice for the world heavyweight title. The first title fight was against Floyd Patterson in 1959, when London lost by KO in 51 seconds of the 11th round. Surprisingly, the 'Blackpool Rock' hadn't fought in the nation's capital since being demolished in three rounds by Muhammad Ali in his last world title bout at Earls Court way back in August 1966.

Brian came to the Bugner fight following a loss, knocked out in one round less than it had taken Ali by Californian banger Jerry Quarry. For that fight, Brian had travelled all the way to the Oakland Arena in California on 3 September 1969. The Quarry v London second bout lasted 2 minutes 30 seconds into the second round, after Brian received a crunching right hand to the head. London was counted out. London had fared much better in their first encounter in 1967, when he lost a points decision to the then up-and-coming Quarry, two years a pro. When it was his time to climb through the ropes to face the 6ft 4in Bugner, it was another losing night, as Joe used a ramrod left jab and snappy right hand to wear down and stop him in the 5th round. After the bout Brian announced his retirement from the ring, ending a career that read 58 fights, 37 wins, 20 losses and 1 draw.

Jubilant Joe on the other hand, took his pro record to 28 fights, 26 wins and 2 losses and announced his eagerness for his next stop in boxing – the USA. The timing of Joe's 'educational' trip to the States in June 1970 coincided with a new Tory Government coming to power in the UK, Mungo Jerry's pop song *In the Summertime* becoming everyone's ear worm – and a chance to see up close that new 'powerhouse' boxer in the USA, Mac Foster.

MacArthur Foster, better known then as Mac 'The Knife' Foster, or Mac 'KO' Foster, was a colossus. He was 27 years old, chiselled out of solid muscle. He was from Fresno, California and by the time of Joe's US trip, Foster was the man in the boxing world many talked about as being a future champion. Mac first took up boxing as a pastime while in the military. He was named by his father Erwin after General Douglas MacArthur. By the time he left the military in 1966, he had served in Vietnam and taken part in many combat operations. He had a reported amateur boxing record of 21 fights, 1 loss, with 17 knockouts and 14 Service titles. When Mac returned to the US, he turned pro and it didn't take long before the Fresno fighter was setting tongues a-wagging and his manager, Pat DiFuria, brimming with confidence that Mac was indeed going to one day wreak havoc amongst the world's elite heavyweights. One incident that helped cement that belief took place two years into the young fighter's pro career.

One Saturday afternoon in June 1968, the imposing 220lb figure of Sonny Liston was in California preparing for his 45th bout and 7th comeback fight after losing to Muhammad Ali back in 1965. His next fight was planned to be against

Henry Clark, set for the Cow Palace in Daly City, California, on 6 July 1968. At that time, it was said there was still plenty of life and menace left in the 'bear' and not many fellow heavyweight fighters were keen to climb through the ropes and face the massive fists of Sonny. That apprehension was still felt even with Liston having the added 'softener' of using pillow-sized sparring gloves inside a training ring. Novice heavyweight, Mac Foster, was one who did take the risk though and volunteered his sparring services.

That day, Sonny Liston was working out in the Lewis and Barberi boxing gym in Oakland and the sparring ring was surrounded by fight people, including Mac's manager Pat DiFuria and gym owners Dave Lewis and Ed Barberi. Foster donned the gloves and slipped through the ropes and with the 'confident encouragement' of DiFuria, ripped into the 'bear', knocking Sonny down onto one knee in the second round. Some reports suggested that Sonny received Mac's right hand cruncher when he was momentarily distracted, but the damage was done, as all bug-eyed bystanders in the gym saw Sonny's legs buckle and touch the mat.

From the earliest times, news in the fight game – especially juicy news like Liston hitting the canvas – travelled fast. By the time the gossip had spread country-wide, the talk was of Sonny being flattened and knocked 'clean out' by a two-year, 12-fight novice. Sonny was probably far from knocked out and picked himself up and completed the session. However, Sonny surely wasn't happy about his 'touch-down' that day, which came by way of a novice, who was presumably paid not to put a whupping on his paymaster.

At the time, Foster himself was preparing for his thirteenth fight, which was verbally agreed to take place at the Selland Arena on 9 July in Fresno, California. It was planned to be against the very fighter that Muhammad Ali's aborted January

1970 exhibition was meant to be with, heavyweight Billy Joiner from Cincinnati, Ohio. In a 30 June 1968 *Fresno Bee* article, it was stated that no contract had been signed for the Foster v Joiner fight. For whatever reason, the Foster fight was put on temporary hold.

Joiner had lasted seven rounds with Sonny Liston in the 'bear's' previous bout in May of that year. He had a return bout against Liston the following year in March 1969, losing by a 10-round points decision. He was the first boxer to last the distance with Liston since Eddie Machen managed the same losing feat nine years earlier in 1960. Billy would eventually make that trip to California to face Mac Foster, but it would take another three years for the meeting to take place. On Thursday 29 July 1971, Joiner entered the ring at the Olympic auditorium for a 10-round contest against Foster. The fight lasted until the 5th round, when Joiner was caught by a left hook flush to the side of the jaw, with the punch knocking Billy down and out. The ten-second count was tolled over the downed fighter by referee John Thomas.

Back to 9 July 1968; Mac's replacement in the Selland arena was Curtis Bruce, based on the east coast in Newark, New Jersey. Bruce travelled a long way for an evening's work, but it didn't take long for him to pick up his paycheck after Foster unleashed his powerful punches and stopped Curtis in the 3rd round.

Even from his pro beginnings back in 1966, Foster talked about being the heavyweight champ by the end of 1970 and by early 1969, Mac was receiving high praise from former world heavyweight champions such as Rocky Marciano. By the end of that year, Foster (born 27 June 1942) had built up a fearsome reputation, with an unblemished record, including impressive double inside the distance wins over former Ali title challenger Cleveland Williams and a one-round knockout over the rated Thad Spencer. After the Spencer win in May 1969, his beaming manager, Pat DiFuria, was quoted in *The Fresno Bee* saying that he believed Mac was the hardest punching heavyweight in the fight game and possibly the hardest punching heavyweight ever! By 1970, Mac Foster was gunning for the title and many believed he was a sure bet to be the next champion. In that year, a readers poll in *Boxing Illustrated* included Mac's name among fourteen other heavyweights, as the ninth greatest heavyweight of all time, tying with former champions, James J. Jeffries and Ingemar Johansson. This was an amazing poll rating as Foster wasn't a world champion, only a number one contender. In that vote, Mac was in great company, as the top five spots were Muhammad Ali (1), Rocky Marciano (2), Joe Louis (3), Jack Dempsey (4) and Jack Johnson (5). Of course, nothing should be read too much into polls, but it gives some indication of how much boxing fans and the fight fraternity itself held Mac in high esteem. (George Foreman and Cleveland Williams also tied into 9th spot with Foster. Jerry Quarry wasn't included in the fourteen fighters nominated.) The ex-marine was confident of being the next champion and he believed he had the strength and 'battle recipe' to topple Joe Frazier. All he needed was to get the 'Smoke' inside a boxing ring to prove it.

Mac's 24th fight took place a couple of months before Bugner's US tour began, on 9 April 1970, and it was another one round blast-out. Mac flattened 6ft 6in 238½-lb 'giant' Jack O'Halloran two seconds before the end of the round at the Olympic Auditorium in Los Angeles. Out of Mac's 24 straight knockout victories, Jack added to his tally of fighters that didn't reach passed the 3rd round to sixteen.

Mac's beaten opponent, Jack O'Halloran, from Boston, was no loser though, as he would not only go on and beat Muhammad Ali's brother two years later, but after his boxing career finished, the giant became known to movie goers the world over as 'Non', a villain in the *Superman* movies.

In June 1970, Mac 'KO' Foster was booked to share top billing for the first time in Madison Square Garden, with former title challenger, Jerry Quarry. Before the fight, the *Ring* ratings placed Jerry four places below the top-rated challenger Foster and many experts had already written him off as a future champ after his defeats to Ellis, Frazier and Chuvalo in 1968 and 1969.

That was the ratings, but in the reader polls, another in *Boxing Illustrated* (published in 1970 but covering 1969) Jerry was voted for the second year running the readers' favourite active fighter in the world. In that poll, the list of fighters amounted to almost 100, all the way from Flyweight up to Heavyweight and included names such as Joe Frazier, Sonny Liston, George Foreman, Dick Tiger, Emile Griffith and of course Mac Foster (Foster was voted 7th). Jerry took the top spot because his fights were mostly action-packed and he came with an exciting style, along with good looks and charm that made him an excellent attraction to both fight fans and TV audiences alike. (At the end of 1970 Quarry would be voted favourite again in *Boxing Illustrated* but sharing the laurels. This would happen after the Ali v Quarry bout and Ali would tie Jerry for top spot.)

Quarry had already proven his courage after he stood toe-to-toe with Smokin' Joe Frazier in a title fight in June 1969. Quarry's bravery was rewarded with a damaged right eye, which ended the fight at the end of the 7th round. Jerry proved that night to be a quality, gutsy fighter and one who had lost none of his popularity, with the tear-up adjudged the fight of the year by *The Ring* magazine.

Many felt Quarry brought a touch of glamour to the boxing game, but he always came to fight. Once inside a ring, it didn't take him long to sense any weaknesses in an opponent, then, he would pounce on any opportunity, which would usually leave his foe lying dazed on the canvas, staring up at the overhead ring lights. However, up to that point, Mac Foster hadn't shown many weaknesses in the ring, only a willingness to brutalize every man that was put in front of him.

Initially, there was talk of Quarry taking on George Chuvalo in a return bout in the Garden, but eventually Quarry and Foster signing contracts to face each other in New York. The June bout with Foster would be Jerry's first since his 19 March bout against George 'Scrap Iron' Johnson.

In 1970, Ali wasn't the only fighter having problems outside a boxing ring. It seemed for top fighters, boxing was the easy part. The politics of the fight game were something else and sometimes created bigger problems for them than simply punching each other on the nose. The Foster v Quarry fight was no different, as it hit snags well before the two boxers climbed through the ropes in New York. The two West Coast sluggers were already said to be signed to meet in California. The Olympic Boxing Club based in Los Angeles, stated they already had a signed contract for them to meet under their promotion. The Olympic had staged Foster's last fight against Jack O'Halloran and had also staged many of Quarry's previous bouts, but the California State Athletic Commission threatened to suspend both fighters, if they fought in New York.

One month before their bout was to take place in New York, George Foreman's trainer/manager, Dick Sadler, was quoted in *Boxing News* saying that if Mac Foster pulled out of the fight, he was eager to put Foreman in with Quarry. However, as the controversy persisted, both Quarry and Foster eventually went ahead with their fight in the 'Big Apple' and a temporary suspension was imposed by the Californian Commission.

On the evening of Wednesday, 17 June 1970, 15,915 fans turned up in Madison Square Garden, bringing along with them a live gate of $165,123 and expectations of an explosive night of fighting. They wouldn't return home disappointed. Foster brought his line of impressive straight knockout victories to the New York ring, while Jerry turned up with a fighting record of 43 fights, 35 wins, 4 losses and 4 draws.

Joe Bugner, then in America to begin his stateside tour of 'fight factories' had the marvellous opportunity of seeing those two top-rated fighters clash inside the Mecca of boxing. Joe's manager Andy Smith and boxing man Micky Duff assisted the youngster in having a close look at these American heavies, meeting the two fighters at the weigh-in as well as sitting ringside at the fight.

Jerry Quarry came to the 10-round fight as an underdog according to the bookies and physically, it looked like it was a mismatch. At the weigh-in, Foster was heavier and taller than Quarry. At 210lbs, Foster looked a sure bet against the 196-lb Quarry, who turned up sporting a wispy moustache. Foster also enjoyed a massive 9in reach advantage, plus the confidence of never tasting defeat in a pro ring.

Minutes before the two fighters entered the ring and started throwing leather, there was a 75th birthday celebration for legendary ex-heavyweight champion, Jack Dempsey, who was also ringside that night. Huge screens hung above the ring showed some of Dempsey's biggest fights against Georges Carpentier and 'Giant' Jess Willard. In his fighting days, the press called Jack the 'giant killer' after he demolished Willard on 4 July 1919. Fifty-one years later, Jerry would try to do the same, but to an undefeated fighter who came along with his own 'giant' reputation. The Dempsey birthday tribute concluded when heavyweight champion, Joe Frazier, presented Dempsey with a gift in the ring. (Incidentally, Dempsey's birthday was still seven days off, 24 June, with Mac Foster's 28th birthday following three days after Jack's on the 27th.)

Quarry was the first to enter the ring in an eye-catching turquoise robe, Foster entered decked out in a maroon number. When the two fighters came together to listen to referee Johnny LoBianco's instructions, the size difference between the two fighters was apparent, the 6ft 2in Foster seem to tower over the shorter Quarry.

When the first bell sounded, it was little surprise that the powerful Foster gained the upper hand after a brief 'feeling-out' period. In the early going, a solid right uppercut and left hook knocked Quarry momentarily back against the ropes, but the Bellflower Belter soon regained his equilibrium. However, Foster's huge 81in reach helped him gain the advantage in the first round. There was plenty to think about for Quarry as the bell sounded. His corner, which included Teddy Bentham and Quarry's brother Jimmy, encouraged Jerry, who was an expert counter-puncher, to lull Foster into making mistakes and then unleash his own arsenal.

In the second round, Quarry did just that, when he rolled under Foster's high guard and fired off some solid uppercuts followed by left hooks to the body, which not only rattled Foster but roused the New York fight crowd. Surprisingly, Foster's retaliation mainly consisted of misses as Jerry ended the second round landing another solid left hook to Mac's midsection.

By the third round, both fighters were fully warmed to the task and the strikes began to get a touch more serious. It was Foster's ramrod jab that kept him narrowly ahead. Quarry picked up some slight damage to his left eye after Foster's left fist perpetually slammed into his face. Two minutes into the third round, Quarry brought the crowd to its feet with an impressive flurry of lefts and rights only to be caught himself by a perfectly timed and placed right hook. Foster's punch crashed against Quarry's unprotected chin and the timing and tenacity of the shot momentarily turned Jerry's steely legs to rubber. The crowd went wild as it looked like Quarry was heading for the canvas, but he somehow regained his composure.

As the bout progressed, the fight plan of both fighters was set. Foster seemed content to let his powerful left jab do most of the work and damage, while Quarry stalked, attempting to turn the boxing match into a gun-slinging brawl. The toe-to-toe tactic with Smokin' Joe Frazier exactly one year earlier in June 1969 hadn't work for Jerry, but it appeared he wanted to see if that same risky approach would work against Foster.

In the fourth round, Quarry started to turn the tables on Mac's effective and powerful jab. Jerry landed a solid right uppercut followed by a left hook to Foster's jaw, but picked up a tasty left hook to his face in the process. However, Quarry began whipping in gut wrenching uppercuts to his opponent's muscled torso with explosive force and in the last few seconds of the round, Jerry landed a peach of a left hook, followed by a sharp right. At the sound of the bell, it was clearly Quarry's round.

By the end of round five, Quarry was finally turning the boxing match into his apparently preferred type of encounter, a toe-to-toe fight. After landing a solid left hook to Foster's body and sensing the ex-marine was hurt, Jerry went in guns blazing, with Foster attempting to return the favour. A fabulous right uppercut from Quarry knocked his opponent back on his heels. Foster's long left-arm jab was now employed as a defensive tool rather than an offensive weapon, but his attempt at defence didn't stop Quarry ripping in another sharp, powerful left hook to the body. The punch seemed to take all the wind from Foster's lungs and as the fifth round ended, it again clearly belonged to Quarry. After five rounds, the referee, LoBianco and one judge had Quarry ahead in the fight, while one judge had Foster leading, winning the first three rounds, with Jerry picking up the fourth and fifth.

The sixth began, like all the others, with Quarry stalking and Foster pumping out his left jab, but midway through the round, Quarry unleashed another impressive barrage of punches, which knocked Foster back against the ropes. Jerry piled in with more hurtful punches and the onslaught knocked Foster partially out through the ring ropes. As Mac tried to regain his balance and composure, Quarry pounced again like a tiger on a wounded deer. The punches landed at a furious pace as Foster's arms dangled at his sides. The ex-marine's survival instincts attempted to kick in, but it looked like his only chance of keeping his dangerous opponent off was by getting hold of his Vietnam M16. This was a different type of combat and Quarry wasn't about to stop throwing leather. A left, a right and another left sent Foster to the Garden canvas and as he was going down, referee LoBianco pulled a menacing looking Quarry away from his stricken foe. As the timekeeper reached the count of three, LoBianco waved his arms and signalled the fight's end. Quarry was a TKO winner in 2 minutes 5 seconds of the sixth. The cheers from the fans echoed throughout the famous arena.

The jubilant victor, who had already seen his younger brother Mike win on the undercard, was congratulated by his brother, Jimmy, father, and thousands of fans afterwards. His spectacular win was more than impressive, it was a shock – many fans had turned up at the Garden believing he was going to get destroyed. The stoppage win now catapulted Jerry up the ratings, with *The Ring* not only naming him fighter of the month (September issue) but also replacing Mac's name at the top of their contender list with Jerry's.

He certainly lived up to being voted the world's favourite active fighter – even if one just went by the live gate figures. According to *Boxing Illustrated* his fight with Foster was the highest dollar gate for a non-title fight. Quarry broke his previous record, when he beat the behemoth Buster Mathis in Madison Square Garden the previous year.

Jerry was riding high and after that spectacular victory, there was immediate talk of a return fight against Joe Frazier. Jerry himself expressed his desire for a return fight with George Chuvalo who held that controversial stoppage win over him the previous year. However, it turned out that George was mooted to fight another George, George Foreman, the former 1968 Olympian. Then the winner of that bout would likely face Quarry in a final eliminator for the world title.

It must have been a fabulous experience for Joe Bugner to attend that big fight inside the Garden, but he would have many other fascinating experiences during his stateside tutorial. Whilst still in the Big Apple, Joe visited one of the busiest boxing training facilities in the world on West 28th Street. The gym was run by experienced trainer/manager Gil Clancy and even though Clancy was spotted in the corner of Mac Foster during the Quarry fight, his longtime prized pupil was former world welterweight and middleweight champion, Emile Griffith. At the time of Joe's gym visit, Griffith was on a comeback after losing a world welterweight title shot the previous year against the equally impressive Jose Napoles by a points decision. In his last fight on 4 June in Copenhagen, Denmark, Griffith spoiled the 54-bout undefeated run (including one draw against Don Fullmer) of European middleweight champion, 'Great Dane' Tom Bogs in front of 10,000 partisan fans. Griffith floored Bogs in the 6th and 10th rounds and scored a well-deserved points win. Emile was also slated to take on the great Dick Tiger in his next bout the following month. While Joe spent two days at the gym, he received many pointers and words of experience from the former world welterweight and middleweight champion who would go on to have 112 fights.

During Joe's time in New York, it was believed that he completed his morning jogs in and around Central Park. Clancy's gym visit came with another bonus. During his time there, Muhammad Ali turned up and Joe sparred a few rounds with him. The former world champion was in pretty good physical condition, as there was still much going on behind the scenes to have his boxing licence returned. It was thought, if permission was ever given for him to fight again, the former champ would quickly shelve his early retirement and resume his career. During Ali's three-year exile, it wasn't unusual to walk into a boxing gym in the US and find the 'Greatest' working out. Whenever Ali was in Miami, it wouldn't be long before he climbed up those creaky old wooden steps that led onto the first floor boxing facility of the 5th Street Gym. In early July 1969, while in Los Angeles, Ali was found in another local fight factory, sparring with three young boxers, one being a 10-fight novice called Ken Norton. On that sunny day in the practice ring, Ali went a few rounds with heavyweight Kenny and a report in the *Daily Press*, Va., on 9 July 1969 stated that the ex-champion refused to pop a gumshield into his mouth that day, saying that he was so fast, nobody could get near enough to hit him.

Only four years later, in 1973, Ken Norton would receive the chance of a lifetime and get to fight Ali for real. That fateful March 31 night in San Diego, Ali did wear a gumshield and it ended up smeared in blood, after Norton hit Ali's head with a crunching power punch. The shot smashed Ali's jaw and surgery was needed to repair it. When Ali moved to Philadelphia, he would also be regularly seen working out in a facility called the 'Champs Gym' which was only a short drive from his home.

On that June day in 1970, inside Clancy's gym, Bugner completed 4–6 fast-paced rounds with the former champion. Afterwards, Ali sang the praises of the Brit boxer, with the former 'Louisville lip' even picking up a slight bruising to the side of his jaw after tasting Joe's rapier left jab.

In addition to the sparring with Ali, during his boxing Grand Tour Joe would receive another tutorial when he went two sparring rounds inside Bufano's Gym and Pool Hall in Jersey City, with none other than the big ole bear himself, Sonny Liston. By that time in 1970, many experts believed Liston was way past his fearsome best, after he had been well and truly flattened in 1:08 of the 9th round by Leotis Martin in December 1969. But swapping punches with even the battle-weary former world champ must have been an incredible confidence booster for the 20-year-old. Joe didn't manage to floor Sonny, as Mac Foster had done two years previously, but his slick boxing skills certainly impressed the handful of privileged ringside spectators that got to watch him coping with Sonny's brute strength, power and intimidating presence that day. Their brief two-round sparring session took place only days before the Liston went in against 6ft 5in heavyweight Chuck Wepner at the Armory in Jersey City on 29 June 1970.

During Joe's visit the frustration behind the scenes of trying to organize a fight for Ali continued and it seemed every piece of good news was followed by bad. The good news came just days before Quarry's blasting out of Mac Foster, on 15 June 1970, when the Supreme Court decided an objector to military service could now include 'strong moral and ethical' reasons. Ali's lawyer, Bob Arum was convinced these changes covered Ali position.

Ed Dooley, the Chairman of the NYSAC, said publicly that if the courts changed their stance on Ali's position, they would immediately reinstate his New York boxing licence. Harry Markson from Madison Square Garden also joined in the growing optimism, by saying they wanted to put on Ali's first fight if his licence was returned. The news must have given Ali a boost too, despite him initially not wanting to publicly comment about the legal change. Anyway, the case in the Supreme Court wasn't resolved for another year, in June 1971. This was June 1970 and those behind the ex-champion, maybe with a touch more enthusiasm, were still trying to get a city to put on an Ali fight, without success.

Not long after the good news about the defence of ethical objection, came the bad. A story broke about another attempt to get a fight between him and Frazier being scuppered. This time, those behind Ali tried to get permission for the bout to proceed in Seattle, Washington. It was hoped that they could organize a fight for some time in September, but on Friday 26 June, the Washington State Athletic Commission voted 2–1 against allowing the fight to take place. This was in addition to another avenue already blocked. Earlier in Washington, on 10 June, Supreme Court Justice Hugo L. Black refused Ali's lawyers request for him to travel over the border to Canada for eighteen hours to face Frazier in Toronto.

Despite the refusals, promoters still remained optimistic that yet another proposal, this time in Detroit, would proceed. Two groups in the city, had even gone as far as reserving the Cobo Hall for the fight to take place on 21 September 1970. It was reported that there had been no initial objection by the state governor or Michigan boxing commission, so the people behind the promotion remained hopeful that the fight would proceed without (official) objection.

So while the toing and froing continued behind the scenes for Ali, he seems to have struck up a friendship with Bugner. Twelve days after the Quarry v Foster fight on 29 June, both turned up to watch Sonny Liston's encounter with Chuck Wepner at the Old Armory in Jersey City. It was reported by *The Ring* magazine that prior to the bout Ali almost caused a mini-riot when he turned up unexpectedly, with some in the 4,012 crowd making a bee-line for the popular ex-champion. While Ali was in the centre of the storm, promoter Willie Gilzenberg gave up trying to introduce him from the ring. Fighters and ex-fighters that eventually did get a mention were Bugner, along with the man who had passed on some privileged boxing knowledge to him back at Clancy's gym, Emile Griffith. Also introduced was New Jersey ex-fighter, 'Two Ton' Tony Galento who caused a few 'storms' himself back in his fighting days, especially when in front of nearly 35,000 fans in Yankee Stadium, he knocked the then defending heavyweight champion Joe Louis on his backside back in 1939.

The Liston v Wepner bout drew a gate of $37,600, but it was here that Bugner would witness again the brutal and sometimes gruesome realities of his chosen profession. Wepner already had a reputation as a 'bleeder' and was well known for having his face stitched up after fights, but the 'bear' caused some serious damage that night, savaging the 228lb Wepner and turning his face into a crimson gory mask.

Referee Barney Felix, who had also been the third man in Liston's losing title fight against Ali/Clay back in 1964 had seen enough by round nine and stopped Wepner receiving more facial damage. According to the report in *Boxing Illustrated* (September 1970) Wepner suffered cuts over each eye and cuts to his lip and also a cut inside his mouth. It took 72 stitches to pull his ripped skin together.

Incredibly, Wepner and his corner still protested about the referee's intervention – they wanted the fight to continue. Liston, who weighed 219lbs on the night, raised his tally to 54 fights, 50 wins and 39 knockouts and he paid tribute to his opponent, saying he was the bravest man he ever fought.

Sonny was reportedly paid $13,000 for the fight and said afterwards that he wanted to fight Jerry Quarry next. His keenness may have come about after it was reported that a syndicate was willing to put up $40,000 for a Liston v Quarry bout and talked about a fight taking place in Atlantic City. Soon after, Liston's next bout was then mooted for August 8 but the opponent had changed to Oscar Bonavena and that fight was planned for Buenos Aires. That bout also sadly didn't materialize. Four months after the proposed Bonavena date, Liston was found dead in mysterious circumstances in his Las Vegas home. The different theories about Liston's end are legion. Ali, Bugner and the 4,012 paying fans who turned up at the Armory that June night had witnessed Sonny's last ever fight.

By early July 1970, Bugner had likely become well acclimatized to his temporary life and boxing tutorials in the States. One week after attending the Liston fight with Ali, Bugner was in Miami Beach, sparring a few rounds with former WBA heavyweight champion Jimmy Ellis in the 5th Street Gym. Bugner not only impressed Ellis and Angelo Dundee with his Adonis physique and eye-catching boxing skills, but also sections of the Miami press. The July 8 issue of *The Miami News* printed a story about Bugner being a future ring star and – almost inevitably – a new Great White Hope!

Bugner was asked to take part in a public charity sparring exhibition with Ali in South Carolina. This was great news for Joe; it also meant he would get to find out first-hand about the type of frustration Ali was going through. The boxing exhibition was meant to take place only one day after the Bugner story broke in *The Miami News* on Thursday 9 July 1970. Promoter Reggie Barrett had joined a long list of others who attempted to get the retired champion permission and somewhere to box again. Originally, it was hoped for Ali to spar in the 4,000-seat County Hall in Charleston, to box six exhibition rounds with KO artist Jeff Merritt from Miami. When Merritt cut his six rounds down to three, it was hoped that young Joe could be 'slotted in' to do the remaining rounds. The event was meant to raise money for a group of underprivileged children and another opportunity for Ali to finally get back through the ropes and ply his trade again, albeit in a charity exhibition.

Incredibly, the planned public workout was also said by some to be some kind of 'warm-up' for Ali, if his bout with Frazier still went ahead in Detroit in September. Well, the exhibition, 'warm-up' was definitely on, then, you guessed it, the exhibition, was off.

This time, the Charleston County Council voted to refuse the promoter permission to use the city venue. Mayor John Palmer Gaillard Jr also said he had received protests and complaints from residents who didn't want it. Probably that was why they pulled out. Then a speedway site three miles out of town was proposed as a potential venue, but talks fell through and the whole venture was cancelled, leaving the promoter and presumably the three fighters disappointed.

Of course it wasn't only the promoter who lost out but also the children who would have benefited from the proceeds. Fight fans were losers too, as they were denied the opportunity of seeing a future boxing star, Bugner, go in against Ali. A public exhibition would have impressed Bugner's buddies and fight fans back home, but sadly, it didn't happen.

Again, any hopes of Ali entering a boxing ring were dashed at the last moment. All the promising talk had come to nothing, despite there still being a 'chance' of him facing Frazier in Detroit later that year. Ali was unconvinced though, saying he was now sure no promoter could get legal permission for him to box again.

Ali always made the point that he was not the one going around America trying to get people to allow him to resume his career. It was the promoters who were constantly trying to pin down a city and venue for him to fight again. If the opportunity arose, he made it clear that he would take it and come out of retirement.

Ali returned to Philadelphia and later in July, Bugner returned to England. It was reported in *Boxing News* that Joe had sparred a total of 40 rounds with various top US fighters, including the recovering heavyweight champ, Joe Frazier. A couple of months after his US training tutorial and return to the UK, Bugner's next paid fight was against the man Sonny Liston bloodied and defeated back in June, Chuck Wepner. Promoters flew the 'Bayonne Bleeder' all the way over from New Jersey to test

Joe at the Empire Pool, Wembley on 8 September 1970. Many thought the fight with Wepner was a big step up for Joe, but promoters knew he had a sparkling ring future ahead of him, when he passed his latest test with flying colours. He stopped Wepner on facial cuts in the 3rd round and took his pro record to an impressive 29 fights and only two defeats.

5

ATLANTA COMMITS – NEARLY

Debates raged around the world as to whether Ali should be permitted to fight again. *Boxing Illustrated* even held a reader ballot – 'yes' or 'no' – if Ali should fight Joe Frazier. The same magazine and others received bundles of mail from fans around the globe, all split on their views of an Ali return.

Plans for the Ali v Frazier fight ranged from putting it on in a giant cargo plane, with 200 spectators paying $1,000 each to board and watch it, to the bout taking place in a bull ring in Tijuana, the border city in Mexico. However, the plane idea never got off the ground and the bull ring idea was all bull. The courts wouldn't allow Ali to travel the four miles across the border.

At least the Ali v Frazier fight planned for the Cobo Hall on 21 September 1970 seemed promising, for now. According to a report in *Boxing News* a contract had already been signed for the fight and the Cobo Hall had been set aside for that date. What was also promising was that the boxing commissioner of the state, Chuck Davey, had already previously defied letter and telephone protests back in 1967. This was when Ali boxed six exhibition rounds (three apiece) with heavyweights Alvin 'Blue'

Lewis and Orville Qualle's in Detroit on 15 June. Then, Ali had already been stripped by the WBA and NYSAC of his titles, immediately after refusing to be inducted into the army in April. The Detroit exhibition date was significant, as it was only days before Ali went before the Federal court in Houston, Texas, for the draft case on June 20. (After that date, the WBC along with the British Boxing Board of Control still initially continued to recognize Ali as champion.)

Now, there were two groups, one headed by a former Detroit news columnist, Edgar 'Doc' Greene and another headed by a former boxer and long-time referee in Detroit, Lou Handler. They hoped to put on an Ali v Frazier fight in the same venue as Ali's exhibition bouts back in 1967. The promising start changed drastically when Chuck Davey, after initially making positive statements about the fight proceeding, eventually told the hopeful promoters that he didn't believe a licence would be approved by the state commission. Both groups withdrew their proposals before they were even considered. Even when a group of eighteen prominent leaders in the city, ranging from the politics to law and the Church, protested and demanded the fight proceed – it still didn't happen.

It had been the same old same old in October 1969, when Ali's friends, Gene Kilroy and Major Coxson, along with the former champion himself appeared at a press conference at Philadelphia's Bellevue Stratford Hotel. Coxson waved a copy of a valid boxing licence for Ali to take part in a bout at the Jackson Coliseum in Mississippi on 15 December 1969. Entrepreneur Coxson hoped to promote the bout under the banner of 'Major Coxson Promotions Inc' and it was also hoped that it would be Joe Frazier in the opposite corner. Mississippi had an athletic commission at the time but it was still an unlikely place for heavyweight champions or ex-champions to practise their trade. So unlikely in fact, that the last time a heavyweight champion fought there in a *real* fight, was when boxing was illegal in most states, including Mississippi, in the late 19th century. John L. Sullivan, bare-chested and bare-knuckled, fought illegally on farm land in Richburg, Mississippi, on 8 July 1889 against the tough Jake Kilrain. They fought each other under the scorching heat of the Mississippi sun for 2 hours, 16 minutes and 25 seconds, until Kilrain didn't come out for the 76th round.

The illegal bare knuckle brawl brought the two fighters big dollar purses. The state governor of Mississippi, Robert Lowry, offered $1,500 for their arrest. Eventually both fighters received jail sentences for fighting illegally and the fight would go down in history as the last bare knuckle world title fight ever held. (Sullivan appealed the sentence and eventually received a $500 fine. The contest was fought under London rules, which was a combination of boxing and wrestling.)

By the 1960s, times had changed in Mississippi, but it still hadn't miraculously become the epicentre of the fight game and still wasn't a place that seemed to attract world champion Joe Frazier. Even though Joe was chomping at the bit to get Ali inside a boxing ring, when interviewed by the *Philadelphia Daily News* in October 1969 he was dubious about the whole idea of travelling down to Mississippi for the 'exhibition'.

So Joe was the first to put a damper on the hopes of 'Major Coxson Promotions'. The second came soon after when it came to light that the copy of the 'valid' boxing licence that Coxson waved around was only a 'tentative' one and it would remain tentative until the Mississippi athletic commission approved the application. The killer blow came when the commission unanimously voted to reject the application. The $70 licence that only a few days before was as valuable as gold dust, became just dust. Mississippi was added to the growing list of states in the US that refused Ali permission to box and as described, some of the proposed fight arenas were as far removed from New York's

Madison Square Garden as you could imagine. In the end, it didn't make any difference – as each and every proposal ended up being cancelled. Although it was clear many in the US wanted to see Ali back in the ring, he was still a hot potato when it came to actually putting one's name to authorization. A sporting hero Ali may have been, but his draft conviction caused not only massive controversy, but massive outside pressure to stop him ever plying his trade again. Publicly at least, Ali seemed to accept his fate either way.

The continual rejections still didn't stop promoters pursuing every avenue. One such promotional group was based in New York, called 'Sports Action Inc'. In 1970, Sports Action was a subsidiary of a company called 'Tennis Unlimited Inc' and the chairman of both companies was a 30-year-old New York Attorney, Robert Kassel. The president of both companies was Michael Malitz. Their publicity guru and coordinator, Hal Conrad, was one of the main individuals who had tried for years to get a city to stage an Ali fight, especially an Ali v Frazier fight, but all his attempts had failed. Sports Action had been involved in the television side of heavyweight boxing for years but their first closed circuit promotion was Joe Frazier's fight against Jimmy Ellis back in February.

According to some accounts, it was Hal Conrad himself who first suggested the possibility of Atlanta – why not? He and others had more or less tried every other city in the US and come up short. However, in 1970, it was Robert Kassel who made the initial call about the chances of obtaining permission for Ali to fight in the southern state capital and the fight they wanted was, of course, Ali and Frazier. Kassel already had connections in the city, meeting his first wife there and being a one-time law student in the city's Emory University. His father-in-law Harry Pett, a businessman, also lived in Atlanta. So in August, Kassel made that fateful telephone call from New York to Atlanta and spoke to his father-in-law, asking if he knew of anyone in the city who could help him get Ali permission to fight again. As an incentive, Kassel mentioned that if anyone could gain that required permission, they could be involved in what could be a potentially very profitable promotion. Kassel was flying a kite but Harry knew of one prominent person in the city who could possibly help. He was a state senator, who lived in Atlanta, Leroy Reginald Johnson.

Forty-two-year-old African American Leroy Johnson was a powerful and influential politician in the state of Georgia. He had a long list of career achievements. His effective style was to use friendship and smooth diplomacy to achieve his aims. Johnson's background was certainly impressive. He graduated from Atlanta's predominately black seat of learning, Morehouse College, studying there at the same time as Martin Luther King Jr. Johnson graduated in 1949, King graduated a year earlier. Two years after graduating, Johnson also gained a Master of Arts Degree at Atlanta University, with a Major in Political Science. At first he became a teacher until he gained a further LLB degree at North Carolina School of Law in 1957 and became an attorney. His political career took off in 1962, when he was elected state Senator for the 38th District in Fulton County. He became the first African-American to be elected to the Senate since Reconstruction and in January 1969 he was the first appointed by the Lieutenant Governor of Georgia as a Chairman of a standing committee in the state. His career resumé was certainly impressive, but just as impressive were his 'people skills' – which helped him as he climbed the ladder.

According to a November 1970 article in the *New York Times*, a short while after making the call Kassel flew down to Atlanta for a meeting with Johnson. Within a short time, it was agreed that the senator would join Kassel in the attempt get Ali a licence and a place to fight in Atlanta. A company would be set up to help make that possible. The corporation would be called 'House of Sports Inc' and Johnson would be president, Harry Pett vice-president. Another influential gentleman called Jesse Hill would be an executive consultant. In 1970, Hill was vice-president and Chief Actuary of the Atlanta Life Insurance Company and was President of the National Insurance Association. Hill, also an African-American, was a leader in the school integration program and encouraged voter registration within the black community. Like Johnson, he carried with him a long list of career achievements and was well respected in both city and community life.

Either at this point or earlier Leroy discovered that Georgia was another place that didn't have a state-controlled boxing commission, so there were no state laws governing the sport. Leroy found out that the decision of allowing boxing matches to proceed was solely down to the city chiefs. This would be the Mayor of Atlanta and board of city Alderman. The day after the meeting with Kassel, Johnson made contact with the Mayor, Sam Massell.

In Atlanta's 1969 city elections, Sam Massell became the 53rd Mayor, with his term starting in early 1970. Massell was white, but won the race with help from the black community, winning in the final runoff against Rodney Cook. Leroy Johnson did not run for Mayor in the 1969 elections but supported Massell in his bid. They had a good working relationship, so he was probably optimistic about Massell supporting his idea of an Ali fight. Johnson met with Massell and portrayed all the positives for Atlanta in allowing the fight and expressed a few of the downsides for the boxer himself if he was never allowed to resume his profession.

It's highly likely the Mayor wanted to keep his new job and would have been well aware that staging an Ali fight in the city would be controversial. Johnson's request put the Mayor in a predicament and it was reported at the time Massell wasn't keen initially, but he didn't have to be a boxing fan or Ali fan to see the potential kudos (and revenue) coming from a major international event such as an Ali v Frazier 'superfight' in the city.

In July 1970, Georgia held the second Atlanta International pop festival, despite objections from many, including state governor Lester Maddox. It attracted over 200,000 people. (The 1970 festival would be the last held.) Another sporting event that attracted thousands and big bucks took place in Augusta, about a two-and-a-half hour drive from Atlanta. Augusta was of course the annual home of the Masters.

Massell already had a firm grasp of the legalities of the draft, as he once had a working role on the draft board during the Second World War. He would have known better than most that legally, there was very little that could stop someone that had been charged for draft refusal – but was free on bail – taking part in a prize fight. Massell eventually agreed to support the idea of having Ali's return in Atlanta, but that agreement came with the promotion aiding the city in some way, by having organizers make a sizable contribution to one of the city programs.

House of Sports Inc believed the championship fight would help display Atlanta in a positive light to the rest of the US and the world and it would help show that Atlanta was indeed, what it promoted itself to be – the most progressive city in the South. Despite Ali's problems with the Government, a 'super-fight' between him and Frazier could also help Atlanta attract other international sporting events and help in the aim of becoming a major centre for big-league sporting occasions.

Next, Leroy, as President of House of Sports Inc, had a meeting with the Athletic and Building Committee of the Aldermanic Council (city aldermen). The private discussions ended in permission for an Ali v Frazier fight to proceed at the 5,000-seat Municipal auditorium in the city on 26 October 1970. On 12 August, a boxing licence was issued, valid until 11 August 1971. The $5 licence was issued by the city athletic commission.

Events were moving quickly, but Leroy Johnson wanted to win the blessing of state governor Lester Maddox. This was a mighty big ask at the time, as it was only nine months before that the governor had blocked an Ali fight in Georgia. That was back in December 1969, when another group, also from Atlanta, had tried for Ali v Frazier. Maddox had publicly declared at the time that Ali wasn't welcome, unless he 'did the right thing' and went into the army and served his country. Then, and only then, would he be welcome to fight in the state. Lester had reacted to the whole Ali/Frazier/Georgia idea with 'Phooey!' (Earlier in August 1969, there had been yet another proposal for an Ali fight. Then, the manager of the 9,000-seat coliseum in the city of Macon, Georgia, Bill Lavery, had been approached by some out-of-state promoters and asked of the chances of staging an Ali bout. The city mayor, Ronnie Thompson, and city aldermen shot it down.)

Leroy Johnson had already gone a step further than those promoters in 1969 by winning the support of the Mayor and city aldermen, but now he was going to attempt to win the blessing of state governor Lester Garfield Maddox. Although the executives of House of Sports Inc were aware that the governor couldn't legally stop them, they knew, looking at what had happened in the past, Maddox was an extremely influential person. He could turn a slam dunk into an awkward and effective full-court press.

In August 1970, Maddox's term of office as state governor was coming to an end, but it would still cover the period of a proposed Ali bout in October. At that time, Lester was campaigning for the position of lieutenant governor, as state law, at that time, disallowed him from another term as governor. Whoever won the final elections, set for early November, would begin their term in office in January 1971. Included in the early gubernatorial campaign were Democrat Jimmy Carter and white supremacist, J.B. Stoner. Although both Stoner and Maddox were great advocates for segregation, Maddox himself claimed to be no racist or extremist. In July 1970, Maddox walked off and led others away from a public political platform when Stoner was in mid-speech, expressing his pro-white, anti-black and antisemitic views. Maddox declared he would never appear alongside extremists again; but his criticism and walk off that day was not only directed at Stoner, but also at the Socialist candidate who was in the same forum.

Georgia was steeped in a history of segregation and slavery. Even going back one hundred years before the American Civil War, Georgia, one of the original thirteen British colonies, was the first to ban slavery in 1735 and then reintroduced it sixteen years later in 1751. Africans were shipped right into the port in Savannah, Georgia, to work as slaves on the plantations. Many in those southern slave states found the antebellum aims of Reconstruction hard to accept and the resistance to it helped give rise to the white supremacist movement called the Ku Klux Klan. The Klan would be born, then fade, rise and fade twice. Maddox was born on 30 September 1915, the same year that the second of three organized movements of the Klan was founded. It also happened in the very place they wanted to put on Ali's fight – Atlanta. During the 1920s, there were reputed to be almost 5 million Klan members throughout the US.

Over time, the numbers in the Klan gradually decreased, but a third Klu Klux Klan movement arose in 1946. During the 1950s and 1960s, the Klan was opposed to the civil rights movement, which meant they detested the Civil Rights Act signed by President Lyndon Johnson on 2 July 1964. From that point, discrimination based on race, sex, colour, religion or a person's national origin was unlawful. At the time, Maddox owned a whites-only eatery in Atlanta called the 'Pickrick', which had been in operation since 1947. He stated, as proprietor, it was his right to refuse entry to whoever he wanted, but that proved difficult when the new Civil Rights Act passed into law. Maddox became notorious for standing outside of his restaurant with a pickaxe handle keeping out those who he believed were 'integrationists'; African-Americans were refused entry. Inside the eatery, there was a water fountain with a sign atop reading 'Make a Wish and make a gift for segregation'.

A short while after the Civil Rights Act was signed, Maddox closed his restaurant, rather than be forced by law to change his strict segregation rules. Lester claimed the closure meant 66 people lost their jobs, of which 44 were African-American and he pinned the blame on the President, the Government and the Communists. His defiant stand attracted a huge amount of publicity and it appeared the attention certainly didn't harm his political aspirations. Although Democrat Maddox had failed on two previous occasions running for mayor, one year after standing outside his restaurant with a pickaxe handle, in 1965 he announced he would run for the 1966 Democratic Primary for the governorship of Georgia.

Maddox wasn't your average US politician, in that he didn't come from a wealthy background. He dropped out of high school in the 10th Grade, but Maddox had something unique going for him. It appeared (by the accounts I have read) Many in Georgia simply 'liked Lester' – as he had the type of personality that touched everyday people from all political persuasions. In the words of Randy Newman, 'He may be a fool but he's our fool/If they think they're better than him they're wrong...' (*Rednecks.*)

Anyway, while most of his political opponents had big budgets for political campaigns and rallies, Maddox travelled around Georgia in an old station wagon, meeting the people face-to-face and not leaving before nailing up a multitude of signs, which read 'This is Maddox Country', before moving on to the next town and doing the same.

Lester caused a big surprise when it was him that eventually walked through the doors to become state governor of Georgia.

However, his views on segregation never changed throughout his life and he had his own arcane ideas about the difference between a segregationist and a racist.

Maddox became governor after he and his Republican opponent, Howard 'Bo' Callaway, failed to gain a clear majority. The decision on who became Georgia's 75th governor was made by the state's General Assembly and they backed Democrat Maddox. He began his term in office on 11 January 1967.

Despite some people's resistance to desegregation, Atlanta still prided itself on being a living and working example of the New South, which meant it had worked hard to leave behind the pre-civil war days of an economy once based on slavery. In Atlanta the demographics of the city had changed dramatically. Back in 1920, the black, or African-American population stood at 62,796, which was about 31.2% of the total population, with registered black or African-American voters standing at roughly one in ten. By 1970, the black or African-American population had increased more than four-fold to 255,051, which represented approximately 51.3% of the total population, of which just under half were registered voters. Even though Maddox was governor of the state, Atlanta had been transformed from a place of complete white political control to a form of power sharing between black and white born of that increase in black votes.

So how was Leroy Johnson going to approach Lester Maddox for his support, or at least acquiescence? Tucked in his mind was something that may have aided his mission. In later interviews, Leroy Johnson recalled how he approached Lester with prior knowledge of a well-publicized case that involved someone in Maddox's family. (I don't want to mention his name, or his precise relationship to Maddox, as I feel it's not necessary for the purposes of this story, so let's call him Mister.)

Mister had gone before the court in June of that year charged, along with an accomplice, of attempted burglary at a garage in Fulton County. He had just completed a long probationary period for two previous burglaries that had taken place in Cobb County back in 1965. When that case came to court, in January 1966, Judge Albert Henderson, also handed out a fine. When the 1970 case came before the court, Mister was sentenced to a further five years' probation, another fine, and was required to spend a few hours each weekend in prison for the next six months. It seemed he had received a break from the judge – handed another chance to straighten his life out, when many thought a long spell in prison was going to be the likely outcome. The case was problematic for Lester Maddox, because of his close relationship with Mister. Just prior to Mister's arrest in March, Lester had announced his intention of running for lieutenant governor in the autumn elections. Adverse publicity couldn't have come at a worse time.

Leroy Johnson could see that the 'second chance' lifeline handed to Mister could be applied to Ali. The Senator knew that free enterprise zealot Lester Maddox didn't care too much for people living on state handouts. If Ali's livelihood was snatched permanently away from him, would he not one day add to the government's welfare line? These were the tools Johnson possessed to help him gain the governor's blessing.

That said, Leroy Reginald Johnson still had his work cut out. Some accounts say the meeting got off to a rocky start, with Lester saying Ali's appearance in the city would attract trouble. Leroy had to employ his full repertoire of skills and insider knowledge that day to obtain Lester's support but by the time the meeting had finished, Lester, to the surprise of many, had changed his mind. It seemed the reasons for blocking an Ali fight in 1969 were shelved or forgotten. He wouldn't oppose the fight. Amazingly, at last, all the required permissions and city agreements were finalized within one week.

House of Sports Inc would concentrate primarily on the on-site promotion and Sports Action Inc would work on the national and international closed circuit and TV outlets that the fight would attract. Now, with licence and permit secured and no objection from the city Mayor or the state governor, executives from House of Sports Inc and Sports Action Inc broke the good news to Ali and his team.

It goes without saying that initially, Ali, although maybe hopeful, approached this latest fight plan with less than 100% certainty. He had heard all the talk before and had grown tired of the constant rejections. Memories of the past fight refusals in Georgia were still clear in his mind.

There was another problem and Leroy Johnson spoke about it later in an interview in *Jet Magazine* (November 1970). He claimed that he was led to believe that if they obtained a licence for Ali, the other name on the official permit, Joe Frazier, would be committed to the fight – he wasn't. Despite that, executives from House of Sports and Sports Action still remained optimistic of pulling the championship bout off. They invited Ali to fly down from Philadelphia to Atlanta for a press conference to announce the fight in the city auditorium on 26 October, with the opponent still being Joe Frazier.

Only one day after Ali's licence was issued, on the morning of Thursday 13 August, executives from both companies turned up at the Marriott hotel to announce in a press conference that they had followed all the state laws and there was nothing stopping them bringing the eagerly anticipated Ali v Frazier bout to Atlanta. According to a report in the *Atlanta Constitution*, Leroy Johnson had met with Lester Maddox prior to the press briefing, which took place at 11 a.m. that morning. In that meeting, Leroy Johnson also expressed his gratitude to the governor for supporting the fight. Leroy stated that every man had a right to change his mind and he was happy that Lester had changed his.

Thirty minutes later, Ali entered the room and joined Johnson, Kassel and others. In the last couple of years, the former champion had trod down similar paths, with nothing actually materializing from all the talk. Maybe that's why in this press conference, despite the organizers' enthusiasm and the valid permit, Ali was reserved and said very little. When he did say something, he spoke quietly, saying that he was 'ready for this latest attempt'. House of Sports did turn up that day with a few people that added additional weight to that licence. There were a few prominent city Aldermen and Vice-Mayor, Maynard Jackson, (presumably representing the Mayor, Sam Massell) who were publicly supporting the bout – some of the very people who could have stopped it.

Leroy Johnson informed the press that the only thing that they needed now was Joe Frazier's and Ali's signatures on a contract. Robert Kassel expressed the positives for Atlanta. He said that $50,000 from the proceeds of the event would be donated to help combat the city's drug problem. Ali was keen to keep on that subject, saying that he wanted to help kids and if his fight in some way contributed to alleviating the drug problem in the city, then he was glad to be part of it.

Newshounds were still keen to ask, after such a long layoff, how Ali could realistically whip himself back into fighting shape with only two months' notice to face a merciless fighting machine like Joe Frazier. Ali tried to reassure them, saying if he trained flat out he would be ready. However, he added that he would only begin serious training after everything was finalized – meaning after the contracts were signed, with a commitment from the Frazier camp.

Afterwards, Maddox was asked about his decision and he praised and supported the ex-champion. As far as Maddox was concerned, as long as Ali's bout against Frazier was 'clean' and 'fair' – it was 'on with the show!' Ali flew back to Philadelphia knowing the promoters had managed to obtain a licence for him; but the same thing had happened in Mississippi back in 1969, when a tentative license was displayed, and in the end, that had come to nothing.

The politicking started in Atlanta almost as soon as Ali walked out of the room. The day after Maddox said he wouldn't oppose the fight, while on a TV show on Friday 14 August, he said that he had changed his mind. He claimed he hadn't been made aware of everything about Ali/Clay's draft refusal case and now said he would ask the city not to allow the fight to proceed. This sudden change of heart by Maddox was an irritation to the promoters, but they were confident it was unlikely he could achieve his goal of halting the fight by swaying city officials.

Leroy Johnson's diplomatic but firm response was to say that the fight was now a legal event and he was hoping Maddox wouldn't try to convince others (the city Aldermen) to stop a legal event taking place. Johnson was expecting both of the fighters' signatures to be on a contract immediately. He already had Ali's commitment and had sent off by registered mail to Frazier's attorney, Bruce Wright, copies of the fight permit for the city auditorium and boxing licence. Leroy hoped this was sufficient proof to Frazier's team of their sincerity and commitment to the promotion. All they wanted now was Frazier's signature. The copies of the permit and licence duly arrived at Bruce Wright's office, but it appeared Wright took more notice of Lester Maddox's objections than any papers. He said any deal struck would have to be face-to-face and not only that, he wouldn't even consider proceeding with the fight without the state governor's approval!

Wright also stated that Yank Durham was the man who ultimately decided who Frazier fought next and he wasn't in

Philly, but in Lake Tahoe in Nevada, where Joe was performing in another show with his band in one of the casinos. Yank Durham didn't believe a word coming out of Atlanta and the copies of the fight permit didn't cut much ice with him. According to Yank, Joe was now already committed to meeting Bob Foster in Detroit in November and as far as he was concerned, he would be concentrating on Joe's next real fight, the one in Detroit, not one a group of businessmen were hoping to put together in Atlanta. He wanted to see physical proof of Ali climbing inside a boxing ring and actually fighting before he would commit Joe.

Undeterred, Leroy Johnson said both he and Jesse Hill would travel to Philadelphia and meet with Frazier's legal team face-to-face to hammer out a deal. The meeting in Philly was planned to take place one week after the press announcement in Atlanta on Wednesday 19 August and Leroy announced that if everything was agreed, they would consider staging the fight at the 50,000-seat Atlanta stadium. He said the final choice of venue would be made in the coming days.

It is not known if that proposed face-to-face meeting between executives from House of Sports and Yank Durham actually took place in Philly, but maybe Yank saved them the journey. What was confirmed in the *Atlanta Constitution* on the day of the planned meeting was that Yank told Leroy by telephone that the Ali v Frazier fight in Atlanta was a non-starter, as he just didn't believe Ali would be allowed to fight in the city.

The use of the Atlanta Stadium for an Ali fight also seemed a non-starter. First, the chairman of the Athletic and Building Committee, George Cotsakis, publicly stated that there was no guarantee that the massive stadium would be approved by the aldermen for fight. And the costs of hiring the stadium would be vastly higher than for the smaller indoor venue.

Yank's telephone call to Leroy Johnson definitely ruled out using the 50,000 stadium, as it was only a fight between the two undefeated 'super-champs' that could potentially fill it.

So after Ali returned to Philly, he may have been optimistic about the fight in Atlanta, but a fight with whom? And could he really back up his talk and return to fighting form over a two month period? Up until then, Ali was thought to have kept to a regular fitness schedule, jogging and visiting various boxing gyms, but fighting competitively demanded so much more. Regarding fitness, it just so happened that it was only a few days after returning from Atlanta that he would visit somewhere that would bring his dream of one day possessing his very own training camp facility closer to reality.

In the woodlands of New Jersey, there was a summer camp called 'Kamp Olympik'. The complex was the brainchild of Ali/ Clay's USA fellow team member and gold medal winner from the 1960 Rome Olympics, Don Bragg. Don won gold in the pole vault. Don, who was raised in Penns Grove, New Jersey set up the summer camp in his home state, primarily for inner-city kids. When Ali visited the camp in mid-August 1970, it was one of his earliest visits. He liked Don's country complex so much, on more than one occasion Ali asked Don if he could purchase it, but Don was not for selling. Both Don and the kids would love it though, when Ali turned up, with the former champ sometimes donning the gloves and going a few playful rounds with the boys. The fun pit-a-pat sparring sessions weren't only confined to the boys, Don himself seldom let the opportunity pass by of going a few minutes with the 'Greatest'. The 6ft 3in former Olympians would hop and skip around each other, throwing playful punches, watched by a platoon of starry-eyed kids looking out for the Ali shuffle. Don's camp was a paradise for kids, with rope swings hanging from trees, log cabins, and streams to swim in. Don called the camp 'Tarzanville' so Ali naturally called his supremely athletic and finely muscled sparring partner Tarzan. Ali loved the woodland camp and its clean air, which probably evoked memories of him staying and working out at Archie Moore's 'Salt Mines' training camp in Ramona, California. Then, Ali/Clay was in between his first and second pro fights in the fall of 1960. Archie had rocks placed around his camp, with legendary fighters' names painted on them. Back then, Ali vowed to one day have his own camp. And he did: in 1972, work began on a log camp training facility up in the surrounding hills of Deer Lake, Pennsylvania. Giant rock boulders were placed around the complex with famous fighters' names painted on them, just like Archie's place. The original paintwork was carried out by his sign painter father, Cassius Clay Sr.

While Ali was at Don's camp in August 1970, he took an urgent phone call. His wife had gone into premature labour back in Philadelphia. The news sent Ali and a member of Don's family on a breakneck car ride from New Jersey to the Medical College of Pennsylvania back in Philly. They arrived just in time for Ali to be there for the birth of not one healthy baby girl, but two. Ali's wife, Belinda give birth to twins Jamillah and Rasheda on 21 August 1970.. Ali and Belinda now had three daughters, their first being Maryum, then two years old. Ali's son, Muhammad Ali Jr, would be born in 1972.

6

ALI AT MOREHOUSE COLLEGE

House of Sports Inc, agreed the best way to provide Frazier and Yank Durham the proof they needed was for Ali to take part in some public boxing exhibitions in the city. Obtaining Frazier's signature on a contract for the 26th was still a priority, but if it didn't happen, then the exhibitions could be followed up with a tune-up fight against a top contender on that October date. Leroy Johnson stated that executives from Sports Action Inc were in charge of deciding opponents for Ali. He said that there were a few being considered, one being the Argentinian tough guy and number one WBA heavyweight contender, Oscar Bonavena.

Presumably, by having Ali take part in various public boxing exhibitions, then taking on a world-rated fighter, this would not only convince Frazier's camp but would also make the Ali v Frazier fight a bigger attraction. If the former champion managed to topple someone of the calibre of Oscar Bonavena, then the public would clamour for more.

First though, were the exhibition bouts, which would be a test to see if a fight could proceed without protest or cancellation. Not only that, it would be a way of finding out how much 'ring rust'

Ali had accumulated. A fighter's working life is short and three years is a terribly long time for any boxer to remain inactive. Time can change everything and quickly within the boxing world, not just over years. One minute a fighter could be a top contender or champion and in a split second, the same fighter could be picking himself up from the floor with all his dreams in tatters and his ratings gone. One didn't have to look any further than Mac Foster's last fight to see evidence of that.

Although Ali was a supreme athlete, it seemed a massive risk for him to return after such a long layoff and go in immediately with champion Joe Frazier, as Joe was knocking everyone flat that climbed in the ring with him. Ali would now be venturing into a new boxing division of fresh, young talent and one that was going through dramatic changes. Mac Foster had been knocked out of title contention by Quarry and the man that flattened Sonny Liston, back in 1969, Leotis Martin, had dropped from the ratings and then boxing altogether as he was forced to retire with a detached retina. The man (Chuvalo) who beat the man (Quarry) who beat the man (Foster) had just recently fought against former 1968 Olympic heavyweight champion, George Foreman on 4 August 1970 – and Chuvalo received a shellacking.

The 10-round fight inside Madison Square Garden didn't get past the third round after Foreman unleashed his brutal long-armed power punches and stopped the Canadian. The $50,000 paycheck Chuvalo reportedly received was small compensation for his plummeting down the ratings. In the *Boxing Illustrated* list of top heavyweights for the period ending 2 August 1970, which was just two days before their fight, Chuvalo was rated 3rd, while Foreman was rated 10th. After George's demolition job in the next ratings, four weeks later, Foreman was number 6 and Chuvalo was dropped to 7th.

After Chuvalo's loss, a medical adviser to the WBA advised him that his career should now come to a close as the punishment he received was in his opinion, making him a 'medical risk'. The teak-tough Chuvalo didn't follow the advice and only eleven days later he travelled all the way to Yugoslavia and scored a knockout win over Massachusetts heavyweight Mike Bruce in two rounds in front of 5,000 fans at the Kosevo Stadium in Sarajevo. After this George went on to have a further fifteen bouts in a career that lasted another eight years. Chuvalo was indeed a brave warrior, who had 93 professional fights in a career that started way back in 1956. Unfortunately, his points loss against Ernie Terrell in 1965 for the WBA heavyweight title and his attempt at Ali's crown in 1966, which also ended in a points loss, would be his only shots at world heavyweight titles. (His losing fight against Joe Frazier in 1967 was a non-title bout as Frazier was still climbing the pro ratings in only his 17th fight.)

Foreman's stoppage win over Chuvalo boosted the former Olympian's record to 22 straight wins, which now included 19 TKO/KOs. The buzz was now about him facing the man Chuvalo beat under what some still called 'controversial circumstances', Jerry Quarry. The Big Apple loved Quarry and a potentially explosive fight with Foreman at the Garden was an exciting and lucrative opportunity for both fighters to ponder over.

So while the top heavies were being reshuffled and considering future high-profile fights, the House of Sports and Sports Action Inc were still trying. They needed Ali's first public exhibition to go ahead without controversy, without conflict. For them, this ruled out the city auditorium, as its 5,000-seat capacity and central city location meant there was more chance of protesters slipping in, with the potential of either stopping the show or making it a very uncomfortable night. The last thing they needed was adverse publicity.

Executives from House of Sports came up with a masterstroke – Ali's exhibition wouldn't take place where war veterans or other protest groups would likely show up. They decided on a small, almost secluded hall in the grounds of Martin Luther King Jr's Alma Mater – Morehouse College – where the gymnasium there could sit up to 3,000 spectators. With the agreement of Morehouse President, Hugh Gloster, the college gym hall would be the place where Ali would finally lace on the gloves in public again, since those two exhibition bouts in Detroit, way back on 15 June 1967. After all the past postponements, the organizers must still have been waiting for the hitch.

On Friday, 28 August, Robert Kassel and Mike Malitz, announced in New York that Ali would box an eight-round exhibition at Morehouse College in Atlanta on 2 September. His opponents on the night would be gym mates, Rufus Brassell and Johnny Hudgins.

Rufus's resumé was 17 fights, which began in 1963, 14 wins and 3 losses. Unfortunately, his most notable fights were his second-round loss to Jerry Quarry in March and a one-round loss to the sledgehammer fists of George Foreman. It was a powerful left hook delivered by Big George that bowled Rufus over at 2:42 into the fight, with referee Earl Keel stopping the bout after Rufus's fourth visit to the canvas, despite the first visit being ruled a slip.

Johnny Hudgins fight record up to that point was 25 fights, 13 wins, 9 losses and 3 draws. His most notable bouts were a 10-round split points decision win over KO puncher, Ted Gullick, but he lost the return bout four weeks later by knockout in the ninth round. That fight was only days before the New York press conference on 19 August. Hudgins also faced KO artist, Jeff Merritt, in March of that year, but lost by a second-round stoppage. (This was the same Jeff Merritt who was meant to box Ali alongside Joe Bugner in the cancelled exhibitions in Charleston back in July.)

It did seem Brassell and Hudgins liked facing the big hitters of the heavyweight division, with Brassell already having taken on Quarry and Foreman. Twelve days before Ali's proposed

October 26 comeback fight both were on the same fight bill. Hudgins faced the pulverizing punching of Earnie Shavers. Their fight took place in Earnie's home state of Ohio, in Canton, but the fight didn't reach past the first round after Shavers unleashed a powerful combination. On the same bill, Rufus was stopped in nine rounds by former amateur champion and undefeated pro-heavyweight at the time, Dave Mathews, also from Ohio.

Another fighter to share Ali's ring rebirth was Philadelphia-based George Hill, but he wouldn't be announced until one day before the show, with the three fighters slotted into eight rounds of exhibition boxing. The boxers chosen were meant to give Ali only a good workout; none had been picked who would take advantage of the former champion's potential ring rust.

In the words of Bob Dylan, time is a jet plane, it moves too fast. Heck, it was only just over 12 months before, in April 1969, that Ali had been giving that 40-minute lecture at the Georgia Tech, in Atlanta, informing the students that he was finished with boxing. Now, he was going back to another college in Atlanta – to box three guys in one night! Most fans in the States would get to see the 'Ali v 3-show', as ABC TV would be filming the night's action for a future transmission.

Ali stated that he only had ten days to prepare for his 'sparring night', his time limited by the new additions to his family. He worked out in Philadelphia for much of the time, running in the morning and using the 'Champs Gym' for his bag and ring work. Then, according to a report in the *Atlanta Constitution* (30 August) he arrived at the 5th Street gym in Miami on the very same day as the New York press conference on Friday 28 August to cram in more training. His sparring workouts began the next day. It was a certainly a last-minute training schedule, with sparring sessions also planned for the Sunday and Monday, before leaving for Atlanta. While in Miami, Ali completed his early morning roadwork around Miami's Bayshore Golf Course.

The 5th Street gym was the same place Ali/Clay used after Archie Moore's 'Salt Mine' training camp facility in 1960, but it was also the gym he had been occasionally using during his long layoff. Exactly one year previously, in August 1969, he spent a week there, helping his buddy, then WBA title holder Jimmy Ellis, prepare for his 27 September title defence in London against Henry Cooper. After that training week in 1969, *The Palm Beach Post* had reported Ali had left for Atlanta on Thursday 28 August to check out potential sites for the growing chain of his franchised 'Champburger' restaurants. Now, one year to the very day of flying to Atlanta, Ali was back in the same Miami gym working out, but this time preparing for his own fight, albeit an exhibition. As in 1969, on completion, the plan was to fly once again to Atlanta, but this time, the flights ending wouldn't be for 'Champburgers', but for a champion's return. Hopefully his workouts with Ellis in August 1969 weren't an omen, as the Ellis v Cooper bout ended up being cancelled.

Ali carried out his final gym workouts in the afternoon, with fans crammed in every pocket of space to watch him punch both bags and sparring partners. Sometimes there was as many as a hundred people passing through the doors of the tiny sweat box gym.

During Ali's few days in Miami, Angelo Dundee reeled off the names of various sparring partners who would help him complete his last-minute preparations and his main sparring partners were two of the boxers marked for the exhibition bouts in Atlanta the following week, Brassell and Hudgins. During one sparring session with Hudgins, Ali stood against the ropes and allowed Hudgins to blast away at his torso with clenched and hefty sparring mitts. As each punch sank into the former champion's midriff, Ali's eyes widened and he said loudly, so everyone in the gym could hear the joke, that for a split second he thought he was fighting Joe Frazier.

It was also during his time in Miami that Jerry Quarry was first mentioned by Ali publicly as a possible opponent for that date in October in Atlanta. Quarry was already set to fight Stanford Harris in Miami Beach on 8 September and there was press talk of him then facing Ted Gullick on 24 September in Cleveland. For whatever reason, that date was changed to 22 October. Ali claimed that fight wasn't going ahead, which would leave him free to face Quarry on 26 October. Nothing was certain at that point though. In an article in the *Fort Lauderdale News,* Ali was quoted as saying that George Foreman could be brought in to be his first comeback opponent! Already on the list of course, was Oscar Bonavena.

Ali arrived in Atlanta one day before the exhibition on the morning of Tuesday 1 September and took part in a press conference inside the city airport. Before he turned up, Ali had already been given the news that he had another opponent to face besides the three boxers. Before Ali left Miami, Murry Woroner announced that he had filed a $5,000 lawsuit against Ali in Florida for comments he made on a TV show back in May, which Woroner claimed were slanderous.

On the day of the press conference, Ali looked unperturbed by it all as he sat alongside Leroy Johnson, who maintained the Frazier fight was still a priority and remained a possibility. Ali was asked if his limited workouts in Miami Beach and Philly were enough to get him through the eight rounds planned for the following evening. He answered quietly, saying he was keen to find out himself, but he remained adamant that he wasn't going to go into serious training until a fight with Frazier or anyone else was 100% certain for the October date.

Ali's very first step into the ring in Atlanta would take place on the anniversary of the ending of the historic Battle of Atlanta, when General Sherman and his Yankee army overcame the resistance of Confederate troops and took over the city on

2 September 1864. Two years previously, Morehouse College held the final funeral service of Atlanta-born Martin Luther King Jr. On 4 April 1968, King had been assassinated on the balcony of the Lorraine motel in Memphis, Tennessee. His body was eventually returned to his birthplace and a service was held for him at the Ebenezer Baptist Church. The funeral service was attended by many leaders from the political and religious communities and the sporting world, with famous names in boxing turning up including two former heavyweight champions – Floyd Patterson and Muhammad Ali. One man who didn't attend was state governor Lester G. Maddox. After the service, a wood-panelled antique farm wagon pulled by two mules took King's casket four miles through the streets of Atlanta to Morehouse College accompanied by an estimated 200,000 people. Once there, an outside service took place in front of Harkness Hall.

So it would be at the spiritual home of the renowned civil rights leader and on the anniversary of the ending of that historic battle that Ali's career would finally rise from the ashes.

On the evening when Ali turned up at the college gym, he was surprisingly only about 9lbs heavier than his last paid encounter against Zora Folley, 42 months before. Ali claimed it was the roadwork that had melted much of the excess poundage away. Exhibition boxing was nowhere like a real fight, but the former champion was still in for a good workout and the estimated crowd of between 2,200 and 2,700 who managed to get into the college gym were in for a treat.

Ali had agreed to do eight rounds, after Angelo Dundee had been overruled as he thought six rounds was more than enough for his first semi-combative encounter in public for over three years. Dundee knew the audience was crammed with Ali fans who had come to see something special. Brassell and Hudgins would go two rounds apiece, while Hill would pitch in with the remaining four. All the boxers except Ali would wear protective headgear.

In Ali's locker room just before the planned 8 p.m. start, it was almost like the old days, as a string of well-wishers popped in. One visitor was Lincoln Perry, better known as Stepin Fetchit, the comedian and actor. The mood certainly would have been lightened by Perry, as he cracked jokes with the ex-champ. Perry was once part of the Ali entourage in 1965 and claimed to have taught Ali the famous ' phantom punch' that downed Sonny Liston in the first round in their return encounter at Lewiston, Maine in May 1965.

Ali received a rapturous welcome as he walked through the small hall that was reported to be touching a staggering 100 degrees. When he slipped through the ropes, the crowd began to settle down, but they were soon back on their feet when Ali was formally introduced. For them, he was still the champ. The sound of *Ah-lee, Ah-lee, Ah-lee* pierced through the sticky evening air. Rufus Brassell was gloved up and ready, the corner men had left the ring, the TV cameras were rolling and with not one protester in sight, the sound of the bell signalled Ali's return.

It was if he had never been away, as Ali immediately adopted his old familiar style of circling to the left, while snapping out his snake-like left jab. For the first two rounds, it was more of the same, as he waltzed through the initial minutes. It was much the same when he went the next two with Johnny Hudgins, with Ali gliding, sliding and jabbing, while his opponent shuffled forward, trying to land some testing shots. The crowd enjoyed it when their 28-year-old hero slotted in a touch of showboating, while still keeping up the pace. Ali wanted to impress; it wasn't just those in the baking gym that would get to see his performance, but soon a nationwide TV audience that would surely include Joe Frazier.

It was during the final four rounds with the fresh George Hill that the first signs of fatigue appeared to creep in. By the sixth round in total, he became more flat-footed and not so keen to persevere with his 'twinkle-toed' routine. Some in the crowd even became restless as they expected to see Ali in razor-sharp form. At one point, Ali appeared almost 'gun shy' or at least arm-weary as he was caught with a few stinging shots near the ropes. The ex-champion blocked the big ones that came his way, but his fans didn't turn up to see a static Ali, they came to see him turn on that old Ali magic. The punches continued to pour in from Hill, making some in the audience fall silent.

Bundini shouted words of encouragement from the corner and Ali must have heard them, as all of a sudden the exhaustion fell away. Bundini's words were like turning on a light switch, as a blistering combination of punches from Ali landed to both body and head of Hill, which knocked him back on his heels. The sudden change in tempo brought the crowd back up off their seats, as they urged their re-energized hero on to maybe provide a spectacular ending to the evening's exhibition; but Ali wasn't there to knock anyone out. He had come for a workout, not a toe-to-toe slugging match and eased off to stop that round quite possibly becoming the last.

In the eighth and final round, although Ali was now seen to be more than a touch tired, he went out and put the finishing touches to the night's performance. For some in the crowd, they still craved some kind of sign-off and they got one, when the ex-champion performed his famed shuffle. Ali's unique, flashing movements in his white ring boots made it appear both feet were swishing inches above the canvas and for a few split seconds, he seemed to be in flight. The fans loved it. They all came for a show, and they got one when he performed his signature manoeuvre three times in as many minutes.

At the final bell, the crowd gave Ali a standing ovation. When the ring announcer finally broke through the applause, it was not to tell them Ali was the winner of all eight rounds, but to pose a question: 'Is Muhammad Ali still the champ?' The walls of the gym vibrated as his excited followers shouted back, 'YES!'

Beads of sweat had formed around Ali's face and torso, much of it dripping into small puddles on the canvas. The stifling heat, exacerbated by the lights in the hall and of course the strenuous 24 minutes of boxing had left Ali looking done in. He was flanked by a jubilant Angelo Dundee and Bundini Brown, with Leroy Johnson climbing into the ring and joining the happy trio. Somehow, the Senator still managed to keep a necktie in place and blue jacket on that night, despite the brain-frying temperature.

Ali admitted to being slightly out of breath and tired near the end, but said that over the eight rounds, he had been mostly active, constantly moving and punching. He claimed he didn't get caught with any clean shots, despite being forced on the defensive a couple of times. Ali was happy with his performance but Angelo Dundee was more enthusiastic, saying it looked like his fighter still retained much of his timing and reflexes. He described his fighter's performance as 'remarkable' and 'beautiful'. Angelo believed Ali still possessed sufficient physical tools and motivation for the October date. The 'bricks are still in place' said Angelo.

All three exhibition opponents added their own positive appraisal of the former champ. Brassell said Ali with more conditioning would be ready for Frazier, while Hudgins commented on Ali's speed, which made him difficult to pin down. Ali's final opponent, George Hill, said that the 'shuffle' was enough to distract him, but didn't believe Ali had been weary or tired during their four rounds. It was all part of the show, said Hill.

There were no reported protests for the whole duration, either in or outside the college hall. This must have put the promoters in the same jubilant mood as Dundee and Bundini. Leroy Johnson was now more than satisfied he had the proof Frazier's manager/trainer Yank Durham had demanded. The boxing licence they now had was valid until 11 August 1971, so Johnson was still optimistic of pulling off the Ali v Frazier 'superbout' for the city.

After the tiring workout, Ali stated that at that precise point, he wasn't ready for *any* top fighters, never mind Joe Frazier. However, he did say that if the Frazier fight did go ahead on October 26 two months should be enough to get in fighting trim.

One day after the exhibition, Leroy Johnson flew to Philadelphia with his 'proof' for Yank Durham. It was a wasted trip. Yank Durham said no. He said Frazier wouldn't even be in fighting condition by that date, and as he had previously stated, Frazier had already agreed to defend his title against the world light-heavyweight champion, Bob Foster, in November in Detroit.

But it was Ali who hadn't fought in over three years, not Joe. During the period of Ali's inactivity, Joe had taken part in eleven bouts, won them all and out of eleven of those fights, nine wins came by the short route and six had been title bouts. In hindsight, it may have been a great option for Yank to accept that October date and postpone the Bob Foster bout, as it possibly could have been a step too far for Ali. It was probably too early for a basically retired Ali to tackle Frazier. 'Smoking' Joe, despite having had a few months out himself with his singing tour and recovering from an ankle injury, was still the young Mike Tyson of his era. Facing him in anything less than top physical and mental condition could have been a costly mistake.

If Leroy Johnson had been in this position 12 months ago, it wouldn't have been too unrealistic for Ali to of taken on Frazier, but that extra year made all the difference. As we all know, the Frazier v Ali 'Fight of the Century' was for the future, but the replacements for Ali's October 26 bout that promoters pondered over were not exactly pushovers.

The favourite was the guy Ali thought would be his first comeback opponent anyway, Jerry Quarry. The same fighter that had just blasted his way to the number one spot in *The Ring* magazine ratings by crushing Mac 'KO' Foster in June: the 'Bellflower Belter', or 'Irish' Jerry Quarry – a new 'Great White Hope'.

The other proposed opponent for Ali was Oscar Bonavena, the WBA number one contender. According to a 31 March 1967 *Boxing News* article, the Argentinian was seen as being Ali's next title defence after Zora Folley. Previous to the Folley fight a contract had been tentatively signed by Ali's manager, Herbert Muhammad and a Japanese promoter on 24 February 1967. The signing was for Bonavena to tackle Ali for the title on 27 May in Tokyo, but the fight never materialized after Ali refused induction into the armed forces that April. All bets were off in an instant.

In June 1967, Ali was found guilty of refusing the military draft, fined $10,000 and handed a five-year prison sentence. However, lawyers appealed the decision and as we know, he was free on bail while his case moved through the various courts. The WBC still recognized Ali as champ until 11 March 1969, when the title was declared vacant.

Both fighters of course had one massive advantage: regular competition. While Ali remained on the sidelines. Bonavena had taken part in an impressive 23 fights during the period, his last being a KO win over the respected James J. Woody on 4 July 1970. Four years previously, in 1966, Oscar had given one-year pro Joe Frazier a huge scare, knocking him down down twice in the second round, but Joe got up and battled back and went on to score a 10-round points decision win. The pair fought again two years later in 1968 and Joe picked up a repeat points win, but over 15 rounds in defence of Joe's NYSAC world title.

Oscar's only other losses during that period was another points defeat, to Jimmy Ellis, that took place in Louisville, Kentucky, in a bout that was part of the eight-man elimination tournament to find Ali's successor; and a disqualification defeat to Miguel Angel Paez in January 1970. Out of his 19 winning fights during Ali's inactive years, 15 came by way of knockout or stoppage, with the tough and skilful Gregorio Peralta holding Oscar to a 10-round draw in 1969. His career record up to that point was 52 fights, with 45 wins.

Inactivity was something we already know 25-year-old Jerry Quarry didn't suffer. One week after Ali's exhibitions and only three months after his demolition job on Mac Foster, Jerry was preparing to fight Jamaican Stanford Harris in a 10-rounder set for 8 September 1970. In Ali's inactive years, between his last title fight on the 22/03/1967 to his exhibition bouts on 2 September 1970, Quarry had completed a highly respectable 18 professional contests and took part in 125 rounds of active fighting. Stanford Harris would increase his active round tally to a possible 135 rounds, that is, if the fight went the full route. It didn't – the total was 131 as the fight ended in the 6th. Quarry had trained two months solid for the Harris fight at Gilman Hot Springs in California with his younger brother Mike being one his main sparring partners.

Stanford came to the bout without a high ranking but confident he could pull off a win, saying he had a similar ring style to the man who beat Jerry the previous year, Joe Frazier. Just like the 'Smoke', he was on the short side for a heavyweight, standing only 5ft 9in tall, but he weighed 233lbs and he also had the prized asset of Angelo Dundee working his corner.

The Quarry v Harris fight was set to take place in Miami and the final preparations of both fighters took place in Chris Dundee's Miami 5th Street gym. Stanford used the fight factory's facilities at noon, while Quarry began his training sessions a short while later, usually around 1.30 p.m.

With confidence likely soaring after his win over Foster, Jerry turned up weighing 7lb heavier than that fight, coming to the scales at 203lbs. He was back in the same place he flattened Rufus Brassell earlier in the year, the Miami Beach Auditorium. This was the same venue in which a young Cassius Clay shocked the world by defeating Sonny Liston back in February 1964. Even though the bout was only meant as a welcome paid workout for the boy riding on top of the heavyweight contenders, Jerry's fans still returned home happy, as their favourite fighter was seen in sharp form.

In front of 3,112 spectators, Quarry was too quick and punched too hard for Stanford and apart from catching an occasional left hook, once the 'Bellflower Belter' found his range and unleashed his trademark punches – sharp, fast and brutally hard combination punches to the body, especially the left hook – an early shower was on the cards for Harris. In the sixth round referee Dick Tobin had seen enough and the fight was stopped at 1:14.

Later in a *Jet Magazine* (19 November) interview, Leroy Johnson explained how he, along with Jesse Hill and an excecutive from Sports Action Inc, had travelled to Miami in an attempt to sign Quarry up as Ali's October opponent. When they arrived, they found that a rival promoter had already tried to move a potential Ali v Quarry fight away from Atlanta to Miami. According to the interview, Quarry's father Jack favoured a possible Ali fight in Miami, but of course the word possible became impossible when it came to official permission to set it up.

After the Harris fight, there was other offers on the table for Quarry. According to the *Fort Lauderdale News*, one of them was again from Madison Square Garden, who still wanted to match him in that blockbuster with George Foreman. Jerry was certainly in high demand, but the Ali v Quarry fight in Atlanta was finally sealed when a huge financial guarantee and an ancillary percentage was offered to him. Later, Quarry would say it only took seconds for him to accept the terms.

When the news of the Quarry v Harris fight hit the news stands the following day on Wednesday 9 September, Robert Kassel and Mike Malitz announced in New York that Quarry's next fight would be against Muhammad Ali. The official signing would take place in the city the following day.

7

ALI AND QUARRY SIGN

The financial package that Quarry accepted would be his biggest pay day up to that point; but his fight against Ali would also provide him with his biggest challenge. After the Harris bout, there wasn't much time to rest, as he and his camp were off to New York for the press conference to formally sign contracts and officially announce the Ali fight.

In the short period leading up to the Manhattan signing, Ali had been spotted working out inside Champs Gym in north Philly. He would roll up in his Cadillac. The heavy boots that he wore during early morning runs and sometimes throughout the day to strengthen his legs were set aside. He would change into his work-out togs, sometimes this included pulling on a rubber vest to work up a mighty sweat pounding the heavy and light punching bags. Stomach crunching exercises followed, with his exercise routine taking approximately 60 minutes. In down time, apart from spending it with his family in their splendid Overbrook home, Ali could be spotted out and about on the city streets shooting the breeze with fans.

In the same week as the New York fight announcement, the *Philadelphia Daily News* published a story with a photo of Ali at Don Bragg's woodland camp in south Jersey, saying that he was there days before the press conference, meeting the kids again and taking in the fresh country air. As on his previous visits, it wasn't too long before he was playfully sparring with Don and any kids that volunteered to go a few minutes with him. On that occasion, Don was stripped down to a pair of tartan shorts, while Ali was minus his dress shirt as they squared up. The picture on the sports page of the *Philadelphia Daily News* of the two former Olympic champions must have been tremendous publicity for Don's Kamp Olympik, as it came out on the same day as news reached all corners of the globe of the official signing of the ring return of Ali. That signing actually took place a day earlier on Thursday, 10 September 1970, when the two fighters met at the Hotel Berkshire in midtown Manhattan in the Berkshire room of the hotel, which was crammed with TV cameras and lights, along with a platoon of media people, all competing with each other to obtain the best positions for their questions, photographs and films. There had been a temporary barrier set up to separate the fighters from the newshounds, but it didn't take long before both they and anyone else that had turned up started to scramble through it to grab a better vantage point.

Quarry sat at the podium looking more like a movie star than a fighter, dressed in a casual open-necked black-and-white striped shirt and black waistcoat. Much had changed for Jerry since the days he was paid a few bucks an hour fitting tyres on Greyhound buses.

Ali, on the other hand, who sat alongside Jerry on the podium, looked like a business executive, neatly attired in an expensive-looking mohair tailored suit.

The public announcement was made, Muhammad Ali would meet Jerry Quarry on 26 October at the Municipal Auditorium in Atlanta. The former heavyweight champion would receive $200,000 against 42.5% of net income, while Jerry Quarry, would earn a purse of $150,000 against 22.5% of net income from the worldwide CCTV sales. According to a report in the *Atlanta Constitution,* both fighters would also receive an additional $10,000 for training expenses. The company Tennis Unlimited Inc would underwrite the event (Sports Action Inc was a subsidiary of Tennis Unlimited Inc) and Sports Action Inc would partner with House of Sports Inc on the promotion. President Michael Malitz of Sports Action predicted a $5 million worldwide closed circuit take on the October event.

Senator/promoter Leroy Johnson sat between the fighters on the podium, with the questions from the press coming faster than Ali's jabs. Ali answered quietly, so much so that his voice was sometimes barely audible above the surrounding din. His quiet demeanour seemed to surprise many, but Bundini Brown, who was also present at the signing, said his voice was quieter because Ali pondered over each and every question before he answered.

The forest of microphones picked up Ali saying that the October fight should be for the world heavyweight title, as far he was concerned, as he was still champion, demoting the official champion, Joe Frazier to a 'good contender'. He also claimed that Quarry was a better fighter than Frazier, even though Joe had already defeated Jerry – albeit on an eye injury.

Ali also went on to inform everyone again that it was the promoters, and not he, who were trying to get a fight organized. But the recent permission obtained in Georgia was a victory for justice. Although Ali was in a sombre mood that morning, he still cracked a few jokes in the room; he mentioned age was definitely catching up with him, as his grey hairs had increased from one to six during his layoff.

Many simply asked if the fight would actually take place. Leroy Johnson tried to reassure everyone. Jerry Quarry backed up Johnson's words, when he said that all the previous rumours of Ali fighting again had been all talk, but he now believed 'for sure' the fight would go ahead. The confidence was pretty much confined to those sitting on the podium that day, as many others still felt the fight wouldn't take place. One person who didn't share the fighters' and promoters' optimism was the manager of Joe Frazier, Yank Durham. Durham went public about what he thought of the Ali v Quarry fight actually taking place in October. Durham said he was so sure the fight wouldn't happen he had even placed a bet on it not taking place. The exhibitions that Ali took part in eight days previously cut no ice with Durham either, as he said they meant nothing compared to pulling off a real fight in a large public venue. Yank claimed he hoped he was wrong and was more than keen to lose his money, but he added he didn't even think Ali could realistically regain his past form. According to Durham, he had seen Ali working out recently in a boxing gym and was unconvinced he could get back into fighting shape by the October date. However, if the fight did come off and Ali still had a licence, or permission to fight, he was more than keen to get Frazier and Ali together.

During the press signing, Jerry mainly listened as Ali spoke, but the sun-tanned Californian exuded confidence. He had good reason; apart from the fabulous purse he was signing up for, he would also be the first fighter the former champion would face in his entire professional career who was actually younger than himself. Jerry was a touch over three years Ali's junior. On top of that, his regular ring activity could give him a decided edge, especially if Jerry dragged the fight into the later rounds, where stamina had a knack of making any superior boxing skills obsolete. While Ali had lived the life of a roaming city college lecturer who slotted some boxing training in between talks, Quarry had been living his life as a full-time professional fighter. The training regime required for any top boxer, or any top athlete for that matter, to remain at the premium level was intense, to say the least. Competitive, regular fighting also meant a boxer being conditioned not only to handing out punishment, but also receiving it. Quarry was certainly battle-hardened, while Ali was not.

There was no doubt the ex-champion was still in pretty good physical shape – yes, he was in brilliant physical condition for a retired fighter or a college lecturer, but to come straight back and face the world's top-rated fighter was still a massive ask. Most fighters returning from a long layoff would take a few fights against moderate opposition before fighting a top contender or champion. Jerry said that with regard to the time-frame Ali had been given and his inactivity, it was doubtful he himself would attempt such a thing. Ali of course still had that court case lingering in the background, so time wasn't something the promoters or Ali himself thought they had plenty of.

The bout was set to be over the championship distance of 15 rounds, so although the fight couldn't be for the official world title, it was as close as you could get. After all, Ali was the man that beat the man (Liston) that beat the man (Patterson), so he had a good reason to believe and tell everyone that he was still champion. Quarry said that he would view himself as world champ if he beat Ali.

The extended 15-round championship route chosen for Ali's comeback was thought by most to be a definite advantage for Quarry, even though the only time he had actually travelled that distance was in losing to Jimmy Ellis two years earlier. Surprisingly, Ali had only travelled the 15-round distance twice himself, when he beat George Chuvalo in 1966 and Ernie Terrell in 1967.

Ali said he scaled about 225lbs, which meant he would have to shed some poundage before the October fight date. He also claimed his training in the run-up to the fight would have at least five interruptions, saying he had other outside commitments that he had to honor. The weight loss and interruptions were something even Ali said would give Jerry a physical advantage, Ali was correct in saying that it had only been two days ago that Jerry fought in a *real* fight and was probably ready to go another ten or fifteen rounds that night.

Quarry would be the first white American boxer the former champion would face (excluding the computer 'fight' with Rocky Marciano) since way back in April 1962. That was when Clay/Ali fought tough journeyman George Logan from Boise, Idaho, inside the Los Angeles Sports Arena in a one-sided fight. The bout was stopped by referee Lee Grossman in 1:34 of the fourth round and took the then 196½lb Ali/Clay's record to thirteen straight wins.

What didn't seem to get much press attention that morning at the press conference was that on the same day of Ali's Morehouse exhibitions on Wednesday 2 September, Quarry had filed a lawsuit for breach of contract and damages against his former manager Johnny Flores. A few weeks earlier, Jerry had received a $1,000 fine from the California State Athletic commission for going ahead with his bout against Foster in New York and he blamed Flores for the contract mix-up.

Reporters present didn't seem too interested in Jerry Quarry's woes outside of the ring though. It was Ali who received most of the attention, some asking why he even wanted to fight again. One reporter pointed ou that it was only a few months before that Ali had said he never wanted to fight again. Why was he wanting to do so now? Ali replied that some men who had committed dreadful crimes in America could still earn a living while free on bail, so why shouldn't he be allowed to earn a living while his case went through the courts? Ali's point was valid enough, but boxing history indicated that a successful return was unlikely.

After the contracts were signed, House of Sports Inc still remained optimistic about the Frazier-Ali fight eventually taking place in Atlanta, but now the month of December was mentioned; that was of course, if both Ali and Frazier won their next bouts. Something else happened soon after the signing that could ultimately put a spanner in the works for those Atlanta hopes.

On the week after the Ali v Quarry press conference, Federal Judge Walter. R. Mansfield listened to Ali's lawyer Michael Meltsner argue the case that the ex-champion had been a victim of discrimination by the actions of the NYSAC in refusing to renew Ali's boxing licence. Meltsner reeled off a list of names of people that had either federal or military convictions against them but were still licensed to box in New York, while Ali had been refused. In the Commission's defence, they argued that Ali hadn't yet served his sentence, while others had done so before being licensed. The Judge came down on the side of the ex-champion, saying, among other things, that refusing Ali a licence was 'without merit'.

After the case, Ali's lawyer said they would be looking for Ali to fight in New York as soon as possible. This must have been some welcome news not only for Ali, but also for the Frazier camp, who could see Joe's meeting with the former champion moving ever closer. That decision though, did not mean Ali was immediately licensed to box in New York, as the commission still had a right of appeal. If for some reason they didn't proceed with an appeal and were to abide by the Judge's decision, Ali would still have to go through the formalities of reapplying for a licence and turn up for a medical, etc. One can only speculate on how House of Sports received that news – it was likely bitter-sweet as they were hoping to put the Frazier fight on themselves in Atlanta, not lose it to promoters in New York.

8

QUARRY: A CAREER RESUMÉ

The fight between Quarry and Ali was signed, sealed and ready to go. So who was Jerry Quarry, why was he so popular with fans and how did he compare with his October opponent?

We already know that he was propelled to *The Ring* magazine's number one heavyweight spot by virtue of his impressive defeat of Mac Foster. In the WBC ratings at the end of August 1970, Quarry was rated number two contender, while in the WBA ratings Jerry was placed at number three. Oscar Bonavena was rated top contender by both.

Jerry was first introduced to to the noble art at three years of age after his pop laced a pair of kiddies boxing gloves on him and both he and his brother, Jimmy, one year older, received 'lessons' from father Jack in the backyard. In a 1969 article in the *Arizona Daily Star,* Jerry's father was quoted as saying that one of the reasons he taught his sons the rudiments of boxing, was that boxing was the one knowledge that he could pass onto to them. Those boyhood battles in the backyard continued under the watchful eye of father Jack until in 1955 Jerry first walked into a makeshift boxing facility in Pacoima, California, one of the oldest neighbourhoods in the northern San Fernando Valley region of LA. He was 10 years old.

The gym was run by youth worker, boxing enthusiast and future pro co-manager Johnny Flores. It was here that Jerry's amateur competitions began and even as a kid he showed exceptional talent, winning the yearly Junior Golden Gloves title every year from the age of 10 to 13. When he was still a teenager and two months before professional world champ Muhammad Ali flattened Sonny Liston in 2 minutes, 12 seconds of the first round in May 1965, Jerry Quarry won the National Golden Gloves senior Heavyweight Amateur title in impressive circumstances.

The 38th national Golden Gloves tournament was held in the Kansas City Municipal Auditorium in March 1965 and Jerry was faced with the prospect of fighting five opponents over a four-day period to get his hands on the title. Almost every opponent outweighed and looked down on the six-foot, 185lb Quarry – but he caused one smashing upset after another, knocking out every man that was put in front of him. His first opponent went out in the first round, his second went out in the second and his third opponent went out in the third. Jerry spoilt the symmetry with his final two opponents, both were flattened in the second. According to a news report in *The Los Angeles Times* (6/04/1965), both suffered broken jaws, with his semi-final 6ft 6in opponent, out long after the 10-second count. (Some accounts say it was only his opponent in the final that suffered a jaw fracture.)

Quarry hit the sporting headlines around the country and took home the prestigious heavyweight title, and the five straight knockouts set a record for the tournament. Jerry also won a special award for being the most outstanding fighter of the whole competition. His knack of knocking out 'giants', and looking dazzlingly impressive while doing it, won him fans and attention country-wide. According to a 1965 report in the *The Manhattan*

Mercury (Manhattan, Kansas, 21 March), Jerry took part in 125 amateur bouts, with 112 wins, 7 defeats and 6 draws.

So going by some reports, Jerry had more amateur bouts than Ali/Clay, whose own amateur career ended in 1960, with a record of 108 fights, with 7 losses. The main difference between the fighters during their amateur days is of course that Clay/Ali won a gold medal in the 1960 Rome Olympics as well as a string of other amateur boxing honours, including national AAU and Golden Gloves championships.

Quarry became the national Golden Gloves heavyweight champion five years after Ali/Clay won the same title in the same weight category back in 1960. When Quarry won that amateur title, Ali was already the heavyweight champion of the world.

Before those 1965 amateur championships took place and just prior to when Floyd Patterson fought George Chuvalo on 1 February 1965, Ali talked publicly about the need for a 'Great White Hope' among the heavyweights to generate more worldwide interest (and more dollars) in the fight game, as black fighters were dominating the division.

In an interview in the *Lubbock Avalanche-Journal* (Lubbock, Texas, 20 January 1965), prior to the Floyd Patterson v George Chuvalo bout Ali said he wanted Canadian Chuvalo to win, so when he fought him, he would have a white challenger who could up the take.

The fight took place in Madison Square Garden in New York. Two weeks before the bout and on the same day Ali dipped his bus into a ditch, Ali turned up at Chuvalo's training camp in Monticello, New York, with two empty buckets and a mop. He wasn't planning on doing any cleaning himself, he presented them to George and called him a 'washerwoman', in reference to his arm-swinging fighting style. On top of the 'washerwoman' title, Ali also stated that he hoped the Canadian, Chuvalo, would knock out the 'rabbit' (Floyd Patterson) in their upcoming bout.

As it turned out, Ali's greatest challenges and greatest purses came in bouts with black fighters, not white; his epic encounters in the 1970s against Frazier, Foreman and Norton.

In the Patterson v Chuvalo bout, Ali's hopes were dashed after the Canadian lost on points; but only one month after the Patterson v Chuvalo contest, Jerry went on his 'knockout spree' in the national amateur competition and many believed that he was the man that Ali had been hoping for. A white heavyweight with knockout power such as Dempsey or Marciano was a rarity, but smelling salts, broken jaws and hospital reports from Kansas City were enough proof for many that Jerry had the punching power, style and natural ability that would take him all the way to the top.

Not long after Jerry's spectacular success in the Golden Gloves, it was planned for him to continue his mayhem against other bigger men, but this time in the pro ranks. Jerry's Hollywood looks, steel-hard body and down-to-earth persona did him no harm in the popularity stakes as he embarked on a punch-for-pay career.

Jerry's original boxing mentors were father Jack, Johnny Flores and his brother, Jimmy, who followed him in his quest for fame, glory and riches. They guided the promising young fighter, who would reach 20 only days after having his first professional bout on 7 May 1965. In a touch over the same period of Ali's two title victories over the 'bear' (Liston) and the 'rabbit' (Floyd Patterson) Jerry took part in 13 fights, with 7 of those ending up by KO or TKO. The majority of those fights happened in the Olympic Auditorium in Los Angeles, with 14 fights in his first year as a pro. The first hiccup came along in his 13th bout, when he drew with fellow heavyweight prospect Tony Doyle. According to the fight report in *The Ogden Standard – Examiner* (Utah) Jerry entered the bout as 10-7 favourite. In the 4th round, Quarry floored his 6ft 4in opponent, but Doyle from Salt Lake City, Utah, battled back, cutting Jerry's right eye in the eighth round and bloodied his nose to gain a well-deserved draw over 10 fast-paced rounds. Afterwards, both fighters said they wanted a return fight and their wish would be granted; they would get to fight each other on two more occasions, in 1971 and 1973.

There would be other draws along the way. The following year, Jerry would be involved in two more and both to the same guy, Tony Alongi. Their first 10-round draw was held at Madison Square Garden, while the second was in the Sports Arena in Los Angeles.

Their second match was followed two months later by a points loss for Jerry to master ring tactician Eddie Machen. After that defeat, some fans and 'boxing experts' changed their opinions and wrote off the chances of Jerry winning the ultimate prize in boxing, but the drawn contests and one loss were great learning experiences for the youngster. By the time of the Machen loss in 1966, Jerry had only recently turned 21 and the slight blemishes on his record would have been thought by those really in the know as only minor setbacks. By the end of that year, which was only his second in the paid ranks, Jerry had taken part in 24 fights, with 20 wins, one loss and three drawn contests. The future still looked promising and 1967 was the time that the competition was stepped up for the hard punching Californian. That year, Quarry took on former world champion Floyd Patterson on 9 June 1967 and that fight also ended up as a draw over 10 rounds, with both fighters hitting the canvas during their torrid encounter. The exciting fight was watched by 20,000 inside the Memorial Coliseum in Los Angeles. This was the year that Ali was forced out of boxing and an elimination tournament began with the WBA to find his successor.

The eight-man series would be screened by the *Wide World of Sports*. Quarry was entered into the competition with Oscar Bonavena, Floyd Patterson, Jimmy Ellis, Thad Spencer, Ernie

Terrell, Leotis Martin and Karl Mildenberger. The two omissions from that group were former champion Sonny Liston and Joe Frazier, but the 'Smoke' would eventually fight the overall winner.

By the end of 1967, Leotis Martin, Karl Mildenberger, Oscar Bonavena and Ernie Terrell had all been eliminated. Floyd Patterson also joined them after an October 1967 return fight with Jerry. The Quarry v Patterson II bout, drew a gate of $78,000 and was another exciting encounter with Floyd hitting the canvas in the second and fourth rounds of a still closely fought 12-round fight. Jerry won by a majority points decision, which took him into the semi-final stage of the competition, which, for him, would begin early in 1968.

His 1967 fight total was six fights, (five wins and one draw) stopping or knocking out three of those opponents, Al Jones, Alex Miteff and Billy Daniels. By the end of 1967, Jimmy Ellis already had victories over Leotis Martin and Oscar Bonavena, which meant he had an assured place in the final while Jerry Quarry still had to face Thad Spencer, who had earlier defeated Ernie Terrell. The winner of the Quarry v Spencer bout would face Ellis for the vacant WBA crown.

At the time, Spencer was rated number two contender by *The Ring* magazine and was favoured to beat the Californian. Jerry hadn't read the script. The two fighters entered the Oakland arena on 3 February 1968 and they were greeted by the thunderous applause of 12,110 paying fans. The bout was set for 12 rounds, but the fireworks began early when Spencer hit the mat in the fourth. Spencer went down again in the 10th and then in the final seconds of the final round, Jerry slung leather at Spencer at such a furious pace his punching onslaught forced Thad on the defensive. The punches left Spencer dazed and staggering against the ropes. Referee Jack Downey stopped the fight, despite there only being three seconds left before the final bell. Jerry was ahead on all three scorecards at the time of the stoppage, It had been a fabulous win for Jerry as he upset the odds and assured himself a shot at the vacant WBA heavyweight title against Jimmy Ellis. The moment of truth finally arrived on Saturday 27 April 1968 when the Quarry v Ellis encounter took place at the Coliseum Arena in Oakland, California.

Jerry came to the title fight at the very same age as young Cassius Clay did back in 1964, both being a mere 22 years old when they received their respective championship shots. Clay/ Ali, as everyone knows, caused a massive upset and won the title. Jerry, on the other hand, went into his title fight as the favourite.

The Quarry v Ellis fight was set at the championship distance of 15 rounds. Ellis turned up with the same man Ali used to have in his corner during his own championship days, Angelo Dundee. On the night, Ellis also emulated his former school buddy, Ali, by winning a world heavyweight title, snatching a majority points decision. It was later reported that Quarry had suffered a back injury going into the bout, but the fighter didn't use that as an excuse and said only that 'the better man won'. He took home his reported $125,000 purse, licked his wounds and ended up taking an extended rest. It was then, a couple of months after the Ellis defeat, he nearly lost more than a fight – his life.

According to a report in *The Los Angeles Times* (5 June 1968) the incident happened that month when the Quarry family rented a property on Olive Street in Newport Beach. When Jerry, his brother-in-law, and younger brother Mike went for a swim, they hit trouble in a rough sea about 200 yards from the shoreline and it was Jerry who found himself sinking under the surf. Panic-stricken, Mike, managed to swim ashore and call the alarm. Life Guards and the fire services were quickly alerted, but fortunately a nearby surfer heard the commotion and grabbed a board and braved the waves himself, reaching and saving an exhausted Jerry.

On 11 November 1968 Quarry returned with a fifth round stoppage win over Bob Mumford in Phoenix, Arizona, and only eight days after that Jerry beat Willis Earls over 10 rounds by a points decision in San Antonio, Texas. Those quick-fire wins were part of a four-bout winning streak, which included three KOs before he was pitched in against the behemoth Buster Mathis 24 March 1969. Mathis, from Grand Rapids, Michigan outweighed Quarry by almost 40lbs (196lbs to 234½lbs) and was taller by almost three inches. The fight would be Jerry's second visit to Madison Square Garden in New York, but the first at the new MSG venue, which opened in 1968.

It was Buster Mathis and Joe Frazier's fight on 4 March 1968 that had marked the first title card in that new venue. That bout was for the then vacant NYSAC version of the heavyweight title and both boxers had turned up to the arena with undefeated records. They also arrived to the unwelcome sight and sound of pickets, marching up and down outside of the entrance holding banners declaring that it was Ali, not the winner of their bout, they recognized as the real heavyweight champ. The pickets may have bugged Joe a touch, but it still didn't stop him beating Buster by an 11th round TKO. The Buster v Joe heavyweight title fight shared top billing with Emile Griffith's losing world middleweight title defence against Italian Nino Benvenuti.

One year after the Frazier loss, the giant Mathis was on a six-fight winning streak and he came to the Quarry bout as favourite in the betting. The sheer size and fight credentials of Buster didn't intimidate Jerry though. In front of 15,078 fans, the 'Bellflower Belter' stormed in against 'massive Mathis' and busted Buster up. His left hook was the most effective weapon, even though it was his right hand that knocked Mathis down in the second round. The punches came from every angle and continued in combinations right up to the final bell. Jerry smashed his way to another highly impressive upset victory, this

time winning almost every round on the judges' scorecards in the
12-round fight.

New York became Jerry's new home from home. With the
ancestral roots of the Quarry clan being in Ireland, and with an
eye to the large Irish population in New York, Jerry was sometimes
introduced as 'Irish' Jerry Quarry – the man who beat giants in
the ring and who was now in line to fight undefeated Smokin' Joe
Frazier for the NYSAC version of the heavyweight title.

By this time, many were calling Jerry the best white
heavyweight to come along since Rocky Marciano. Despite this,
Jerry again approached the Frazier fight as a betting underdog,
which was set for New York's Madison Square Garden on
23 June 1969. Up to that point, all three of Joe's opponents in
title defences turned up as betting outsiders and it was only the
rated and powerful Oscar Bonavena who lasted the distance,
while both Manuel Ramos and Dave Zyglewicz failed. (The
Mathis bout was for the vacant title.)

Prior to the fight, both fighters carried out some of their final
sparring/publicity sessions outdoors at Duffy Square, the northern
part of Times Square in central Manhattan. The meeting of the
two warriors was one of those occasions when even non-boxing
fans were talking about who was going to win. Jerry or Joe? Ali
was quoted in newspapers as saying he thought Quarry would
cause an upset and defeat Frazier.

Many others also believed this would be the case, but there
was one interesting fact that came from the annals of boxing
history that didn't bode well for Quarry's chances. Up to that
point, no defending heavyweight champion had ever lost their
title to a challenger inside the famous Madison Square Garden
arena. (Madison Square Garden arena, should not to be confused
with the Madison Square Garden Bowl. The 'Bowl', which was
sometimes called the 'Jinx Bowl' – or 'graveyard of champions'
– was a 72,000-seater outdoor arena situated in Long Island,

New York, while Madison Square Garden is in Manhattan. Madison Square Garden Bowl was owned by famous promoter Tex Rickard and was the place where between 1932 and 1935 Max Baer, Max Schmeling, Jack Sharkey and Primo Carnera all lost their world heavyweight titles.)

In the Madison Square Garden arena on Monday night of the 23 June 1969, 16,570 fans turned up to see if Jerry could cause another startling upset and turn the tables on hot favourite Joe. The fight was beamed to 125 cinemas around the country. As we know, it wasn't to be, as the 'Smoke' stopped Jerry on a cut eye at the end of the seventh. The fight had been tremendously exciting though and ended up being named the fight of the year by *The Ring* magazine. Despite the injury, loss and disappointment, it wasn't long before Jerry was back in the ring again, with two KO wins quickly following, one of which was a second round KO over Brian London.

The year of 1969 was rounded off with his seventh fight in 12 months and his third after the Frazier fight, but it ended up with that controversial defeat to George Chuvalo. After that loss, Jerry was written off again by many, but the new decade of 1970 saw him return and eventually achieve his spectacular victory over Mac 'KO' Foster.

Now, as number one heavyweight contender, he was going to face the most controversial former heavyweight champion since the late, great Jack Johnson.

9

TRAINING

The exact date Ali returned to Chris Dundee's 5th Street gym in Miami, Florida, to begin his main preparations for the Quarry fight is not known, but according to the book, *The Greatest: My Own Story* by Richard Durham, Ali and his camp flew down to Miami immediately after the New York signing, which was Thursday 10 September. However, some newspaper reports at the time suggest Ali was home in Philly at the beginning of the following week. This was when he received news about Judge Mansfield's ruling against the NYSAC on the 14th. By Wednesday the 16th at the latest, Ali was spotted back inside the 5th Street gym sweat-box, completing his daily workouts. On the next day, news broke that the NYSAC were not going to appeal the Federal Judge's decision. So Ali was now free to apply to have his licence in New York reinstated.

The following week tickets for the Ali v Quarry fight went on sale and the prices were set at $100 ringside, $50, $25 and $15. That week, as the tickets went on sale, Ali broke off training and flew to New York to complete the physical in the medical offices of the NYSAC boxing commission. His weight was said to be still hovering around the 225lb mark. During the medical, Dr Edwin Campbell decided to check his cardiac reserves, asking the former champ to carry out some fast push-ups on the spot, but that was toned down to doing some fast knee-bends, after Ali cracked he didn't realize he came up to New York for a workout. After the joking and formalities were completed, Ali's travelling assistant jubilantly talked about Ali's return bringing the sport back to life – that Ali would be soon floating like a butterfly and stinging like a bee again.

Surprisingly, the next day Ali wasn't found back in Miami resuming training, but he was in Chicago to help fight promoter Irv Schoenwald publicize various closed circuit outlets for that city. That was the type of interruption Ali had talked about and there was more to come, but prior to his travels he said he was pleased with the way his training was going.

On that same day, Ali was in Chicago, another interruption was coming from Georgia. State governor Lester Maddox held a press meeting about a coming drugs conference, but during that briefing, the *San Bernardino County Sun* reported that Maddox stated he would do everything he could to stop the Ali fight going ahead.

As Maddox was there primarily to announce a conference about stamping out drugs, the link was quickly made to the $50,000 promised by promoters to help fight drug addiction in the city, which of course would not be forthcoming without a fight. Maddox said the offer was a bribe and meant very little if the city was going to honour someone who had refused to fight for his country. He claimed he could organize something that would raise $25,000 more than the promoters' offer.

His incentive for putting a kibosh on the event must have been the pressure from war veterans. He said the planned fight was an offence to all those who served in Vietnam. Another incentive was surely Maddox's penchant for self-publicity, simply for being seen to be doing stuff. The state governor stated he would consult with his Attorney-General, Arthur K. Bolton, to see if they could put a halt to the bout. When Maddox spoke about stopping the fight, his words were not just confined to Atlanta or Georgia, they stretched worldwide and were hardly going to inspire confidence in those financing the fight.

With the former champion's New York licence set to be issued the following Monday on the 28th, Ali's initial reaction to Maddox's statement was to say that if the fight was somehow scuppered in Atlanta, then promoters could shift the bout to New York. According to an article in the *Atlanta Constitution*, a New York promotional outfit, not named at the time, hoped to do just that.

Another firm but diplomatic response came from Leroy Johnson. He rejected the charge of bribery. He then reassured everyone, including Ali himself, that they had covered all the legal bases and not even Maddox could stop the fight from going ahead. Mayor Sam Massell also chipped in and said that the governor lacked any legal authority to stop an event sanctioned by the city. There must have been more than a few jittery moments for the promoters, but they passed when the Attorney General, Arthur K. Bolton, stated that there was nothing Maddox could do to stand in their way. The Attorney General's reply came in the same week Ali's licence was reinstated in New York. He reiterated that the jurisdiction over a boxing event in Atlanta was a matter for the city, not the state.

Lester Maddox, who received Bolton's reply in writing, accepted that there were no further avenues to pursue. All he could do was publicly denounce the fight and that was about it. The state of Georgia had exhausted all legal avenues, so he wasn't interested in the fight, apart from hoping the 'unpatriotic' Ali receiving a good thumping on the night.

After Ali had fulfilled his promotional commitment in Chicago on the 25th, he flew back to Miami the following day and resumed training. He stayed in the Sea Gull hotel on the beach front and trained diligently every day.

Inside the wood-floored 5th Street gym, there was one training ring, two heavy bags, one light bag, a couple of large mirrors, a 'rubbing' table, no air conditioning – and of course, an array of top-quality sparring partners. All professional fighters initial preparations are similar, with morning roadwork followed by gym sessions afterwards, sparring, hitting the heavy and light bags and calisthenics. That disciplined routine would be followed until near the time of the fight. In the big title fights, this is when the main press build-up would begin and the training sessions would be tapered down. Ali's and Quarry's preparations were no different.

The former champion's morning runs and sometimes his gym sessions were carried out with the aid of that trusty rubber vest of his. After those sessions, he would lift it up and watch a flood splash to the ground. Angelo Dundee stated that when Ali first arrived in Florida, he was up at 4.30 a.m. every morning, doing his runs around Bayshore golf course, which lasted for 45 minutes at a time and would be gradually increased to about an hour. Ali's weight loss program limited him to one main meal a day, usually grilled steak or grilled chicken with vegetables. Each gym session would begin and end in the experienced, gnarled hands of his Cuban masseur, Luis Sarria. Apart from sparring, Ali also used the training ring for shadow boxing. Ali didn't use this exercise primarily to hit an imaginary opponent, he was using his legs, the sparring ring was converted into his own dancefloor. He glided and shuffled around the circumference occasionally punching through the stifling air at an imaginary target.

In down time he would sometimes read the many letters that arrived daily from around the world. Some fan letters no doubt warned him of the dangers of facing top-ranked Quarry and counseled he should have taken on an easier comeback opponent. During the early weeks of training, he was often in a sombre mood, with the showboating and jokes witnessed in build-ups to earlier fights a rarity. Ali had to be serious this time, as he wasn't only fighting one man but a cohort that wanted to see him fail. He wanted to show America and the world that he couldn't be humbled.

However, the leaner and fitter he became, the more chance people got to seeing glimpses of the old 'Louisville lip'. After one sparring session, Ali said Quarry had never faced a fighter like himself, the fastest heavyweight champion ever. If he could get back to his 'dancing weight', there was no way Quarry could even touch him with a decent shot, never mind beat him.

Ali's sparring help included the then second-ranked contender in the world light heavyweight division, Vicente Rondon, (Rondon would become WBA light-heavyweight champion in 1971), heavyweights Willie Johnson, Rufus Brassell and Johnny Hudgins.

Incidentally, both Johnson and Rondon would fight each other in a bout at the Miami Beach Auditorium during Ali's Miami's training period, on 6 October, and Rondon would score a fourth round TKO win. Jimmy Ellis and Alvin 'Blue' Lewis were another two fighters in the gym around the time of Ali's preparations and they both would have sparred with Ali.

'Blue', the 6ft 3in solid punching machine, had taken part in the exhibitions against Ali in 'Blue's' home city of Detroit, way back in June 1967. Lewis would have used the vital experience and training in the 1970 Miami Beach workouts in preparation for his own coming fight in Detroit, which was then mooted to be against Cleveland Williams on 21 October 1970. It just so happened his last bout was against Billy Joiner back in July, with 'Blue' picking up a points win over Billy at Madison Square Garden.

Ali's brother Rahaman, who had recently turned 26, would also help in his brother's preparations. He not only resembled his brother facially, he also was on a boxing comeback and was undefeated. Rahaman's comeback had already began. On 11 August 1970 he fought and beat Tommy Howard in the Miami Beach Auditorium. This was the first fight for Rahaman in 4½ years. So Rahaman had been inactive longer than his brother, but he needed to be in shape as it was said he was going to get a slot on the undercard of his brother's comeback fight.

Rahaman Ali (Rudy Clay) had his first pro-fight on the undercard of another one of his brother's fights. His pro-debut night was already rather special though, as it was his brother's first world title bout back in 1964. Rudy/Rahaman fought Chip Johnson and won by a points decision over four rounds. (On that memorable night, Cassius/Ali became the second boxer born in Louisville, Kentucky, to become heavyweight champion. The first was Marvin Hart, born in a Louisville suburb called Fern Creek and who won the vacant title against Jack Root back in 1905. Eventually, the city would boast four heavyweight champions: Hart, Ali, Ellis and Greg Page.)

On Thursday 1 October 1970 Ali completed 14 rounds of non-stop sparring, using four different partners, Rondon, Hudgins, Brassell and Johnson, with Ali sometimes receiving clips to the chin and whacks to the body. That stiff test was in preparation for the 15 rounds Ali would potentially have to travel against Quarry. As in the Morehouse exhibition, the number of rounds set for the Quarry fight didn't sit too well with Angelo Dundee. He was quoted in the *The San Bernardino County Sun* as saying that he believed 12 rounds was the preferable distance for Ali's first comeback, but he was overruled again.

Jerry Quarry chose his home State of California to prepare for the fight of his life, his fight headquarters being at the Massacre Canyon Inn, again at Gilman Hot Springs, which was about 80 miles outside of Los Angeles. This was the setting that he had used for his preparations in some previous fights and he claimed he had never lost a bout after working there. Quarry would complete five miles of roadwork each morning and over 80 tough rounds of sparring in total. He was focusing on speed, sparring with light-heavyweights. Just like Ali, he would include calisthenics in his training schedule, but his included special neck strengthening exercises to help absorb head punches.

As with Ali, his younger brother would also help in his preparations. Mike Quarry, who was one of the best upcoming light-heavyweights in the world at the time, had a similar hit-and-run style to Ali, so he was an ideal sparring partner. Mike would also assist in his brother's roadwork, clocking the miles – over 100 – before leaving for Atlanta. At that point, Mike had taken part in 23 professional fights and was undefeated.

Quarry genuinely respected Ali for standing up for his beliefs and felt it was wrong to deprive him of his livelihood while still on bail. He had high regard for Ali as a fighter, but the former champion's recent public exhibition at Morehouse had left him unimpressed. In an interview with the *The San Bernardino County Sun* at Gilman Hot Springs, Jerry said he had watched those exhibitions on TV and what he saw enhanced his belief he could pull off a crushing win. He declared that Ali's sparring partners at Morehouse were nowhere as good as himself.

Many of those supporting Quarry felt that Ali would eventually tire as at Morehouse, falling flat-footed. They were backing Quarry to cause a huge upset and some even predicted six rounds was enough time for him to complete the job. Jerry though, wasn't getting ready for the Ali that he saw on TV, but rather, the pre-exile version; that's why he was preparing for all possibilities, including training to go the full 15-round distance. Jerry hoped Joe Frazier would be at ringside. Despite suffering a few days of flu, Jerry's training ran on schedule and he said he expected to come in for the Ali fight at a lean 195 pounds.

Quarry's training may have been going well, but the contract issue he had with Johnny Flores over the Mac Foster fight in June wasn't going away. According to a report in the *The Indianapolis Star* (6 October 1970) the financial penalty Jerry received from the California State Athletic Commission still hadn't been paid and this resulted in another suspension. As it turned out, it would be a long two years before Quarry fought in his home state again and that would be during his 1972 campaign. In April of that year, he would return and deploy his devastating left hook to knock out Eduardo Corletti in 2:58 of the first round inside the Forum, in Inglewood.

Training for the Harris bout in early September meant Quarry couldn't have been too far off peak fitness already. In that situation, over-training was a danger, which could end up with a boxer leaving all his fight inside the gym when the day of the contest arrived. This may have been why on Thursday 8 October, only a few days before leaving for Atlanta, Jerry had a break from the daily physical grind and turned up at a health club in Beverly Hills for a meet-and-greet with the press. Famous movie star and former World War II hero, Audie Murphy turned up that day to add some glitz to the occasion and he was full of praise and support for the top heavyweight contender.

While there, a relaxed and confident Jerry at first seemed more interested in talking about golf than boxing, saying that he had already booked a golfing break at the Catskills in New York after the fight. He spoke confidently of slowing down the once nimble-footed, inactive former world champion with his left hook and constant pressure.

Quarry was asked about the differences between Ali and Mac Foster. Although Ali and Mac were the same age, 28, and physically similar, with Ali standing a touch taller at 6ft 3in to Foster's 6ft 2in, it was Ali's speed that was the difference. Jerry said he would be bringing plenty of his own speed to the fight and was more than confident of spoiling Ali's comeback party.

On 12 October Jerry and his camp finally left California on a flight to Atlanta. On the same day, but back in Miami, Ali was still working out at the 5th Street Gym, but it would be his last day of serious sparring before moving camp himself.

On that day, Alvin 'Blue' Lewis was going through the sparring rounds with Ali and at one point Ali instructed 'Blue' to pound his midsection with his clenched 16-oz gloved fists, Alvin obliged and started thumping away at Ali's body. One particular hefty punch apparently caught Ali unawares and the shot dropped the former champion to the canvas. Many of the bystanders and fighters at the gym that day thought the knockdown was just another Ali prank for the benefit of the visiting press. But Ali said the punch and knockdown was genuine and he had been winded. His surprise tumble appeared real enough and it just so happened the BBC were there that day and film of Ali hitting the deck would be shown on David Coleman's *Sportsnight* programme in the week before the fight. The 'surprise' punch Ali received meant he left for Atlanta with a bruised rib.

One wonders if either man was reminded of a press day back in 1967 at the Detroit Press Club before the exhibition between Ali and Lewis. 'Blue' was there on that day and Ali asked him to hit his raised palms with his jab. As 'Blue' raised his fists to clout Ali's open mitts, Ali shot a fast, straight right (a tap really) to the unprotected midriff of 'Blue' that caught him by surprise and left him clutching his belly.

Ali carried out one of his last press interviews before heading north to Georgia and was full of anticipation and optimism, saying that all the former ring legends, from Jack Johnson to Joe Louis, would have considered him crazy for attempting such a comeback with only a few weeks' notice. According to Ali, all the previous champs would have demanded at least six months preparation, not six weeks. Ali even turned the 'Blue' Lewis knockdown from a negative into a positive, saying that it would help him prepare for every conceivable punching scenario that Quarry might attempt. In Ali's mind, his training was similar to what astronauts did before flying off to the moon – checking out everything that could go wrong before launch day. He had to prepare for super-hard punches, so he used a hefty puncher, like 'Blue' Lewis, who at that point in time had 27 fights, which included 24 wins and 14 by KO/TKO. Ali had to prepare for the feeling of being winded and practise coming back from the nausea after being hit by body shots. He had to recondition not only his body but his head, both inside and out.

Inside a training ring, it seemed that on occasions, Ali was more interested in receiving punches from his paid hands than punching them back. The former champion had always been known to go easy on his sparring help and only occasionally would he unleash hard punches. His reasoning for his lack of punching was that too many of these guys who worked for champion boxers had been seriously hurt and he didn't want to pummel a man just so he looked good in front of the cameras. His aim, so it seemed, was to 'preserve' his sparring partners, not punch them out of a job. For Ali, the 'art of boxing' was all about movement and ring-craft and as long as he could maneoeuvre either himself or his opponent into a punchable position, that was all he needed. Punching someone hard on the nose could be left for the night of the fight, when he got paid.

As the questions continued from the press, Ali could be quick to talk about some elements of his fight preparations, but his replies to certain questions were short, especially ones about his position in the courts, as that was in the hands of his legal team. When a reporter asked him if his comeback could be equated to that of the 'great' Jack Johnson, Ali said the fight would be a 1970 rerun of the 'Great White Hope', reversing roles so that he would be in the role of champion Jack Johnson and Quarry would be the returning ex-champion, Jim Jeffries. In the famous Johnson v Jeffries title bout back in 1910, it was the returning champion who received the shellacking. The active fighter was the one that won, Jack Johnson. Sixty years on, there would only be one active fighter slipping through the ropes on the night and it wouldn't be Muhammad Ali.

Or maybe Ali was referring to the time Jack Johnson fought another 'Great White Hope', Jess Willard in Havana, Cuba, but in that 1915 fight, it was the 'Great White Hope' who won, beating Johnson in the 26th round of a 45-round contest. Or maybe, Ali was just bamboozling everyone for the love of it.

Ali ended one interview with the BBC sending a message out to the young man he had sparred with earlier in June, Joe Bugner. He looked into the camera and stated Bugner would be a future boxing star and predicted, as it turned out accurately, that they could one day meet in the ring.

The day before leaving for Atlanta, Ali was again back in the gym, looking trim and fit, but just concentrating on shadow boxing and light and heavy bag punching. After his final workout, Ali stepped on the scales and they tipped at a sleek 215½ pounds. He said by fight night, he would probably be lighter than when he fought Liston in 1964, so there was no way Quarry could pull off a victory. Ali claimed he was now faster than ever. He boldly proclaimed that the condition he was now in and the way the weight was dropping off, he could 'dance' for 20 rounds if need be. His dress pants had to be kept up with a cord.

On the very day of leaving Miami for Georgia Ali received a gift at his hotel. When the box was opened, it didn't contain a lucky horseshoe but a small, dead black dog. The 'gift' came with a 14-word written note warning him to stay out of Georgia, as draft dodgers like him were likely to suffer the same fate as the box's contents.

10

HYPE, HISTORY AND HEADACHES

When Jerry became National Golden Gloves Heavyweight champion in 1965, it wasn't too surprising that certain sections of the press started dubbing him a 'Great White Hope'. Jerry may have initially accepted being labelled thus as being good publicity, but it didn't take long before he was quoted in the press as wanting to drop the racial reference.

Two years into his career and the first time he fought Floyd Patterson in June 1967, the Mayor of his hometown, Bellflower, in California, held a 'Jerry Quarry Day' and Jerry had the name 'Bellflower Bomber' bestowed on him. The 'Bellflower Bomber' was already known as the 'Bellflower Belter', and the 'Great White Hope' stories continued. Then came the Ellis title loss in April 1968. In a later interview, Jerry said it was after that fight that he no longer wanted to be known as a 'white hope'. Jerry spoke of how he didn't like the reaction of fans after his title loss. Some fans who had previously applauded him turned their backs and didn't treat him well. Jerry spoke of how at the beginning of his career many spoke of the financial rewards that could be gained by being cast as a 'Great White Hope'. Now he considered the tag 'stupid' and said if he fought for the heavyweight championship again, it would be for himself, not to please others.

Regarding labels, there was plenty of focus in the press before the fight on Quarry's Irish roots. If he had become champion in 1968, he would have been the first 'Irish' American to win the title since 'Irish' James J. Braddock, who beat Max Baer back in 1935. There was also mention that he would have been the first fighter born in California to manage the feat since James J. Corbett back in 1892.

When Jerry got his second opportunity to fight for a world title, against Joe Frazier in 1969 at Madison Square Garden, a few blocks away at the Alvin Theater on Broadway James Earl Jones was starring in the play, *The Great White Hope*. Jones portrayed a boxer called Jack Jefferson, a character based on the first black heavyweight champion, Jack Johnson. The show played to packed audiences every night. How could any harried hack resist making the connection to the Joe versus Jerry scrap? Back in his home state of California, on the day of the Frazier fight the headline in the sports pages of *The San Bernardino County Sun* pointed out that Joe would be facing the 'Great White Hope' Jerry Quarry. Again Jerry lost and again, you would have thought, the defeat would have spelled the end of the soubriquet – but then along came the Ali fight. This time, it wasn't just some sections of the press casting Jerry as a 'Great White Hope', but Ali himself. Even though the stage play had run its course in New York and finished at the beginning of 1970, a nationwide promotional campaign for the screen version started. The film would have its US theater release on 11 October 1970, 15 days before the Ali v Quarry fight.

Twentieth Century Fox and cinema houses around the country had placed adverts in every city newspaper about this soon to be released movie. Also in those same newspapers, people would find adverts for locations for the CCTV outlets for the approaching fight. Flick through the pages of those same newspapers and the sports sections were full of stories about Ali's return. The timing of the film's release couldn't have been better for drawing attention to the fight. The original stage play was written by Howard Sackler, who had spent much of his youth in Cuba, where Johnson lost his world title against Jess Willard. Ali attended the Broadway play on a reported four different occasions and the similarities between Johnson and himself were not hard to see. Both were outstanding heavyweight champions and both were highly controversial and outspoken. Their actions outside of the ring brought them trouble with the law. In Johnson's case, it was a trumped-up violation of the Mann Act. Both fighters were handed prison sentences, both received fines from the courts and both spent years out of the fight game in the US. Johnson was sentenced to a year and a day in prison and fined $1,000, but while out on bail in 1913, he fled the country and didn't return for seven years. During his exile period he took part in 13 fights, one of which included him losing the heavyweight title to Jess Willard in 1915 in Cuba. When he returned to the US on 2 July 1920, Johnson was sent to jail and served his full sentence. Actually, both would serve time in prison, as Ali served a few days behind bars in Dade County Jail in Miami in December 1968 for an old traffic violation. At the time, Ali called his short spell 'inside' good training if he was going eventually to have to serve the five-year sentence hanging over him.

Ali claimed he had received an offer to play Papa Jack in another proposed film, but said he refused the role because of the love scenes. According to *The Holy Warrior: Muhammad Ali* he refused a $400,000 fee to portray Jack Johnson in a film.

For the stage play, James Earl Jones spent several weeks boxing training under the watchful eye of former NBA World super-lightweight champion Mushy Callaghan. Jones even brought his weight down to a similar poundage to Johnson's and had his head shaved to look like the 'Galveston Giant'. Jones was already a fan of Johnson, collecting mementos of the fighter's life and career.

Ali had visited the rehearsals of the play and sparred a few friendly rounds with the Jack Johnson lookalike in a makeshift boxing ring situated on the stage. Although James Earl Jones possessed only the rudiments of boxing, seeing a version of Jack Johnson exchanging punches with Muhammad Ali would surely have given Murry Woroner thoughts of another 'Mystery Fight of the Century'. He had the 'super computer' and movie wizardry to carry it off too.

There were also of course links with and similarities between Ali and James J. Jeffries. One was that they were both 'matched' in Woroner's NCR 315 computer. Another was that they were both undefeated world heavyweight champions who returned after a long absence. According to one boxing record archive, Jeffries had 2 drawn contests and 2 no-decision contests in a 23-fight career before the Johnson bout. Their reputations also made them both return to the ring as favourites in their respective comeback bouts.

Ali didn't seem to believe 42 months of inactivity would really affect him, but the one newspaper headline that really summed the fight up was 'Can Ali Defy Boxing History?'

Time and the fight game itself were not kind to ex-champions attempting to return to their trade. James J. Jeffries had been out of the ring for almost six years and lived the easy life on his alfalfa farm, allowing his weight to balloon up to 300lbs. His comeback ring opponent, on the other hand, had remained active and was in sleek fighting condition.

Their famous fight took place in Reno, Nevada on 4 July 1910, with Jeffries reducing his weight down to 227lbs in preparation for the bout. When the bell rang in the temporary outdoor arena, 15,760 people witnessed the 'Great White Hope', James J. Jeffries smashed around until 2:20 of the 15th round of 45-round contest. The crushing defeat came despite Jeffries having a previous splendid record and having twice defeated fellow ring greats Bob Fitzsimmons and James J. Corbett.

In the period of Jeffries' six years of inactivity after he fought Jack Munroe on 26 August 1904, Johnson had taken part in an incredible 38 contests. In the first he knocked out 'Denver' Ed Martin in two rounds and in the last destroyed Stanley Ketchel in 12 rounds on 16 October 1909.

After looking at Johnson's activity sheet and in hindsight, it seems Jeffries' favouritism was based on hope rather than facts. Never mind, after the loss Jeffries went back to his alfalfa farm with his share of a $101,000 purse and never fought again.

Going back even further to the great boxer, John L. Sullivan, he suffered a similar fate to Jeffries. From his start in 1879, Sullivan kept active in each and every year until after he stopped Jake Kilrain in that last bare-knuckle championship fight (London rules) in Richburg, Mississippi, in 1889. Three years later, when he defended his title again under the Marquess of Queensberry rules, he was knocked out in the 21st round by James J. Corbett. John L. Sullivan never fought again.

Maybe it was in the Sullivan and Corbett era that 'a heavyweight champion can never come back' became a mantra, but heavyweight history is littered with comeback kings who never made it. After Corbett took the title off Sullivan in 1892, he only had two further bouts to 1897. Then when he fought Bob Fitzsimmons in that year, he suffered a knockout loss in round 14 and ceded the world heavyweight title. Corbett took part in only one bout in the next three years before attempting to regain the title in 1900. The next time he went in against new champion, James J. Jeffries, but lost again by knockout in the 23rd round. Incredibly, Corbett would go through another three-year period with only one competition bout before he had

A famous image of Muhammad Ali in his prime aged 25 – though not yet in his prime as a boxer, as history would prove – taken in 1967 by Ira Rosenberg. (Library of Congress)

Opposite and above: Jack Johnson, vanquisher of the 'Great White Hope', James J. Jeffries, in the 'Fight of the Century' on 4 July 1910. Johnson became the first African American world heavyweight champion at the height of the Jim Crow era. (Library of Congress)

Two years after the 'Fight of the Century', and due to its fallout, distribution of all prizefight films was banned. This remained the situation until 1940. Here, legendary heavyweight champion Jack Dempsey (right) converses with John R. Kilpatrick, president of the Madison Square Garden Corp, before a 1939 hearing regarding a bill to lift the ban. (Library of Congress)

The Ku Klux Klan's heyday may have been in the 1920s (opposite and above), but it had a resurgence in the middle of the twentieth century. To the right, two children can be seen flanking the KKK Grand Dragon in Atlanta, Georgia, in 1948. Georgia state governor Lester Maddox would ride to power in the 1960s on a wave of segregationist rhetoric, though his personal views were not identical to those of the KKK. Today the Klan still exists, even in progressive Atlanta. (Library of Congress)

Above: The civil rights leader Martin Luther King Jr was born and raised in Atlanta. He entered the city's Morehouse College at age fifteen, and can be seen here third from left in the front row. (Library of Congress)

Below: The Capitol, Atlanta. When Martin Luther King Jr died, the governor of Atlanta, Lester Maddox, refused to allow his body to rest in state here due to a flimsy rumour that the building would be stormed. (Library of Congress)

Lester Maddox exhibits some irritation about something the *Atlanta Constitution* has printed (left). He gained notoriety as a restaurant manager in the 1950s when he stated that he would sooner close his restaurant than serve African Americans (and did). When he ran for the governorship of Georgia on the Democratic ticket, some Republicans voted for him as they considered him less likely to win against their candidate; however, he swept to power as the state legislature was dominated by Democrats.

Elijah Muhammad, civil rights activist and leader of the Nation of Islam, gives a speech in 1964. To the left is a young Cassius Clay; it was in this year that he would win the world heavyweight championship and take the name Muhammad Ali after denouncing his 'slave name'. (Library of Congress)

Left: Lincoln Theodore Monroe Andrew Perry, better known by the stage name Stepin Fetchit. Perry was a close friend of Ali. Known for playing 'the laziest man in the world' on screen through the 1930s, his fame faded when he began to be seen by African Americans as a derogatory representation, an 'Uncle Tom' figure. That view has now been modified: Fetchit is viewed as a clever trickster. (Perry himself was certainly clever enough to be probably the first million-dollar black film star.) (Library of Congress)

Below: Atlanta Municipal Auditorium, now the Dahlberg Hall, the venue for Ali's fight with Jerry Quarry. (Courtesy of Keizers)

Opposite: The futuristic lobby of the Hyatt Regency in Atlanta, scene of the fight after-party. (Courtesy of Karen Mardahl)

Quarry and Ali sign the contract for their fight. (© AP/Rex/Shutterstock)

Ali pinches the cheek of his mother Odessa after the weight-in for the fight. Cassius Clay Snr is to the right. (© AP/Rex/Shutterstock)

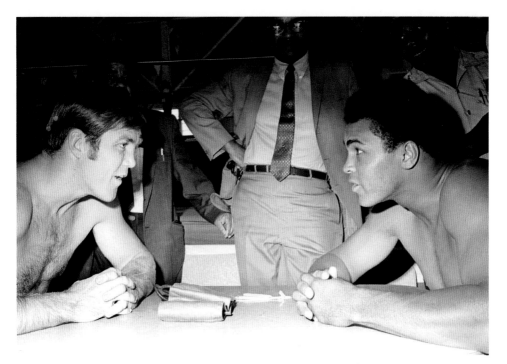

Quarry and Ali size each other up after undergoing physical examinations at the training centre in Atlanta. (© AP/Rex/Shutterstock)

Ali makes a point in his own inimitable style during a news conference inside the ring before the fight. (© AP/Rex/Shutterstock)

Quarry hits Ali with a left in the second round, knocking Ali back; it wasn't all one way. (© AP/Rex/Shutterstock)

Ali connects with a hard right. (© AP/Rex/Shutterstock)

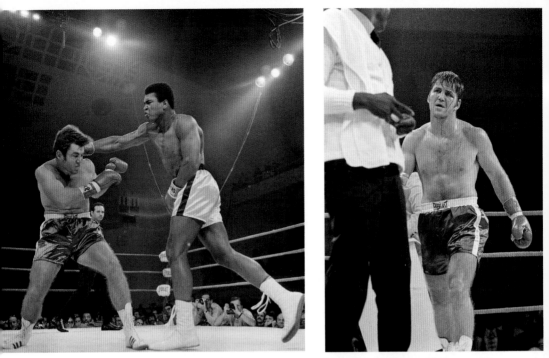

Above left and right: Quarry struggles as Ali comes to dominate. (© AP/Rex/Shutterstock)

With Quarry's eye bleeding from a cut that required eleven stitches to close, his team opt not to answer the bell for the fourth round. Referee Tony Perez waves to signal the end of the fight; Ali is declared victorious. Drew 'Bundini' Brown has his arm round him, while his trainer Angelo Dundee reaches out to him from the right. (© AP/Rex/Shutterstock)

Ali meets President Jimmy Carter, ex-Governor of Georgia, in 1977 at a White House
dinner celebrating the signing of the Panama Canal Treaty. (Library of Congress)

Ali meets Rosa Parks – the woman Congress described as 'the First Lady of civil rights' – in
1994 at a Brotherhood Crusade dinner held in their honour. (Library of Congress)

Foreman, Frazier, Ali; will there ever be such a rivalry in the heavyweight division again? (Author)

Ali ignites the Olympic flame during the opening ceremony of the 1996 Summer Olympics in Atlanta. (AP/Rex/Shutterstock)

Ali sketches a scenario for the impossible fight that every boxing fan has thought about at one time or another: Ali–Tyson. (Author)

Ali's home on the day after his funeral. (Author)

another go against Jeffries for the world title, but he was stopped again in the 10th round. James J. Corbett called it a day.

Jack Dempsey was an extremely active fighter. According to his record, Jack had a total of 75 bouts, which began in 1914 and in the first five years of his career, he jammed in 67 of those pro bouts. This included crushing Jess Willard in three rounds for the world heavyweight title on 4 July 1919. Then, from 1920 to 1923, Jack took part in just five fights. His next fight wasn't until 1926, when he defended the world title against Gene Tunney and lost the fight and title by a points decision. Jack slotted in a KO win over Jack Sharkey before fighting Tunny again the following year in 1927, but when he did, he lost on points in his last fight.

James J. Braddock was another fighter who in the early days crammed in a multitude of bouts until he won the title. From his pro start in 1926, until he beat Max Baer for the world heavyweight title in June 1935, he fought an incredible 85 pro bouts. Then after he beat Max, he didn't fight again for two years. His first defence of the world title was a losing one against the 'Brown Bomber', Joe Louis. Braddock was counted out in 1:10 of the eighth round on 22 June 1937 and became a former champion. Braddock only fought one more time before hanging up his gloves.

The great Joe Louis himself, who beat Braddock in that 1937 fight, went eleven years without defeat but after knocking out Jersey Joe Walcott in June 1948 the 'Brown Bomber' announced his retirement in March 1949. In September 1950, Louis made a comeback after being out of the ring for 27 months and went straight in against new champion, Ezzard Charles. Louis also went in the bout as favorite, but lost by a points decision and failed to regain his title. Louis continued his comeback, but it only lasted 13 months, after he was crushed and knocked out in the eighth round by young, undefeated contender Rocky Marciano in October 1951.

Floyd Patterson, was the only heavyweight champion who managed to return successfully, but the difference between him and the others is that he never retired or suffered a potentially damaging long layoff. Patterson remained active in every year since turning professional in 1952 until he lost the world title in 1959 against Ingemar Johansson. It could be argued that one of the factors going against him in his losing title defence in 1959 was that after he won the title against Archie Moore in 1956 he took his foot off the pedal as regards ring activity was concerned, taking part in two fights in 1957, only one fight in 1958 and two fights in 1959, one of which he lost by a devastating TKO in the third round against Johansson. It was exactly 12 months from him losing the title to him regaining it against the same boxer.

Floyd was only 24 years old when he lost the title in June 1959 and 25 years old when he regained it in June 1960. For young Floyd, it would have been a case of finishing one training camp, then after the loss and some rest, straight into another camp. He never really suffered the handicap of a long period of inactivity before he regained the title.

In 1970, one fighter in the 5th Street gym around the same time 'Blue' Lewis was thumping Ali's midsection was former WBA heavyweight champion Jimmy Ellis. As previously mentioned, after Ellis beat Floyd Patterson in Stockholm in September 1968 he went through 16 months of inactivity and didn't fight again until February 1970. During that time, he was still in training camp for fights that didn't come off, so he would have completed many rounds of sparring, including those with Ali himself. However, some say a hundred training rounds don't equate to five rounds in a real fight. To be fair, Ellis's opponent on his return was rather special, Joe Frazier, but in that same 16-month period of Jimmy's inactivity Frazier had fought Oscar Bonavena, Dave Zyglewicz and Jerry Quarry, all in title bouts and all wins. I am not saying if Jimmy had stayed active he would have beaten a super-champ like Joe, but it might have been a different fight than the one-sided battering fans witnessed in February 1970.

So boxing history didn't bode well for Ali's ring return. And behind the scenes, the Atlanta promotion was facing yet more problems.

The main income from the event was going to come from the sale of approximately one million closed circuit cinema seats, but there were some outlets facing pressure not to screen the fight and some regional promoters had second thoughts. For example, the CCTV planned for the Palace Theater in Albany in New York was threatened by opposition. In Spokane, Washington, the trouble didn't come from pressure groups, but the city council itself. At first, they refused promoters rental of the city-owned Coliseum as a venue for the CCTV operation. That decision was based primarily on Ali's draft situation, but after legal advice by the promoters, the decision was finally overturned.

The fight was going to be beamed as far away as Russia and Australia, with Russia having for the first time ever a live boxing match brought by satellite from the US. Tass, the official news agency in Russia, was not only quick to criticize the US Government's treatment of Ali, but also relayed stories about how the American people would be charged exorbitant fees to watch the fight in cinemas, while everyone in Russia would get to see the fight free of course, courtesy of state-funded television.

Controversy continued over the NYSAC's return of Ali's licence. Nat Fleischer, the editor of *The Ring* magazine stated that the New York State Athletic Commission should have appealed the decision. He wrote in the magazine that the Commission had never issued a boxer's licence to anyone who was on bail with a felony charge, except Muhammad Ali.

ALI AND QUARRY PREPARE
IN ATLANTA

Jerry Quarry and some of his party arrived in Atlanta on Monday night, 12 October. The group included his four-year-old son, Jerry Jr and one-year-old daughter, Keri. A team of newshounds were there to greet them. Flight stewardess Helen Funclerburgh had her photo taken alongside the arriving boxer, with the pic hitting many newspapers around the country the following day.

One news guy asked Jerry about his similarities with former heavyweight champion Rocky Marciano, while others asked about his chances against Ali. His answer was was that he was a different style of fighter to Marciano, as 'Rocky' was primarily a go-forward puncher, while he could box as well as punch. Jerry said everybody would find out about his chances against Ali on the night of the fight and added that the 15-round distance wouldn't bother him, as he was in shape to go 20. Jerry spoke confidently about the winner getting a crack at the title and the winner was going to be him. After the questions, Jerry and his people left for a motel about six miles outside of the city called the Matador Inn. The 'Quarry clan' eventually amounted to about 35 members.

Two days later, Ali and his camp flew in to Atlanta from Miami and the ex-champion's first press conference took place at the airport. It was a rather low key affair. Maybe some believed that they would meet up with the same brash, boasting boxer they all remembered from the 1960s. Heck, it was only two fights ago that Ali had a raucous time in the run-up to his bout against Ernie Terrell and he carried those same loud vocals into the ring. Ali snarled through his mouth protector during the fight, 'What's my name, what's my name?' in reference to Terrell continually referring to him as Cassius Clay. Or maybe some in the press expected a bold Jack Jefferson/Jack Johnson type introduction from Ali, as in the movie, *The Great White Hope*, in which Jefferson struts up the street, arms aloft, shouting 'here aah is, here aah is!'

They didn't get either, instead they were faced with a reserved man, almost business-like who came across as very polite and cooperative. A suited and booted Ali sat alongside his father and brother and quietly answered questions, saying he 'would do his best' in the upcoming bout. Ali said he was well prepared mentally as well as physically, as no other previous retired champion had ever successfully returned.

However, fellow camp aide Drew Bundini Brown enlivened the formal press occasion a touch, when he treated them to his own colourful and poetic reasons why Ali was 'definitely' going to win. It's likely that only a few in the room could actually decipher his meaning. According to Bundini, Ali's win would all come down to the moon, space and stars. It would also have something to do with the 'man that created the daffodils', the planets and of course, the perfect human being, Muhammad Ali. Bundini also brought Quarry's alleged fiery temperament into his colourful reasoning, when he equated Quarry's temper to a 'storm' and once that storm was overcome, the winner would emerge. It must have been quite a sight watching the assembled press attempting to scratch down Bundini's stream of consciousness as it tumbled out. He was certainly a jovial character and it was easy to see why Ali liked having him around. By the time Bundini had finished delivering his outer-space reasoning, it seemed the fight was already a foregone conclusion.

The place designated for Ali was Senator Leroy Johnson's private lodge, which was about 15 miles from downtown Atlanta. The lodge was actually a secluded log cabin situated on a lakeside in acres of woodland. Here Ali would rise at 4.30–5 a.m. every morning, ease his heavy boots on and complete miles of roadwork around the surrounding red clay hills. It would also be here that he would relax and consume his one main meal a day.

The actual fight headquarters was the plush 1,000-plus room Regency-Hyatt House Hotel situated on Peachtree Street in downtown Atlanta. The hotel was opened three years previously in 1967 at a reported cost of $18 million. It would be here where many of the fight people, press and super-rich would reside until the time of the fight. The luxurious ballroom would be the setting for the official weigh-in.

The lobby, said at the time of completion to be the largest ever, was surrounded by a box-shaped 'courtyard' that stretched up 22 floors, with glass cylinder 'rocket ships' that shot up and down another sky-high boxed structure within it. On closer inspection, the glass rocket ships were actually elevators. They seemed like they were headed for the stars, as a glass skylight was fixed above. The futuristic elevators were reported to be the first operating in the world at the time and cost around $35,000 each.

Perched on top of the hotel, some 300 feet above the ground was a blue glass flying saucer shaped structure called the Polaris. It was in fact a restaurant seating 200. Eating dinner in the Polaris also came with another unique feature; the structure revolved, so one could slowly take in the panoramic views of the city. Some fighters of yesteryear may have turned their noses up at such surroundings for a fight headquarters, but Ali and Quarry were rarely there. The hotel was the choice of Angelo Dundee and Bundini Brown, as Ali, unlike many top fighters, liked crowds of people around him in the run-up to fights, but in the end it was the countryside lodge they settled on.

Both fighters would conclude their final workouts a short distance across town in a somewhat dilapidated 1930s barn-like structure, called the 'Sports Arena'. The small hall was situated on the south-west side of Atlanta on the corner of Chester Avenue and Old Flat Shoals Road. The venue was mainly used for small-budget wrestling matches and singing bands, its one claim to fame being that a 20-year-old Elvis Presley once performed there in December 1955. By 1970, the building was beginning to show signs of age, the lines of red white and blue bunting hanging along the walls and ceilings doing nothing to brighten the place up.

For almost two weeks in October 1970, the old hall became the temporary training ground for heavyweight boxing's elite and their arrival came with all the international press attention that is always associated with an approaching big fight. The small arena made the pages of practically every newspaper on the planet. Fans who turned up to watch the fighters work out were well-rewarded for their $2 entrance fee and the steadily increasing stream of newsmen that came through the doors were accompanied by ex-fighters and boxing 'experts'.

The old hall was one of the venues that would receive a satellite screening of the bout. Approaching fight night, the hall would be converted into a makeshift film theater after it had served its purpose as a makeshift boxing gym. Home TV and radio coverage would be blanked out in Atlanta during the fight but locals who didn't have a ticket to the city auditorium could still get to see it live if they coughed up the $10 entrance fee to watch it inside the Sports Arena.

The fight itself would take place inside the 5,000-seat Atlanta Municipal Auditorium, situated on the corner of Courtland Street and Gilmer Street. This was another old structure, constructed in 1909, which was also normally home to visiting pop groups and wrestling shows. The relatively small seating capacity of the arena, meant the attendance of the fight would be the smallest for an Ali bout since he fought Sonny Liston the second time in 1965. Then, a hockey rink called St Dominic's arena in Lewiston, Maine played host to 2,434 spectators, which had set a low attendance record for any previous world heavyweight title fight.

Inside the entrance lobby, visitors were greeted by a white bust of the famous Italian tenor, Enrico Caruso. At the time of Jerry and Muhammad's October appearance, the arena was of course owned by the city of Atlanta, but nine years later, the building was taken over and used by the State University of Georgia. (Today it's called the Dahlberg Hall. The last time a boxing match of any importance took place there was 31 years earlier, when surprisingly, none other than Angelo Dundee's brother, Chris, brought middleweight Ken Overlin to face Atlanta favourite 'Belter' Ben Brown for a 10-round contest, which ended in a draw. Overlin's visit to the auditorium was five months before him winning the NYSAC version of the world middleweight title at Madison Square Garden against Ceferino Garcia on the 23 May 1940. Overlin won on points over 15 rounds.)

Three days after the Brown v Overlin 1939 scrap and in the same city auditorium, on Thursday 14 December 1939, the venue hosted the movie premiere ball of one of the most famous films of all time, *Gone With The Wind*. Author of the 1936 novel Margaret Mitchell was from Atlanta. The world film premiere of *Gone with the Wind* took place in city, at Loew's Grand Theater in downtown Atlanta, a day later; 300,000 people crammed the streets on the day of the opening.

When Ali arrived in Atlanta in 1970, some critics believed Ali's boxing skills had gone with the wind. Across town from the auditorium, inside the Sports Arena, fans had their own opportunity to see how far Ali's skills had or had not eroded, when his workouts were scheduled to begin at 12.30 p.m. each day, while Jerry's training time in the hall would begin later at 2.30–3 p.m.

On Thursday 15 October, the day after the former champion arrived, after his early morning roadwork Ali completed eight fast-paced rounds inside a temporary ring – three with Herman 'Bunky' Akins, three with brother, Rahaman and two with Willie Johnson. Ali wore headgear for the session and most of the time he worked on speed and defence, using his feet and reflexes to avoid any damaging punches. Afterwards, Ali was in a more talkative mood than the previous day, telling everyone that he hoped Jerry hadn't been reading all the past press stories about him being out of shape, as he was feeling and looking in great condition. When a tape measure was brought out, there wasn't any notable difference to his physique since his last bout in 1967, except his biceps had grown an inch bigger.

His jovial mood that day may have had something to do with another visit by Stepin Fetchit (Lincoln Perry), who turned up to watch his gym session. The banter continued, and just before leaving Ali scrawled a chalked message on the heavy bag, warning Jerry not to pound it too hard with his fists, as he might damage it.

According to a report in the *Dixon Evening Telegraph* this was also Jerry's first training period in the old hall and the session lasted about one hour. He completed six sparring rounds, four with light-heavy Eddie 'Bossman' Jones, who attempted his own impersonation of Ali's fast-moving ring style and a further two rounds with his equally speedy 19-year-old brother Mike. Jerry impressed bystanders by cutting the ring off on his sparring partners and landing solidly on his faster moving, lighter opponents.

Afterwards, Quarry claimed it wasn't only Ali's style that his sparring hands could imitate, but both were also faster than him. Surprisingly, Jerry didn't wear protective headgear that day. He claimed he didn't need the protection as he had never once been cut during training for any of his previous fights. He claimed he wasn't susceptible to cuts, despite losing to Frazier on a cut and according to the fight reports at the time, suffered minor cuts in a few of his past winning fights.

On Friday Ali went through nine rounds with the same sparring partners. Ali spent most of the time avoiding punches by back-peddling and circling the ring, occasionally unleashing a combination. It was impressively fast and certainly captured the attention of the 100 or so in the hall watching. The *Atlanta Constitution* reported that Willie Johnson was left looking 'groggy' after the session and Akins ended up on the floor outside of the ring, even though this didn't come from a punch, but when he lost his footing.

Ali's brother was the last man to spar with him that morning and he went four rounds. In between sessions, Ali called out to some wide-eyed kids watching from the surrounding benched seats that boxing was a hard way to earn a living. The boys would have witnessed what Ali meant, when in the final two rounds he hardly moved off the ropes, absorbing body punishment from Rahaman's clubbing blows. He allowed his brother to pound away without offering a return shot and when Rahaman slung punches to his head, he usually, but not always, managed to sway out of distance.

It was this tactic of swaying his head back that Jerry's brother Mike claimed would be Ali's downfall. Mike, already showing marks on his face after the previous day's session, declared that if Jerry threw a right hand that happened to fall short of Ali's moving head, he would 'counter' to the body with a fast left hook. He believed reaching Ali's body with 'power shots' would eventually wear him down. Quarry's trainer, Teddy Bentham, said that's exactly where Jerry would be aiming his attack on the night of the fight – to Ali's body – adding that Jerry was probably the hardest body puncher in boxing. Even though Jerry looked sharp in the training ring that day, his amount of ring time was curtailed to a mere four rounds, two with 'Bossman' and two with his brother. Teddy said he didn't want Jerry to peak too soon. So maybe training for Jerry finished a touch early that afternoon, but it still didn't help him catch a thief, or thieves, who lifted a $90 coat. The *Atlanta Constitution* reported that the theft happened while Jerry was going through his training session. His motor was parked outside, with a coat inside and someone took a liking to it and swiped it.

After each daily gym session, Ali would normally be driven back to Leroy Johnson's three-bedroom log cabin out of town. It was here that he spent most of his downtime, but the cabin would forever have a stream of visitors. Press, family, friends, fans and those involved in the promotion turned up. As previously stated, Ali always enjoyed being surrounded by people, even to the point of pandemonium, approaching fights, but the constant flow of characters meant it was difficult to get a private word with him. A cottage that might have held five people, sometimes became temporary home to a dozen or more. Ali would sometimes be found wearing a tracksuit chewing on a toothpick and lounging on a blue-framed couch, chatting to visitors and answering a stream of telephone calls from wherever they came. Dinner would usually consist of a couple of steaks and vegetables, washed down with beetroot or carrot juice. He would also sometimes watch a film projected onto a white sheet hung on one of the wood-framed walls. The curtains of the cottage were normally closed, not just to watch films, but to also keep the glare of sunlight out.

It was fight films those in the crammed cabin would watch, of course. Occasionally, Ali would put on Quarry's losing 1969 effort against Frazier, or his own eight-round exhibition event from the previous month.

Watching himself or his opponent sometimes prompted him to include his own commentary, dancing and jabbing as he talked through the flickering images on the wall. Ali would sometimes study the fight footage of Quarry and then reassure visitors and possibly himself that his opponent couldn't win. According to Ali, Quarry's short-armed counter punching style couldn't work against his own, faster moving style and longer reach. Sometimes, fight films of the old greats including Jack Johnson were shown, but mostly they watched films from the lighter divisions, such as those of 'Sugar' Ray Robinson, Johnny Bratton or 'Kid' Gavilan. Watching the 'Kid's unique 'Bolo' punch on screen gave Ali the thought of trying that punch out during the Quarry fight. Heavyweight Ali still claimed he was faster than those lighter, smaller fighters – except for the legendary 'Sugar' Ray, whom he had idolized as a kid. If it wasn't fight films they watched, Ali would sometimes spool up a good western, or in lighter moments, cartoons.

Artist LeRoy Neiman was one regular visitor to Ali's temporary cabin hideaway. Sometimes Neiman would spend hours alongside keen amateur artist Ali and his talented sign painter father, Cassius Clay Sr painting pictures. Neiman had been commissioned to complete the artwork for the front cover of the official fight program and a number of on-site posters with a limited run of only 500. The visiting artist and the ample downtime inspired Ali to complete a large mosaic-like painting of how he thought the fight would turn out. He was the winner. The art work showed a boxing ring surrounded by circles, which represented the many faces at ringside. Inside the ring was a caricature of a boxer with stars spinning around his head. The referee had a bubble drawn above his head with the words 'Stop it, Ali go to your corner, it's all over now.' Even state governor Lester Maddox had a place in Ali's art work. In one corner of the painting a figure was shown striding towards the ring, with another bubble above his head, with the words 'Stop that fight!'. Next to the figure was the word 'Maddox'. Ali's painting wouldn't be completed until two days before the fight, and when it was, he signed it with the words 'To Leroy from Muhammad Ali'.

Over the first weekend in Atlanta, there was no respite in training, with both fighters using the Sports Arena. On Sunday, 18 October, each boxer scaled well within their fighting weights, with Ali weighing at 213¼ lbs and Jerry at 197lbs. Their now repetitive training routine meant Ali completed another nine rounds, with Jerry going five. Jerry mostly concentrated his ring work on body attacks, calling one of his 'speciality' body punches, the 'Marciano lasagne punch', in reference to Marciano's Italian heritage and his famed brutal attacks to the body.

The slight reprieve in training came a day later, on Monday, 19 October, one week before the fight. While the fighters relaxed away from the the Sports Arena, representatives from both camps came together to formalize some of the rules. Jack Quarry, Angelo Dundee and Hal Conrad from Sports Action Inc thrashed out agreements on how the fight would be regulated.

The absence of a boxing commission in Atlanta meant both parties agreeing to a scoring system used by the NYSAC. This would mean the 15-round fight would be scored on a round by round basis, with the winner gaining 10 points and the loser being awarded 9 points or less. The referee and two judges would score and they wouldn't be named until the day of the fight.

Even though it was also agreed that 8-ounce gloves would be used, they couldn't yet agree on the rule about three knockdowns ending the bout, or whether a mandatory 8 count should be administered after each knockdown. One other important issue that wasn't decided that day was the size of the ring. A large ring was thought to be to Ali's advantage. Most of the decisions would be ironed out behind the scenes over the next few days. With one week to go before the fight, one news report claimed the tickets in the arena were still moving slowly. It said that even though all the $15 tickets had been sold, many of the $25, $50, and $100 were still available.

On Tuesday 20 October, Ali's preparations included his usual early morning roadwork, followed later by his 12.30 p.m. gym session. Ali completed nine sparring rounds and included a few shuffles and a couple of attempts at impersonating 'Kid' Gavilan's 'Bolo punch'. He followed this with a punishing calisthenics routine. After the session, one report had him down to a svelte 209lbs, which was an impressive 4¼ pounds fewer than he weighed on the Sunday. This was an extremely low weight for Ali, even though he was training for speed It was expected that he would come to the fight heavier than that. Ali though, declared he would come in even lower at 205 lbs, which would be 5½ lbs lighter than when he fought Liston back in 1964. Ali said the weight loss was down to more than just training, it was also down to his strict diet, which included vegetables that he had juiced every day. Thirty or more carrots were crushed to form a daily drink.

Sandwiched between both fighters training slots that day, a telephone link-up with 25 US cities took place. Press, 'boxing experts' and ex-fighters were meant to call in from around the country with questions. Unfortunately, the telephone engineers had trouble with most of the connections and many of those trying to get through failed to do so. Many writers at the time said that the hook-up ended up in silent comedy chaos, with David Condon of the *Chicago Tribune* writing that the only voice that came through clearly was that of Howard Cosell!

So in between them receiving the odd call from the 25 city connections, there was a lot of standing around, so much so that a 'weary' Ali, said that he thought maybe the whole thing was an attempt to tire him out pre-fight. On one of the few occasions the phone connections did work, hook-ups were made to former heavyweight boxing champ Jersey Joe Walcott, who called in from New York and – still an idol to millions – Joe Louis, who called in via one of the 'crackling' phone lines from Denver, Colorado. Louis was a co-promoter of a CCTV venture that would be beamed to Denver. When his voice came through Joe was heard to say that he agreed that next week's fight should be for the world heavyweight title as Ali had never lost his title in the ring.

However, he still may have rattled Ali a touch, when he spoke about how he doubted Ali could regain his peak form after only six weeks training. Louis claimed that after a long layoff, the first thing a fighter loses is his 'legs' – meaning a fighter's footwork. Louis said Ali should have a few more warm-up fights before venturing in against Frazier. That comment may have also rattled Quarry, who didn't see himself as a warm up opponent.

In contrast, Walcott's words from New York likely put a smile on Ali's face, when he disagreed with Louis and said the former champion should have no problem reaching top form, as he believed Ali was one of the greatest heavyweight champions ever.

For those who believed in omens, Joe Louis's somewhat negative forecast for Ali could be good. Louis had predicted Ali to lose on numerous past occasions, including his first title tilt against Sonny Liston. Joe was a notoriously bad guide when it came to predicting the outcome of Ali's bouts. On the other hand, as we know, Louis was another ex-world champion who had once made a comeback in an attempt to regain the world heavyweight title. When Louis faced rising heavyweight sensation, Rocky Marciano in his last ever fight at Madison Square Garden, it took place on 26 October 1951. October 26, was the very same date Ali would face Quarry, exactly 19 years to the day. Louis, as with Ali, went into the bout as favourite and both were former champions facing arguably the hardest hitting white heavyweights of their era. In the 'Brown Bomber's' case, the odds makers were proved wrong, when he was crushed by the 'Rock'. Of course the main difference between the comebacks was that Louis was 36 years old when he returned to face Ezzard Charles in September 1950 and one year older by the time he was pitched in against Marciano. Ali was still only 28 years old. Back in 1951, Marciano belted and battered a nation's idol to an 8th-round defeat and the sight of 'old' Joe Louis half hanging out of the Madison Square Garden ring lingered in the minds of fight fans for years after.

Ali's answer to all the doubters never wavered. A Louis type defeat wouldn't befall him because he was better than all the past heavyweights. Apart from having youth and speed on his side, he claimed to be a better boxer than Gene Tunney and have a better defence than Jack Johnson. The ultra-confident former champion said it was unwise to compare any other comeback attempts to his own.

When the telephone connections worked and it was Jerry's turn to speak, he mentioned that he was now becoming bored with going through the same daily routine of 'banging bags' and punching sparring partners. He was ready now for the real thing. He said there would only be one winner in Monday night and that would be him.

As the on-off telephone hook-up continued, 6ft 11in basketball star and fellow 1960 Rome Olympic gold medallist Walt 'Big Bell' Bellamy walked into the hall. At the time, Walt was with the Atlanta Hawks and he was set to play in the big game that Saturday against Boston Celtic. When Ali spotted him, he invited him over and it didn't take long before he went through his routine of 'sizing up' the giant ball player. Ali continued with the telecom-chat, but it didn't last long, as Quarry wanted to start his

3 p.m. training session. Eventually Ali had to cut the last caller short, saying Quarry was waiting for him to leave.

Angelo Dundee hung back to watch Jerry's ring work that afternoon but he wouldn't get to see much as the issue of Quarry peaking too early was taken seriously and Teddy Bentham restricted Jerry's sparring to five rounds. The sparring session may have been short, but it was still impressive. One particular moment caught Dundee's eye when Jerry and 'Bossman' got involved in a torrid exchange of punches in the centre of the ring. Angelo was heard to say that the Californian sure could sling his punches fast, accurate and hard. Jerry apparently heard the complimentary remarks and later assured Dundee that it wasn't only his impressive arsenal of punches that he would be bringing with him on Monday, but ring craftsmanship as well.

Five days before the fight, about 200 people that included fans, legendary trainer/manager, Cus D'Amato, a few members of the Quarry clan and a growing number of the world's press all filed into the Sports Arena. On that day, Angelo Dundee wanted Ali to restrict his ring work to four rounds, but he still ended up completing seven. Ali's father, Cassius Sr, was also ringside that day and watched his two sons going through three rounds together. Ali again spent most of the time with his back against the ropes, absorbing punches. A further four sparring rounds were shared with Akins and Johnson. In those final rounds, Ali upped the tempo, dancing around the ring and shooting out rapier jabs that bounced off the protective headgear of his sparring partners. When Ali used the ring and let his punches fly he certainly resembled the fighter of old and didn't look a day older or a pound heavier than in 1967.

To most, it was an impressive performance, but one guy who wasn't buying it was Cus D'Amato. He said looking great in the training ring didn't mean he could replicate it in a real fight. In D'Amato's opinion, it could be completely different on fight night if Ali found himself under constant pressure. The veteran trainer wasn't convinced the former champion could return to form. He had noticed in particular that Ali's brother was able sometimes to catch him with hooks coming off the ropes. The problem, according to D'Amato's expert eye, was that if the fight went into the later rounds, he didn't think Ali could keep up those slick movements he was seeing in the training ring. He said Quarry would go in with a huge advantage because of being active and being used to the pressure that always came with a big fight.

Jose Torres was another one who thought Quarry's pressure could cause the inactive Ali problems. Torres knew the boxing business inside out, being a former world light-heavyweight boxing champion himself and protégé of Cus D'Amato. Torres still favoured Ali though, but this was not based on what he witnessed in the workouts, it was just about who Ali was. He believed Ali's character and confidence were enough to deflect any leather that would head his way on the 26th.

After Ali's sparring session finished, he gave interviews and had some advice for any kid that wanted to follow in his footsteps. He advised against it, saying that it was only worth it if you became a champion and said he certainly didn't want a son of his to be a professional boxer. At that point, his family consisted of three daughters. It would be another daughter and not a son, Laila Ali, born seven years later in 1977, who would win a world title in 2002 and have 24 fights without defeat during her career.

During Wednesday's press session, Ali was in fine form, saying that he was such a big draw, people from all over the world would be coming to see him and it wouldn't just be a normal fight crowd that would show up. If he could maintain his present condition and form, Quarry wouldn't get past two or three rounds. Most of the press seemed to be in agreement.

They were impressed by Ali's condition and movement in the sparring ring and thought his odds of 2 to 5 on were about right. The bookmakers, of course, based their odds not only on how a boxer performed in the training ring.

One obvious consideration was how the fighters had fared against the same opponents; which in this case meant Brian London, Floyd Patterson, Alex Miteff, Billy Daniels and George Chuvalo. From 1961 to 1966, Ali/Clay had fought each one of the above and knocked out or stopped all of them except Chuvalo, who took him the full 15 rounds in 1966. Incredibly, Jerry crammed all those same opponents into only eight months (From 9 March to 28 October 1967) and that included fighting Floyd Patterson twice! As we know, Patterson held Jerry to a 10-round draw in their first encounter, but Quarry won the return four months later by a points decision over 12 rounds. Brian London managed to last 10 rounds with Jerry, but lost the decision. Jerry knocked out both Miteff and Daniels early in their respective fights and as we know, when Brian London eventually climbed back into the ring with Quarry two years later (1969) he was counted out in the second round.

Chuvalo, as we know, had a previous controversial inside the distance win over Jerry. One concerning thing for the Quarry camp is that both Chuvalo and Patterson (in their first fight) managed to deck Quarry, something that never looked likely when they met Ali.

So based on common opponents and how they fared, it was easy to see how Ali was the big betting favourite, but boxing, especially with the heavyweights, is never straightforward. The factors weighing against Ali were the ones no one could quantify, the physiological and psychological effects of being dumped on the sidelines for so long. Was six weeks intensive training after three-and-a-half years out of the game enough to regain ring savvy?

A boxing ring is somewhere you can find a guy who looks unbeatable on the outside, possessing rippling muscles and looking meaner than an angry pit bull dog, only to later see him get flattened by a mild looking kid – that's one of the attractions of the sport. Ali looked in better condition as each day passed. He was bigger and faster than Quarry and most people expected him to win, but on the night, the odds could be easily overturned just by one heavy thud on the chin.

There was no time for flashy ring displays when Quarry went through with his Wednesday afternoon sparring session. It was brutal, rugged aggression all the way. It was clear that Jerry hit hard, especially with the left hook and he hit with the type of speed that could trouble any opponent. That is, if he managed to hit them at all of course.

One of Ali's favorite sayings was 'hitting hard doesn't mean nothing if you can't find nothing to hit.' That was a very true statement, but a couple of times when opponents did find something to hit, he went down on the seat of his pants from left hooks, delivered by Sonny Banks in 1962 and Henry Cooper in 1963. Quarry, along with Joe Frazier of course, had possibly the best and most effective left hook in the business – it was fast, crushingly hard and accurate as a sniper's bullet. Teddy Bentham had already made it clear that their fight strategy was based on concentrating attacks to Ali's body to eventually wear Ali down and when that happened, Jerry would pounce and unleash every power punch that he possessed.

There was no doubt Jerry would bring plenty of firepower into the ring; but what about his alleged fiery temperament? This was something Bundini had brought up when they first arrived in Atlanta and something the Ali camp seemed keen on exploring further. In a couple of Jerry's losses, especially when he fought the best of the sluggers, Joe Frazier, he tried to out-slug him and failed and when he fought a master boxer, Jimmy Ellis, he tried to out-box him and failed again. It was thought in these two fights, Jerry should have done the opposite and attempted to go in slugging against the boxer (Ellis) and out-box the slugger (Frazier). He ended up trying to beat his opponents at their own game.

In an interview after the Wednesday sparring session, Quarry claimed he would now strictly follow the advice of his corner instead of veering off the fight-plan and trying to fight his opponent's fight. However, earlier that day, when both fighters had come together for the official pre-fight medical, the unpredictable Quarry psyche was seen to crack and his 'Irish' temper flared in front of both Ali and the world's press. The medical had taken place inside their shared training headquarters and was carried out by two black doctors. When Ali spotted them, he jokingly shouted out that it made a change to see two 'soul doctors', while Jerry called out that he was going to need more help than two doctors during their fight. Both fighters were stripped to the waist and sat opposite each other at a small blue table placed in front of the training ring, where the doctors examined them. Publicist Murray Goodman called the double physical examination a first in boxing history, as the normally boring requirement was traditionally carried out separately.

While this was taking place, photographers and press used the opportunity to snap and interview both fighters together, but as the two stared at each other across the table, they started to mildly heckle one another. Ali gently reminded Quarry, that he would be going against the 'greatest fighter ever' next Monday, while Quarry raised a clenched fist to show his opponent how he was going to answer his verbal bravado. When the weights and measurements of both fighters were completed, it was announced Ali was almost 3in taller (6ft 3in to Quarry's 6ft ½in), weighed 12lbs more (on that day) and had a 5½in reach advantage (Ali, 82in, Quarry 76½in). (These are also the 'tale of the tape' measurements given in the official fight program, but Quarry's reach seems to have increased dramatically, as in the Foster fight it was given as 72in.)

While various announcements were made, the needle continued, with Ali's quiet, endless verbals probing Quarry's psyche. Ali repeatedly goaded Jerry by adopting an unblinking hypnotic stare and with a serious, almost inquisitive look on his face, repeatedly asking Jerry what it was that made him believe he had a chance of actually winning. The 'Irish' temper, started to simmer and with a forced grin, Jerry spat back, 'I know I can!' Ali, again, quiet but direct, reeled off the names of those past opponents that he had beaten with ease, knowing Jerry had had tough fights with a couple of them. Jerry, informed Ali that he best forget all those former opponents as it was him that he was fighting on Monday, not Floyd Patterson or George Chuvalo.

It was clear Ali was out to unsettle Quarry. If Jerry was quick to lose his temper now, that fragile temperament could well be carried over into the heat of battle, which could make him lose concentration when he needed it most. At one point, they stood next to each other as the doctors went about their various checks and the exchange continued. Ali asked Quarry to show him 'what he could do' and Jerry placed his fist on Ali's jaw. Ali asked 'Is that all you've got?' At that point, one of Ali's sparring partners, Willie Johnson, chipped in with his own piece of 'advice' that finally brought the temper to the boil.

Willie urged Jerry to check out if his insurance covered burial costs before the fight. That was enough and Jerry unleashed a tirade, all directed at Johnson. Ali joined in the drama, attempting to turn the proceedings into a stage-managed riot. If the whole thing was a ploy by the Ali camp to get Jerry riled, it worked. The aggravation came to a stop when Angelo Dundee jumped in between the two, leaving Ali to walk out of the arena smiling and Jerry steaming. (According to a report in the

Courier-Post of 22 October, when Ali left the Sports Arena that day, he visited the grave of Rev Martin Luther King Jr.) The venomous words from Jerry included making some threats about flattening Johnson in the ring after beating Ali and belittling the sparring partner's ring talents. Jerry said Willie Johnson needed to 'butt out!'

The world's press were all there, recording every word and angry reaction from the Californian fighter. Jerry, still seething, said the last opponent who attempted to 'get under his skin' before a fight was Thad Spencer two years before. Spencer ended up being pummeled around the ring until the referee came to his rescue. In that fight, immediately after the referee's instructions, Quarry informed Spencer that it was now time to shut his 'big mouth'. Jerry raised his clenched fist again and said Ali was in for a similar night.

That afternoon, further announcements came out about the rules for the fight. It was agreed that the three-knockdown rule would be waived. A mandatory 8-count was agreed, meaning if either fighter was knocked down, they would receive an automatic 8-second reprieve, even if they wanted to continue immediately.

Some time later, boxing writer Peter Moss described what happened during Ali's training session the day after the medical showdown. In a feature article in December 1970 for *TV Times* magazine, he described how a whole platoon of the Quarry family showed up, as many as two dozen and spread over several generations. They sat in a single line and watched Ali go through six rounds. Nearing the end of the final round, Ali placed a small square piece of material flat on the blue ring canvas. He planted his feet on the cloth, lowered both his gloved mitts and beckoned his sparring partner to hit him. His punching partner then slung a barrage of punches in Ali's direction, but not one landed. It was an impressive display and by Peter Moss's account, it drove the crowd of paying fans wild that day; except for that one long line of stony faces.

A few days later, Angelo Dundee, in an interview with the *Independent Press-Telegram* (Long Beach, 25 October) even said he felt a touch sorry for Quarry, comparing the boxers with politicians Richard Nixon and John F. Kennedy in their famous TV debates back in 1960. Ali, naturally, was the charismatic Kennedy. Quarry was Tricky Dickie, of whom Chicago Mayor Richard Daley, having watched the debates, said, 'My God, they've embalmed him before he even died.'

Ali could certainly captivate an audience and it was a great time to do it, as the press arriving from around the globe increased every day. After Ali's Thursday training session, in a ten-minute period, he completed quick-fire interviews with press representatives from three different countries. He told the assembled hacks that he would know when it was time to quit boxing – when more than two punches managed to land on his face in one round. Ali stated that he was now in a condition to do 30 rounds, never mind 15 and it was his early morning 90-minute runs that were key. He felt so fit, he thought he might even complete eight sparring rounds on the morning of the fight. He told them the fight would be over early. Ali's father, there that day said his son could end the fight early, but he wanted him to stretch it out to six rounds to be fair to the fans travelling from abroad.

Thursday's 2.30 p.m. start time for Quarry's sparring saw a change of mood; it was straight down to business. This included trading punches with 'Bossman' for three rounds and reportedly going through a few rounds with an unnamed heavyweight. This would be the last day of ring work for Jerry and after completing his tough calisthenics routine, it was only mild loosening-up exercises for the remaining few days. He had completed something around 130 rounds of sparring and clocked up to 8 miles of roadwork each day in preparation for Monday's bout.

Afterwards, Jerry spoke to the newsmen that had gathered in the hall and claimed Ali's reach wouldn't be a factor in the fight's outcome, as almost every fighter he had fought had a longer reach than him. Jerry said that he had only been hurt once in the ring and that was against Al Jones. The quickest fighter he had ever faced was Floyd Patterson. When asked about Ali's situation outside of the ring, Jerry stated that he admired Ali, as not many people would stand by their convictions if they were faced with a five-year prison term.

Later that day it was decided that there wouldn't be one or even two doctors stationed at ringside on fight night, but four! – two white and two black. The 'racial balance' of medics came about after concerns from the Quarry side about the fight being stopped too quickly in Ali's favour if Quarry picked up a slight injury.

There was two other significant statements that day. First came the news that the winner of Monday's bout would be pitched in against Oscar Bonavena from Buenos Aries in Argentina. One press statement said that Bonavena, rated number one by the World Boxing Association, had already signed his part of the contract to face the winner. It's unsure how that news would have sat with both fighters, as both were after Joe Frazier. According to a report in the *Atlanta-Constitution* a clause in Quarry's contract meant that if he beat Ali, he was tied into a return bout. Quarry later denied there was a return clause in the contract

Another voice that was heard that day was that of Lester Maddox. He eased himself back into the Ali picture and the news headlines declaring the people of Georgia should treat the day of Ali's bout as 'a day of mourning' and hoped he would be knocked out for the count of 30. Maddox urged people to boycott the fight. Maddox contrasted Ali's statement about not wanting to inflict pain or death on someone in war, with his actions in coming to Atlanta to inflict pain and punishment on a fellow American citizen and receive a huge sum of money to do it. He said again, that he felt it was wrong to glorify a man who neglected his duty to fight for his country. Maddox urged all the 'patriotic people' of Georgia to show their displeasure about the fight – by this he presumably meant by not showing up for the fight, not turning up to the CCTV outlets or maybe coming out on the city streets and protesting. His words were printed in the *Philadelphia Daily News* on 23 October. It goes without saying that Maddox wouldn't attend the fight.

Jerry, on first hearing Lester Maddox's words, said that he certainly wasn't going to 'mourn' on Monday. In fact, he would have much to celebrate, when he won. City Mayor Sam Massell was heard to sing a different tune to Maddox, calling the Ali v Quarry fight a great event that would shine a positive international spotlight on the sports-mad city and state. The event would be the climax of a spectacular sporting weekend in Atlanta.

The three-day extravaganza would begin on Saturday afternoon, when the Georgia Tech–Tulane University football game would take place and that evening there would be the Atlanta Hawks–Boston Celtic basketball game. On Sunday there would be the Atlanta Falcons–New Orleans Saints NFL game and an international motorcycle race taking place during the same weekend. Then on Monday, the city would host the fight.

Behind the scenes though, there was something allegedly discovered that could have derailed Sam Massell's sporting spectacular. According to the book *Muhammad Ali's Greatest Fight*, an old state law was uncovered dating back to the post-Civil War period, which stated that fights between blacks and whites were prohibited in the city of Atlanta.

Lester Maddox objected to the fight because of Ali's draft conviction, not because of his race. This ancient ruling was apparently kept away from the eyes of Lester Maddox, but even if he had seen it, would he really have acted upon it? Some say yes.

I think Maddox, even in his keenness to put a kibosh on the fight, was too canny even to consider using something as inflammatory as that to stop it. Anyway, as it turned out, the ancient city ordinance was a non-starter.

Some reports said local radio stations were swamped with callers protesting about the fight. One thing that was sure, those opposed to the fight were not just confined to Georgia. Mississippi state congressman, Democrat Thomas Abernethy, publicly stated that the bout involving Muhammad Ali should be ignored.

The objections by certain politicians was in contrast to some everyday fans though. One local resident who visited the daily training sessions was interviewed by *The Los Angeles Times* (25 October). The guy was a construction worker and when asked about Monday's fight, he claimed that it was only the politicians who wanted to stop it. He claimed the working people in the city were happy that the event was taking place and he didn't think there would be any trouble.

Yet there were stories of threats and intimidation. Ali's autobiography, *The Greatest – My Own Story*, tells of bullets flying past Ali and Bundini's ears one night while they stood outside Leroy's countryside cabin. The gunfire was not the only thing they heard coming from the direction of the woods, but also shouted threats, warning Ali not to proceed with the fight. Both Mayor Sam Massell and Robert Kassel also received threats. There were many rumours and insinuations flying around – one was that a bullet would be heading Jerry Quarry's way.

Despite those later claims of gun shots and ring shootings, Teddy Bentham told *The Los Angeles Times* at the time that they didn't receive one threatening phone call at the Matador Inn. But Ali received vicious telephone threats at the cottage; and head of security, Detective J. D. Hudson, did make statements to the press about letters of protest, but he described them as coming from cranks and didn't take them too seriously. Nevertheless, after the police department heard of one particular threat, detective Hudson increased security around Ali and switched the routes of his morning training runs as a safety precaution.

From the moment Ali set foot in Atlanta, he had been extremely polite. His time in the city came with the absence of the brash talk that maybe some expected or remembered him for. Apart from the minor face-off at the physical on Wednesday, Ali was quite reserved and most of his banter came with an air of charm and friendly diplomacy. While in town, Ali even had kind words for the man who said would do his utmost to put a stop to the whole event, Lester Maddox. Ali showed no animosity towards the governor and said Maddox was only saying in public things he believed in; something Ali was known for of course. The newspapers in Atlanta didn't print any controversial headlines, confining their accounts to fair and unbiased reports. A later report in a *Newsweek* article of 9 November made the point, saying the two main city newspapers could well have stirred feelings up, but they didn't. The same could be said for the fight trade magazines in both the US and the UK, with their words confined to the facts.

One can only imagine how things could have turned out if Ali had approached the Quarry fight in the same raucous manner he did with Liston back in 1964. No doubt Ali would have certainly created more interest among the people in the city, but maybe it would have been the wrong type of interest. That approach would have played straight into Lester Maddox's hands

In any case, House of Sports Inc had already gone beyond the amount of security that was required by the city alderman and had hired more police and ushers for the arena on the night.

The popularity of the fight across the rest of the country would be revealed by how many people turned up at the cinemas. Pressure from some protest groups prevented people from purchasing a ticket in some places. That day (Thursday) news broke of one promoter in Scranton, Philadelphia, called Lindy Vicardi, who had to cancel his CCTV operation because of opposition from local veteran groups. A satellite screening of the bout was meant to take place at the Scranton Catholic Youth Center, but opposition had been organized by an American Legion commander who appealed to veteran organizations in both Lackawanna and Wayne Counties. The cancellation came after the district commander, who represented thousands of members in Lackawanna County, called for a boycott. Various other district commanders of other veteran groups echoed Lester Maddox's words and urged people not to attend any of the satellite screenings.

In Ohio for example, one newspaper in Akron, *The Akron Beacon Journal* told how various veteran groups in Summit County planned on picketing the CCTV showing at the local Civic Theater. As the fight drew near, the *Daily Mirror* newspaper in the UK reported that promoters were showing concern about shifting the 900,000 allotted cinema seats around the world.

There was other more technical problems in the run-up to the fight. Angelo Dundee had held out for a 20-foot square ring, but the wrestling ring in the auditorium measured only 18 feet square. No deal said Angelo, so a search was instigated – there wasn't a 20-foot ring in the whole of Georgia. Eventually, one was found but it had to be transported all the way from the US Navy Base in Charleston, South Carolina. Right up to the day preceding the bout, the ring had still not been fully erected.

Despite all the controversy, technical shortfalls, uncertainty, threats of protest, cries of objection, hype and ballyhoo, it all came to down to what Lester Maddox said at the very beginning: 'On with the show!'

On Friday morning, (23 October), just three days before the bout, representatives from the House of Sports Inc and the city

Aldermen met together to finalize all legal requirements. The only change came when the city Aldermen changed the name on the auditorium permit to Muhammad Ali and Jerry Quarry, rather than the original one that said Muhammad Ali and Joe Frazier.

Jerry was a no-show for even light training on that day and spent his time back at the Matador Inn. Sure, Jerry was at his peak and had finished all his heavy sparring the previous day but it still seemed a strange day to miss as 200 or more media guys from all over the world attended the Sports Arena. With them were three or four hundred fans who paid their entrance fee and expected to see something for their $2.

Rumours abounded as to why Quarry didn't arrive for training. Some members of his family were still spotted sitting at ringside. Ali's father was again present at the 12.30 morning training session and he laughed loudly after he was asked about Lester Maddox's remark about the day of the fight being a day of mourning. Clay Sr half-jokingly but also probably accurately said that Maddox was just finding ways to get attention for himself, with all world's press being in town. As regards his elder son's fighting condition, he believed he was in the best shape since the first Liston fight. He also claimed not to have seen him as dedicated in training since that world title bout.

With the fight so near, trading blows in the ring was not in that day's training schedule. Skipping, shadow boxing and hitting the light and heavy bags were enough. However, this changed after a few quiet, but persuasive words from Angelo Dundee, who reminded him of the vast distances some had travelled to see him. So before many of the writers could even reach for their notebooks, the ex-champion was gloved up and had hopped into the sparring ring, ready to change the light workout into a boxing exhibition.

All the ballyhoo, hype and sparring may have ended for Quarry, but Ali seemed to want to wind it up further, deciding to go three rounds with 'Bunky' Akins. The fans, press and the few members of the Quarry family ended up getting to see the full repertoire of his unique pugilistic skills inside the ring and his verbal talent outside of it afterwards. For the first two sparring rounds, he put on a punching display, with his slick in-and-out footwork, making Akins miss most of his own attempted shots. Maybe with the exception of Quarry's family members, those inside the hall enjoyed his ring craftsmanship and unique 'hit-me-if-you-can' movements. Bundini Brown shouted words of encouragement from ringside wearing a tee-shirt with the immortal words 'float like a butterfly and sting like a bee' printed on the back. The sizzling punches made the hard-boiled pressmen pull their folding chairs a touch closer to the ring and sit up.

Then in the third session, just when Ali's ring manoeuvres had captured everyone's attention, he suddenly changed tactics and allowed Akins to pound away at his body. The seconds ticked by as the punches slammed in one after another. Ali faked tiredness and fatigue, first 'slumping' against the ropes, then gasping for breath. He then finished the show by jumping out of the ring, to the applause of the crammed hall.

After his sparring and calisthenics routine was completed, a folding chair was placed in the ring and Ali held court. Wrapped in a white terry towelling robe, with streams of sweat dripping from his head onto the canvas, he sat near the ring ropes and answered questions from the writers and broadcasters, at least a dozen of them coming from the UK alone. When Ali was asked to comment about Lester Maddox's day of mourning statement, he answered by saying he couldn't really comment as he didn't know what Maddox meant. When someone ringside helpfully explained Maddox meant it was going to be a 'black day' Ali had everyone laughing when he agreed and said Monday was certainly going to be that, there were going to be a lot of 'his people' turning up at the fight.

When it did come to talking seriously about the fight, the mental challenge, according to Ali, would be bigger for Quarry than the physical one and he equated Monday night's bout with the one he had with Sonny Liston in Lewiston, Maine, back in 1965. Then, there had also been many threats and rumours of assassinations flying around in the build-up to the fight and now, five years later, a similar thing was happening. Some believed the pressure got to Sonny and perhaps Quarry might suffer a similar fate. The press was well aware that the dramas happening outside of the ropes never seemed to unsettle Ali, while it really wasn't known how Quarry would react. Ali claimed Quarry was only familiar with the sport of boxing, not the kind of maelstrom Ali always brought along with him.

Ali stated that he already had his immediate future mapped out in certain stages. The initial stage would end on Monday night after he beat Quarry. The second stage would come about after he tied Frazier down to a fight and the third and last stage would happen after he reclaimed his world heavyweight title. He also informed everyone in the Sports Hall that he was now stronger and could hit harder than ever before his exile years and that part of his preparation had been studying films of the past great fighters. He thought he could learn something from watching the old timers' styles and techniques; incorporating his version of 'Kid' Gavilan's 'bolo' punch in his ring workouts had been one result and he planned to use it on the night of the fight. The non-arrival of Quarry for his allocated training slot didn't go unnoticed by Ali either: he said that it was the wrong time to be absent.

Ali loved to talk just as much as he loved to fight and he didn't confine himself to boxing. One moment, he talked about how kids should stay in school and get an education, the next how the flights to his fights were sometimes more scary than the fights themselves. For him, flying through a thunderstorm was much worse than 15 rounds.

Although most thought Ali's fear of flying story was just another line, he was partly serious. His apprehension about flying may have sprung from the occasion in 1960, in Chicago, when he was waiting to board a plane to Louisville but the flight was delayed when one of the engines failed. Cassius Clay decided to take the train home that day, rather than chance it.

After the verbal sparring finished, Ali returned to the cottage and spent his evening watching some film footage of Jack Johnson. The film had been brought along by Jim Jacobs, along with a few more cartoons that Ali asked him to bring along.

12

ALI'S PRE-FIGHT WALKABOUT

On Saturday 24 October, it was raining hard in Atlanta. That day, both Ali and Jerry showed up at their allocated times at the hall. It would be their last sessions there, carrying out minor stretching and loosening-up exercises only. After their workouts had finished, the ring they'd used for almost a fortnight was dismantled. The heavy bag was released from its chains and the speed-ball platform was disconnected from its temporary fixing point. The small arena was then transformed into a dance hall and two nights after that, it would be turned around into a movie theater to screen the fight.

With the persistent rain that afternoon, boxing fans in Atlanta may have tuned into television channel 7 at 5 p.m. to watch on *Wide World of Sports* a repeat of the Rocky Marciano versus Muhammad computer 'superbout'. Only a few months before that fans around the country had coughed up a $5 entrance fee in cinemas to watch a 'once-only showing'.

It's not known if either fighter watched the program that afternoon, but maybe it was something Jerry would have found interesting. If he did miss the 'fight', he always had the big football game to go to the following day.

According to a report in *The Bee* (Danville, Va.) Jerry had been invited to the big NFL game between the Atlanta Falcons and the New Orleans Saints in the Atlanta Stadium the day before the fight. However, Jerry was unhappy about a previous press story that claimed he had made some kind of negative racial remark about Ali, so he cancelled the stadium visit. Jerry vehemently denied the accusation. He also felt some in the press had not given him the respect his number one *Ring* magazine rating deserved. According to the same report the result was Jerry remained holed up in the motel on Sunday, along with members of his family. Quarry's withdrawal made some in the press dismiss his chances even more, printing that it looked like the pressure was starting to get to him.

Meanwhile, back at the fight headquarters, inside the Regency-Hyatt House Hotel, the atmosphere could only be described as celebratory; it looked like an Ali victory party was already in progress. The brigade of expensively dressed 'dudes' and their diamond wearing women had been arriving all week and for some, the party really had already begun. The fun wasn't only confined to the Regency-Hyatt House Hotel, as the Playboy club in Atlanta also held a party for the press and media. Hugh Hefner would get a live feed of the fight directly into his own pleasure palace back in Chicago.

Back at Leroy's cottage, one of the many visitors was the man who had been bringing over the regular supply of fight films for Ali to view, film maker and owner of the largest fight film collection in the world, Jim Jacobs. This time, he came to inform Ali of a special film preview showing of the United Artists documentary movie, *AKA Cassius Clay*, which was going to be shown later that evening in the city. Jacobs was one of those behind the making of the film, so he was naturally keen for Ali to attend. The local newspapers had printed stories about the showing and mentioned Ali was going to make a personal appearance, at Loew's Grand Theater, then situated at 157 Peachtree Street in Downtown Atlanta.

When Ali heard that people were expecting him to attend, no problem – he was going, even though that decision probably added a few more grey hairs to Dundee's head. Angelo was adamant that Ali should stay clear of all those crowds, where possible injuries and definite mayhem would occur. The fight was now only hours away and Angelo wanted him clear of over-excited fans. Ali though, always did things his own way and it seemed the more he heard voices telling him to stay away, the more he wanted to go. Besides, he was in the starring role.

Ali showed up for the one-off 8 p.m. screening. It was little surprise that by the time he arrived, a small army of fans and hangers-on had attached themselves to his already large entourage. They were all welcome, as a sea of faces, both black and white, streamed into the theater. The entertaining film included interviews with Ali about his views on war, religion and politics, interspersed with his unique wit and humour.

Maybe it was the film that created Ali's buoyant mood that night, but he became almost the showman of old, rhyming predictions and confidently telling those present that the movie they were watching was only one part of his life – there was plenty more to come. After the movie finished, Ali headed down Peachtree Street along with a troop of fans.

On the same day, Ali went to the fight headquarters of the Regency-Hyatt House Hotel and when he set foot inside, it wasn't long before pandemonium erupted. His buoyant mood inside the cinema was the same at the Hyatt, as Ali told the excited crowd what they would all see on Monday night. He shadow-boxed with the fans, punches zooming inches past their noses. He told them to turn up for the fight early, or they might miss it. The crowd followed him to one of the glass elevators and as it started to rise the ex-champ acknowledged them from on high like an emperor.

Below him was an extraordinary mix of the rich, famous, eccentric and flamboyant. The Hyatt lobby was certainly the place to be seen that day, but not all those wearing the furs and diamonds were pillars of society. Some getting in the party spirit were big-time gangsters and villains; but the good, bad, rich and super-rich all had one thing in common – they came to support their returning hero.

13

PRELIMINARIES ON THE FINAL DAY

On the morning of 26 October 1970, the ballroom of the Hyatt was packed with TV cameras and hacks. The weigh-in for the two fighters was set for 10.00 a.m., the scales standing on the middle of a temporary raised platform. The air was abuzz with fight talk. Hal Conrad, trying to keep some kind of order in the room, had a group of singing students and a brass band from the local university ejected.

One of the press agents stepped onto the scales. This was just a tryout before the gladiators arrived, checking that there were no last-minute adjustments to be made. He noticed he'd lost 50 pounds in weight, even though he hadn't been on any crash diet of late. The scales had been wrongly calibrated. The panic call went out for a replacement set. Fight organizers first buzzed around the hotel and they found a set in the frozen food department. Trouble was those scales were the industrial weighbridge type and wouldn't have registered a reading even if both boxers and the referee stood on them at the same time. A desperate call to a local scales rental company solved the problem. The scales arrived before the fighters did.

Jerry Quarry arrived first, with a posse of about a dozen. He looked nervous, but confident – a good sign. The Californian chatted to his wife, Kathleen and son, while press from around the globe jockeyed for position. Ali turned up five minutes later, wearing casual grey slacks, blue shirt and heavy boots and with another large entourage, which included his father and brother.

Quarry took off his favourite turquoise robe and was first up on to the scales. He stood barefoot and wore a pair of blue Everlast shorts and displayed at least a couple of days of stubble. He came in at a solid 197½lbs. After stepping off, Quarry admitted that Ali had had the edge in all the pre-fight banter, but he wanted the world to know that later that night, it would be his fighting ability that would have the last word. And that was about it. Quarry wasn't in the mood to hang about for the usual prefight photo-shots. All the press got from Jerry was another raised clenched fist and a quip that he didn't need to see Ali's face, as he would be seeing plenty of him later that evening. With that he went back to the dressing room and got ready to leave.

Ali tipped the scales at 213½lbs, only 2lbs heavier than he weighed for his last bout against Zora Folley. He outweighed Quarry by 16lbs. Ali had been predicting all week that he would come to the scales much lighter, maybe that had all been flimflam. When Ali stepped off the scales, he told newsmen that he had completed a three-mile jog at 5 a.m. that morning, just to 'stretch his lungs'. Again, there no way of knowing it that was true. If it was, it was a highly unusual thing to do on the day of a fight.

The absence of a head-to-head photo shot didn't trouble Ali, but some in the press were not about to let it pass without comment. Quarry's father lamely explained Jerry couldn't hang around too long as he was standing in bare feet. Teddy Bentham was more on the money when he said that Quarry was still upset at how some of the international press had tried to turn the bout into a racial thing, instead of what it really was, a boxing match.

The weigh-in was a low-key affair, unlike some of Ali's past arrivals at the scales over the years. There weren't any memorable quotes or photos that morning.

Announcements were made about the officials. The referee would be the same man who bossed the Ellis v Frazier championship bout in February, Tony Perez and the two judges appointed were Billy Graham and Lew Eskin.

After both fighters returned to their retreats a caller rang to say that a bomb had been planted in the city auditorium. The call was a hoax, but the arena had to be shut down and thoroughly searched before reopening later that evening.

Quarry, back in the Matador Inn, spent the final few hours before battle playing cards and watching TV. Ali watched more film footage of turn-of-the-century boxing legend Jack Johnson. There was a packed house for the show: Angelo Dundee, Bundini Brown, Rahaman Ali, Howard Bingham (friend and photographer), Cus D'Amato, Jim Jacobs, two police bodyguards, a film crew and reporters, fans and newsmen from Los Angeles and from New York. Ali talked about dedicating the fight to Jack Johnson.

The movie wasn't watched in silence. Ali told everyone how he was going to beat Quarry later that night. As newsmen scribbled away, trying to catch his every word, he also spoke about how he was out to 'destroy' that famous old boxing saw that a heavyweight champion can never come back. There was another impromptu shadow boxing display, with everyone having to line the walls to get out of the way of the jabs. Sometimes Ali impersonated 'Papa Jack', whose image still jabbed away in the background on the pinned-up sheet.

Ali's pre-fight meal consisted of lamb chops and vegetables and this was followed by a long stroll along the country lanes. Chewing a tooth pick and holding a seven-foot makeshift staff, the pied piper meandered down the roads followed by a posse of camp followers, a film crew and his assigned police security. Cars that approached would sometimes stop, either just to gawp or to get an autograph.

The entourage set off up a winding drive that led to one of the secluded houses. As the troop approached the front of the impressive looking building, the front door opened and out came singer, songwriter and guitarist Curtis Mayfield. Curtis would be playing the Star-Spangled Banner before the fight. Everyone went inside.

By late afternoon, Ali and those following him were back at the cottage, where he eventually had a nap. That nap was constantly interrupted by telephone calls and yet more visitors. Jesse Jackson called by.

When Ali and his entourage eventually left the cottage for the fight arena, they made a slight detour on the way. This was to the front of the Regency-Hyatt House hotel, where a convoy of buses stood, engines idling, loading fans up ready for the short drive to the arena. Ali was making sure all his friends and fans didn't miss the bus and had a seat. Along with the buses there were stretch limos, Cadillacs and customized Rolls-Royces making their way to the auditorium, parking up on Peachtree and Courtland Street. Some were chauffeur-driven and had arrived straight from the airport. Bug-eyed locals had never seen anything like it since 1939 and Clark Gable and Vivien Leigh, Cameras outside of the arena tried to catch the arrival of each attending VIP. A hundred police were on hand that night and after the earlier bomb scare, belongings were searched. As Ali had previously said, it was Ali v Liston II all over again.

Back in 1939, at the premiere ball for *Gone with the Wind* some came dressed in the style of the Old South, long flowing gowns, bouffant hairstyles and high hats; 5,000 people had turned up, including the rich and famous. In 1970, another fashion parade happened. The scene became a glittering spectacle, with silk suits in every colour of the rainbow, 20-inch-wide fedoras cocked to one side. The 'army of soul' dripped in gold and diamonds. Successful and famous African Americans came in force: stars like Sidney Poitier, Harry Belafonte, Bill Cosby, Dick Gregory, baseball's Hank Aaron, Diana Ross and the Supremes, Stepin Fetchit. Along with them came Mrs Martin Luther King, Julian Bond and Dr Ralph Abernathy (President of the Southern Christian Leadership Conference). Atlanta Senator and promoter Leroy Johnson arrived decked out in a sleek tuxedo, as did Robert Kassel from Sports Action Inc. Ali's mother and father were there, with Cassius Sr dressed in a dapper all-white suit and a white topper to match.

Mixing with the great and the good of the entertainment, sports and civil rights worlds was a phalanx of big-shot gangsters who had travelled in from all over the country. From New York came Frank Lucas, kingpin of a drugs empire, allegedly the biggest in the city. In his book, *Original Gangster* he not only tells of how he imported the highest quality heroin from Southeast Asia, sold on the streets of Harlem as 'Blue Magic', but also of the time he turned up in Atlanta to see Ali's comeback fight.

Another dude that made his way past Caruso's bust that evening was Harlem legend Pee Wee Kirkland. Pee Wee was the greatest in his own right, not only as a street basketball player, but as a 'super-criminal'. When he was a kid, he reputedly had so much loose cash hanging around, he carried it around in shopping bags. When some kids his age were jumping the underground to get from A to B, Pee Wee went by Rolls-Royce. A 2008 *New York Daily News* article said he began trading stolen jewelry for heroin and he was soon raking in millions.

His generosity was also legendary – so much so that he was sometimes referred to on the streets as 'the bank of Harlem'. At the time of the fight, Pee Wee was dripping in cash. Many years later, he relayed the story of that night to David Davis of the *Atlanta Magazine*. Pee Wee took along all his buddies after purchasing bundles of ringside tickets and headed a two-dozen-strong motorcade of the flashiest motors money could buy all the way from Harlem to Atlanta. When his band of merry men reached the 'city too busy to hate', Pee Wee didn't just provide his chums with free accommodation, he took over a couple of floors in one of the best hotels.

On fight night, the temperature was about 70 degrees, but the steamy heat still didn't stop Pee Wee arriving in an ankle-length mink coat. A later *Sports Illustrated* article claimed the jewelry he wore that night amounted to hundreds of thousands of dollars. Of course, Pee Wee and Frank Lucas were only two of the super-rich villains that went through those auditorium doors that night. There were many others and they came from all over the country.

Ali's friend and businessman, Major Coxson, had miraculously tied up a large batch of the on-site tickets that had been made available for the Philly area and there was only one way the Major travelled and that was in style. Earlier in the year, Coxson had joined with fellow entrepreneur Stanley Branch and opened an exclusive club called the 'Rolls-Royce Supper club' in Philadelphia. They set up an exclusive fight trip to see Ali in his comeback fight and named the trip, the 'Rolls-Royce Junket'. They organized charter flights from Philly to Atlanta for an 'Ali fight night extravaganza', with the 'Rolls-Royce Junket' leaving on the morning of the fight and returning the next day. Perhaps the parade of exquisite Rolls-Royces on the streets of Atlanta that night persuaded Ali to buy a $30,000 maroon Roller shortly after the fight.

The good, bad, famous and wealthy, alongside 500–600 members of the world's press, all struggled to get to their seats. The $15 upper balcony ones were said to be filled mainly by out-of-state fans. The top-priced $100 seats came with the additional 'bonus' of having their expensive upholstery potentially stained by the blood of the combatants who would be soon hammering each other a few feet away. Civil Rights activist Julian Bond and his wife had third-row seats. Comedian Bill Cosby had one of the best seats in the house as he was part of the CCTV commentary team. Diana Ross had a good vantage point as she was in a fourth-row seat just near Ali's corner.

Police Chief Herbert Jenkins and head of Ali's security, Detective Lt, J. D. Hudson, oversaw events inside the arena, while Superintendent Bob Lane saw to the security outside – none reported any trouble. As police wandered among the crowds and scanned those settling into their seats, they would have spotted many familiar faces. One slick and expensively dressed spectator was immediately recognized by Detective Lt Hudson. He came with the street moniker of 'Chicken Man', but his real name was Gordon Williams. The then 37-year-old Gordon (Chicken Man) Williams had a rap sheet that stretched back years, with offences mainly for gambling and drugs. Williams was a known former lottery kingpin. He owned a sleek property on Handy Drive in Collier Heights, situated in a respectable middle class area in the north west of Atlanta. It was one of his many properties. During that 'sporting weekend extravaganza' from Saturday to Monday, 'Chicken Man' loaned out his luxury pad on Handy Drive to a man who was originally from Atlanta but had moved to New York called 'Fireball'. It was intended that Fireball and an acquaintance known as Frank, also from New York, would use the property as a venue for gambling, and for a birthday celebration party for a fellow New Yorker called Tobe. The big sporting weekend culminated in the Ali v Quarry fight, which was the main attraction for most of the party guests who turned up. Invitations had been sent out by post to some big spenders around the country and were handed out in both New York and Atlanta in the week leading up to the fight. Invitations had also been handed out to some of the party people hanging around the Hyatt all week and were still allegedly being offered at ringside on the night of the fight. The majority of the elite and famous didn't accept an invite; or at least, most of the famous and rich denied they ever attended the party on Handy Drive. Most of the 'big shots' claimed to have been at the party that Muhammad Ali himself would later attend – inside the Regency-Hyatt House Hotel. The basement of the property on Handy Drive had already been converted into a temporary gambling den by 'Chicken Man', who aimed to go there himself after the fight.

As more than 5,000 people began to settle in their seats for the preliminary bouts, the man everybody had come to see entered through a back entrance. When he arrived, he was still surrounded by hordes of fans, but once inside, he squeezed his way through the back corridors of the hall and made his way to a small dressing room where police Sergeant Eldrin Bell was assigned to his protection.

A short hop across town, at the Sports Arena, about 1,800 fans had already lined up around the block as they purchased their $10 tickets at the arena entrance. A large screen had been erected at one side of the hall. About eight city cops managed the crowds and again, there were no reports of trouble.

As per the official fight program, inside the fight arena the order of ceremonies started with Curtis Mayfield setting the crowd alight with his emotional strumming of *The Star Spangled Banner.* He received an enthusiastic ovation.

As the start time for the preliminary bouts neared, a few oversights were revealed. One can only presume it was the lack of experience of the promoters that caused the few last-minute panics. An overhead ring light busted before the start, and ring stools and resin dust were missing. The stipulated 8oz red 'Seyer' gloves that Ali and Quarry would use had to be retrieved from the airport at the eleventh hour.

The problems were sorted by the time of the start of the main event but too late for the first bout of the evening, featuring Ali's younger brother, Rahaman. (Rudy Clay). The only corner stools available were a couple of folding chairs. Canvas chairs for corner stools was one thing, but fortunately for the promoters and Rahaman, a late replacement had also been found for his advertised opponent, who was supposed to be Tom Cohen from Charleston, South Carolina. The replacement boxer was introduced as coming from Freeport in the Bahamas, 'Hurricane' Grant. Grant weighed 199lbs, Rahaman 196¾lbs. It would be Grant's first and last pro fight. The contest was set for six rounds. From the bell to the finish, the two folding chairs would be used twice. Rahaman, although based in Chicago, was introduced as coming from his hometown of Louisville, Kentucky.

Rahaman looked, fit, confident and ready to rumble and it quickly became clear that the 'Hurricane' wasn't nearly destructive or fast enough. From the fight's start, Rahaman went on the offensive, forcing Grant on the back foot. At one point in the first minute, Rahaman unleashed an impressive volley of punches that rocked his opponent. Even in the early stages, the ending looked imminent, as Rahaman belted Grant around the head, but somehow 'Hurricane' managed to survive.

In the second, Grant, mustered up an attack but it didn't last long, as Rahaman countered with a more powerful and sustained attack himself. Rahaman jabbed and hit, while 'Hurricane' ducked, dodged and absorbed, and by the round's end, both had worked up a good sweat. Grant even tapped Rahaman as a mark of respect as he went back to his corner.

At the start of the third, Grant already looked weary and within seconds, after receiving a neatly timed combo, he was dropped to the canvas. 'Hurricane' looked finished, but he slowly rose to his feet. He found himself immediately facing another storm of punches. Grant went on to the defensive. He bent so far down, his nose almost touched the canvas, but that didn't stop the punches bouncing off his head. There was no respite for the boxer from the Bahamas, as a smashing left hook to the head followed by a solid right dropped him again on the seat of his pants.

At 2:40 of the 3rd round, it was all over as Grant gamely tried to get back to his feet. The win took Rahaman Ali's tally to six straight wins. As the victor eased his white towelling robe back on, he offered his commiserations to his beaten opponent. (Rahaman would increase his winning tally on the undercard of Ali's next fight against Oscar Bonavena two months later in Madison Square Garden on 7 December 1970.)

The next bout up was a 10-round fight between Jerry Quarry's sparring mate, Eddie 'Bossman' Jones and a boxer Jerry Quarry beat back in 1968, Willis Earls. 'Bossman' was ranked number three in the world's light-heavyweight contenders, while his opponent was ranked number nine. Willis came from Austin, Texas, and scaled 178lbs. 'Bossman' proved to be the 'boss' in his 28th pro bout when in the seventh Earls was floored three times, the first two knockdowns resulting in mandatory 8 counts, but after the third knockdown, referee Ed Morgan stopped the fight. The ending came at 2:47 of the round and this was a sweet victory for 'Bossman' as it avenged an earlier drawn encounter they had a few months earlier on 30 June in Houston. The win meant Jones was only two fights away from challenging for the WBA light-heavyweight title. His big chance came a year later in August 1971, against recently crowned champion Vicente Rondon, but he would lose the title bout by a points decision in Caracas, Venezuela.

In the penultimate bout of the evening, Ali's sparring partner, Herman 'Bunky' Akins, (206lbs) from Los Angeles, fought Jimmy Brown (189lbs) from Charleston, South Carolina. The six-round contest didn't amount to much, as Brown was reluctant to 'engage' with his opponent. When Akins finally released his bombs, they blasted straight through Brown's retreating defences. After three knockdowns, the fight was ended at 2:55 of the fourth round.

The total number of rounds that the preliminary fighters engaged in amounted to one round less than the Ali v Quarry fight was planned to go and those in the auditorium were anxious for the main event to begin. The tension was rising, but they would still have a considerable wait. The last prelim bout was all wrapped up just before 10 pm, but it was planned that the main event fighters wouldn't leave their dressing rooms until about 10.25 p.m. Those 25 minutes provided many in the audience some additional time to contemplate the social and sartorial undercard – the dazzling fashion show and the display of wealth and flamboyance ringside.

Situated at the front of the auditorium was a large stage with two old, long velvet curtains hanging to each side. On this night they were both pulled wide open. Behind one of the curtains were stairs leading down to a corridor and the fighter's dressing rooms. Both rooms were small but a cohort had crammed themselves into the tight space of Ali's. This made any warming up for the former champion difficult – so much so that most were ordered out, leaving only Ali and his trusted inner circle, along with civil rights activist Jesse Jackson, police sergeant Eldrin Bell and two writers from New York. One was George Plimpton.

While Ali was getting changed into his ring togs, his personalized bulky red body protector that he had been using all week in training was nowhere to be found, so it was his brother's black, more streamlined protector that he eased on. Ali then produced his gleaming, pressed white ring shorts out of his bag and tried them on – then they were off again. He didn't like the way they fitted around the different protector and was convinced a pair of boxing shorts at the bottom of a gym bag, again belonging to his brother, looked better, so it was those he wore. Dundee wasn't happy about Ali's 'missing' red and bulky, foul-proof protector and he had a good right to be. Quarry was a known dangerous and damaging body puncher, many past opponents had weakened under his torso assaults. His concern was that Quarry's sledgehammer shots could also end up below Ali's belt line and the missing guard provided superior protection.

The last time Ali fought a boxer with a murderous body punching reputation was back in 1966, Canadian George Chuvalo. Before that 15-rounder, many 'experts' warned Ali that he must avoid Chuvalo's body attacks, but what happened was the opposite. During the fight, Ali willingly offered his chiselled midsection to the slinging, bludgeoning punches of Chuvalo. The Canadian's mitts pounded into the body of his opponent, but apparently to no avail. Ali not only didn't show signs of wilting, but he beckoned and encouraged Chuvalo to hit him harder. The fight went the full distance, with Ali a winner on points.

There was very little doubt that Quarry's body assaults wouldn't have been too much trouble for a 1966–67 version of Ali, but this was 1970. The last thing he had been absorbing during his multi-state lecturing tours and nationwide TV interviews sitting on studio couches in the past few years was a regular clubbing to the body. Although Ali took part in many gym sparring sessions during his exile years, large 'pillow'-sized 16-ounce sparring gloves would have been used, not the tight fitting, 8-ounce ones that Jerry was pulling on just a few feet away along the corridor.

Ali always did things his own way and many believed the change of ring togs and 'missing' bulky protector was because he wanted to appear super slim. Maybe in Ali's mind, this wasn't the time for bulky protectors and loose hanging shorts – he wanted to look great as well as feel great.

While the crowd waited, Ali decided to turn the screw on his opponent. He slipped out of his room and walked the couple of steps along the narrow corridor to Quarry's dressing room. The mischievous Ali opened the door just enough to pop his head through and deliver a few words about impending doom tor the tensed-up Quarry, before quickly closing the door and scurrying back to his own quarters.

Ali's dressing room would get a visit from a member of the Quarry camp. When it was time for Ali's hands to be bandaged, Willie Ketchum, one of Jerry's corner men, entered the room to supervise the taping. Ali sat on the rubbing table while the bandages were carefully applied around his knuckles and wrists. The banter flowed both ways as both attempted to gain some kind of last-minute, psychological edge before the punches were thrown. Ketchum took pleasure in informing Ali that once 'his man' caught up with him, it would be 'lights out', while Ali informed Willie that catching him would be Quarry's biggest problem.

After the taping was complete, Ketchum made his way to leave the room. As the door opened, the manic roar generated from the thousands outside leaked in. Nothing brings out the primitive, atavistic instincts of normally pleasant and peaceful human beings than a fight, especially one between two giants. Those intense, divisive feelings reached all corners of the globe. Ali had much to prove, but he wasn't out to make haters become lovers, only to prove the haters wrong. To do that, he needed an emphatic win.

The red Seyer gloves that both fighters would wear wouldn't be laced up until both fighters were in the ring, but legend has it that Angelo Dundee penned a few words inside one of Ali's gloves, saying when he thought the fight would end. The inked prediction would be revealed after the gloves were removed at the fight's end.

White tape was also applied around the top of Ali's polished ring boots, encasing any laces that could loosen during the fight. Vaseline was 'needled' into to his finely tuned, muscled body by his Cuban masseur, Luis Sarria, with the lotion making his impressive bronzed physique shine. Those inside the still crowded dressing room pressed back against the walls to allow Ali additional space for some last-minute shadow boxing in front of the wall mirror. The sleek fighting image looking back at him assured him and everybody else in the room that he was more than ready.

Ali slipped on a short hip-length white towelling robe, with 'Muhammad Ali' emblazoned in red lettering on the back. Moments later, the noise outside of the dressing room changed. It grew louder and more intense, with whistles and applause intermingled with shouts, chants and boos. Jerry Quarry was making his way out to the ring.

A touch before 10.30 p.m., from behind one of the huge velvet curtains, Quarry along with his handlers in close formation, emerged before 5,100 people – most of them there to see him get a pasting. It was mayhem, as there was no designated walkway from the stage area to the ring. Quarry squeezed and shadow-boxed his way through the heaving crowd, wearing his turquoise robe. Teddy Bentham led the way with the fighter following and looking anything but intimidated by the pro-Ali crowd. There was no smiling by the sandy-haired battler, just a look of grim determination, as he bent between the top and middle ropes and into the ring.

Minutes later, it was Ali's turn, so with his borrowed shorts and borrowed protector, the former champion, along with his corner men, fans and famous followers, left the dressing room for the same short but chaotic walk. Fans shouted down from the top balcony tier, while many on the arena floor area pushed forward, making it difficult for the former champion to get through. The line of handlers leading Ali through the throng included Angelo Dundee, his doctor, Ferdie Pacheco, Bundini Brown, Luis Sarria and Jesse Jackson. Although hemmed in by his entourage and a floor full of fans, Ali still found room to bounce and shadow box. As he did, his bobbing, weaving, handsome head was above everyone else around him. A quick hop and skip and he was up the ring steps and through the ropes. The moment his feet touched the canvas, the din of the crowd rose to fever pitch.

Ali bounced, skipped and faced away from his opponent, remaining in his corner, while he looked out at the blur of faces that surrounded the ring and stretched up to the top balcony tier. It was as though he was both acknowledging and admiring the army of fans who had come from all corners of America to support him. Jerry's fans and family sat among the sea of Ali's followers.

For some, the highly charged atmosphere was tinged with feelings of apprehension. Even at this late stage they thought something would still go wrong. While they had one eye on the ring, the other was on the exit signs.

Jerry Quarry paced back and forth in his corner and looked grimly across the ring. The only thing facing him was the blood-red lettering of 'Muhammad Ali' on the back of the returning champion.

14

AT LAST, THE FIGHT

The hundreds of thousands of fans who watched the fight live in cinemas across the country would get fight commentary from former American football player turned broadcaster, Tom Harmon, with comedian Bill Cosby adding his own views. Back in the UK, millions of TV viewers would eventually get to hear Harry Carpenter describing the action as it happened, but one day after the event.

Before the start, there were various ring introductions and acknowledgments that fans and the now pent-up fighters had to endure. Standing alongside the ropes, inside of the ring, were some of the people that made the fight possible, Leroy Johnson, Sam Massell and Jesse Hill. Alongside them was New York ring announcer, Johnny Addie, who introduced various stars from the world of boxing. First up was former lightweight champion Ike Williams, followed by former light-heavyweight champion Jose Torres, then the former WBA heavyweight champion Jimmy Ellis, who was decked out in a dapper suit, with red shirt and matching tie. While the ring was filling with former boxing champs, both corners started gloving up their fighters.

This give Leroy Johnson an opportunity to take the microphone and introduce members of House of Sports Inc and Sports Action Inc. He also presented the promised $50,000 check to Mayor Sam Massell in aid of one of the city's drug programs. Massell said a few words himself, calling the fight, 'a demonstration in democracy' and said the financial donation would help 'stem the flow of drugs in Atlanta'.

Then it was everybody out bar the fighters, their handlers and ring announcer Johnny Addie. Ali, still bouncing on his toes in his corner, had yet to glance over at his opponent as his corner men carried out the last-minute checks – gloves tied, robe removed, body greased, mouthpiece in.

In the opposite corner, Quarry was now stripped down to his blue Everlast shorts. Both fighters looked tense. They still had to listen to the formalities of the ring officials being introduced. The four ringside doctors, along with timekeeper, Ernie Snow, judges, Lew Eskin and Billy Graham and referee Tony Perez all received a formal mention.

The time touched 10.40 p.m. as Quarry was introduced and a few jeers mingled in with the cheers, but it was still a relative 'warm' reception considering the hugely pro Ali crowd. Johnny Addie announced the 'Return of the Champion – Muhammad Ah-lee!' Cheers erupted, but before Addie finished his words, Ali turned and finally faced his opponent and while doing so raised one gloved fist in acknowledgment.

Both fighters strode to centre ring for the final pre-fight instructions from Tony Perez. They came together almost nose-to-nose, more interested in their own words than listening to the referee as they used the face-to-face opportunity to continue the heckling that had begun the week before. The traditional face-off that the newshounds were denied at the weigh-in took place seconds before the first bell. Mean glares, clenched teeth and threatening barks were exchanged. The crowd noise was such that Johnny Addie was forced to take the microphone and holler for everyone to quieten down a touch, just so the fighters could properly hear the instructions. Surprisingly, Johnny's plea worked; the decibels temporarily lowered as Perez completed the formalities. For the two fighters it didn't make much difference, as they were focused on each other and were not listening, only talking.

Quarry, with a white towel draped across the back of his shoulders had to look up to his taller opponent, while Ali seemed to focus on something immediately behind Jerry's eyes, as his 'hypnotic stare' pierced through his ring adversary. The master of mind games was heard to utter a few last words, before both touched gloves and returned to their corners. Ali faced out to the crowd again, lowered his head and held both gloved mitts palms-up for a short silent prayer.

Moments before the start, the noise in the hall subsided eerily. It was as if the crowd felt something crazy was about to happen; as the final seconds ticked by, nothing was heard except the timekeeper's ringside bell.

Round One

After the bell sounded, Jerry shot across the ring, looking as though he was going to immediately force Ali into a gun slinging fight. When he reached his opponent, his target glided out of punching distance, leaving him the only option of following his fleet-footed adversary.

Even in the first few seconds, Ali somehow managed to manoeuvre the menacing-looking Quarry into the centre of the ring and unleash a barrage of stinging punches – all aimed at Jerry's chin. A fast straight left and right, followed by a couple of slashing left hooks came Jerry's way. Some connected and some missed, but the speed of the attack was dazzling.

The ex-champion seemed to want to quickly stamp his authority on his aggressive opponent, catching him again with a classy, crisp combination, even though the speed and power of his punches didn't deter his stalking opponent from trying to get inside and underneath Ali's long-armed punches. When Ali unloaded another barrage of shots then glided out of harm's way, he made the fight game look like an easy way of earning a living; but in reality he was moving only inches away from certain head crunching damage.

Jerry, like Ali, was a ring craftsman, but Jerry's speciality was counter punching – feinting an opponent into making mistakes, then attacking with his own shots. He tried this tactic early on, shooting out a left jab which made his opponent retreat, but Ali's unique manoeuvrability meant he had put himself back into a punching position, which resulted in Quarry tasting a fast left fist, followed by another stinging right to the head. The attack though brought Ali within range of his shorter-armed opponent, where Jerry found success in landing a solid left and right. Ali moved again and slung his own left and right; both missed, but the next two connected, spearing straight through the high guard of his opponent, slamming hard and flush into Jerry's face.

Then came a slight hiatus as the fighters fell into a clinch and they remained there until Perez broke them up; but the pattern of the fight had formed quickly and it was no surprise that it was going to be a classic encounter of the matador and the bull.

The 'matador' moved out from the clinch and slung another zinging right hand that glanced off Quarry's head and once again after the short, fast attack, glided back out of range. When he did move nearer his opponent, Ali held both arms out and momentarily placed his gloved mitts on his shorter opponent's shoulders, measuring the distance to the target. A split second later, Ali landed another very sharp, stinging right to the head, which forced Jerry to retaliate with his own fast right, but his ended up shooting past the chin of Ali into the smoke-filled air inside the auditorium.

Ali's fast start was impressive, but maybe it was too fast; the fight was over 15 rounds. Then the action heated up as both fighters exchanged a barrage of damaging shots. Ali connected with another two slicing right hands to the head, while Quarry's own right pushed Ali back on his heels. Again Ali glided away from the shootout Jerry craved, but not before the 'Bellflower Belter' received a snapping left jab to his face. Each punch launched by Ali, whether it landed or missed, brought yells from his army of fanatical followers. On occasions when Jerry's powerful shots slipped past Ali's chin by inches, they gasped and winced.

Ali's white size 13 boxing boots hardly touched the canvas as Quarry could only follow, crouching, shuffling, looking for angles to eventually connect hard and change the early pattern being set in the fight. The sight of Ali's unique skills was certainly a welcome one to any true fight fan, as no fighter in his absence could replicate it. Former WBA title holder and ringside spectator Jimmy Ellis did have a similar ring style, but Ali had something more. He brought along with him something far beyond just silky ring movements and teak toughness. He added a panache, a presence and surprising power that was unique only to him.

If only Ali would stand still for a few seconds, his opponent might find the success he was aiming for, but unfortunately for Jerry, when Ali occasionally did put the brakes on, he went on a blistering attack. A left, followed by two flashing rights knocked Jerry back, with Quarry retaliating with a swinging left hook that missed Ali's chin by a foot.

This first round was not going to be a repeat of the first round Ali had with Patterson back in 1965. Then he used the first session to just move and glide, avoiding punches without throwing any meaningful shots in return. The former champion sometimes used a first round just to weigh up his opponent's strengths and weaknesses, but on this night, on his big ring return, he included zipping, hard punches in that dancing routine.

Worryingly for Jerry, even at this early stage, he was starting to show slight signs of facial damage. A red blotch could be seen over the bridge of his nose, after receiving a constant stream of stinging, straight punches that arrived from a long distance out that constantly pierced through his high guard.

Ali's superior speed and reach were making the difference in the first round and the 'aaahs' and 'whooos' from the crowd started to get louder as the velocity of his flying fists increased. The punches came in bunches, a kind of a 'whiplash' effect as lefts and rights connected to Quarry's bobbing head.

At one moment in the first, Ali threw a volley of shots and missed with every one, but it still didn't stop his fans screaming out as though each one had landed. The punches that had connected were still enough to mark his opponent's face, but his attacks didn't appear to seriously dent the armour or deter the tenacity of tough guy Jerry. What was clear though, was the former champ was winning the round with relative ease. In the last 30 seconds, Quarry threw a fast left and right, similar to the punches that crumbled Mac Foster a few months back, but Ali's unique agility allowed him to shapeshift away from potential trouble. Ali danced to the left, flicking out his trademark left jab, all to the sound of Bundini Brown shouting from behind a ringside corner post, 'All night long' – meaning he was urging Ali to keep the fight at long distance, jabbing and moving and avoiding any close exchanges.

As the seconds ticked down to end the round, Jerry had also picked up red marks under both eyes. The red blotch under one of Jerry's eyes made Angelo Dundee momentarily believe Jerry was cut and he jumped up, shouting out to Ali that Quarry was cut. His brother, Chris, pulled Angelo back down and quietly informed him he was wrong. When the bell rang to end the round, Ali strode back to his corner unmarked.

He won the first three-minute session, and there were two important factors that became evident during it. First, Ali was seen throwing a bundle of sizzling right hands. When he came down off his toes and he set himself, his straight right hands came with such speed that they could easily rip open an opponent's skin. Secondly, Ali was seen to miss with many punches. It was understandable that his timing was off a touch, after being out for such a long period.

Ali expended a huge amount of energy in that first round. There were still another 14 to go. One mistake and even the durable-chinned Ali could be flattened and Jerry Quarry's left hook was a potent weapon; but of course, he had to land it first.

Round Two

Ali was up early to start the second round, again bouncing on his toes. When Jerry eased himself off his stool, both fighters glared at each other, eagerly waiting for the sound of the bell.

When the round got underway, it seemed both were preparing themselves for a long night, as both started slower than the first, with Ali concentrating on rapier left jabs and Quarry still attempting to bob and weave himself under Ali's long arms and into punching distance. When Jerry launched a left hook, the punch landed high up on his opponent's right arm and again, Ali quickly glided out of firing range. Up to this point, it was Ali's long, snaking left jab, 'snapping' right hand and foot speed that defined events.

After one failed attempt by Quarry at finding Ali's chin with his left hook, Ali retaliated with a six-punch combination. The punches came fast but only half landed and they didn't appear too hurtful. After throwing that impressive cluster, Ali stepped back, half expecting a retaliatory attack, but all that came was a shrug from Jerry. It was a gesture to Ali and to all those watching around the world that his opponent's punches were having little or no effect.

Ali continued the swift movements though, with each step accompanied by Bundini's chorus that was meant to both advise and motivate. The former champion glided across the canvas until his back was pressed against the ropes. Ali couldn't go back any further and Quarry steamed in, but the fleet-footed Ali bounced back off those ropes, which forced Quarry to miss with another left hook. After that miss came a slashing left uppercut from Ali that brushed up the right side of Jerry's head. Quarry came back with his own left hook only to fall short again. The 'Bellflower Belter' was certainly slinging his punches with intent, but those power shots could also tire him, especially if they continually hit nothing but air.

'Don't box with him Jerry' came the cry from Quarry's corner. This was an effort to deter Jerry from 'boxing the boxer', as he did in his losing fight against stylist Jimmy Ellis. Jerry's corner was encouraging him to wade in and for him to 'make a fight of it'.

That was easier said than done; 29 previous opponents had already tried to do the same to Ali and failed. Jerry did connect with a straight left to the body but again fell short when he tried to connect with another shot to Ali's chin. Jerry kept shuffling forward, throwing shots and attempting to get one solid punch that would hit Ali flush. It nearly came seconds later, when a powerful shot connected to the right side of Ali's jaw, but unfortunately for Jerry, his opponent was already sliding backwards when it landed, which reduced the impact.

The 'punching momentum' of the battle continued and Jerry landed another hook to Ali's midriff, even though Ali looked unperturbed by it. The former champion fired off his own sharp right hand, which struck Quarry's head, knocking him momentarily off balance. Jerry quickly retaliated with a 'looping' swing with the punch missing Ali's whiskers again by a good foot. 'You're the boss!' yelled a now hyperventilating Bundini, but Jerry still bulled forward and found success with two left hooks to the body that knocked Ali back.

The tempo in the fight and the din inside the hall increased again as both fighters swapped punches centre ring. At one point, Ali was caught off balance by another left, but he immediately straightened himself and struck Jerry with a solid, straight left jab, flush to the face. The connecting punch brought the crowd to its feet as it knocked Jerry back a touch. This moment of success only seemed to enrage Jerry, as he went on the attack, now walking through Ali's stinging punches and landing a right to the body himself and another sharp left to the head. 'Stick him out of distance!' shouted Bundini. Ali seemed to obey, as he quickly darted out of range while still flicking out that long, stinging left jab, which still connected. Jerry landed another impressive left hook, which thudded into Ali's midsection, but the sound of the bell stopped any follow-up.

Quarry had more success in this round, with Ali looking a touch slower, even though most of Jerry's best attacks were still being nullified. If there was any criticism of Jerry in that round, it was that he seemed too reliant on landing his powerful left hook. Up to this point, most of his hooks were being blocked or his opponent managed to move out of hitting range. Unlike Ali, he was barely throwing any right hands, but this was still only the second round and the younger Quarry's strategy was to come on strong in the later rounds of the fight.

Jerry's moment of success came at a price. When he got to his stool, a large lump was visible above his left eye and he was also bleeding inside his mouth. Although Jerry had only shared six minutes in the ring with the ex-champion, he was starting to show the bruising effects of doing so and maybe, just maybe, showed the first signs of discouragement.

Round Three

Ali was up early again from his stool before the start of the third and in contrast to Jerry, looked relaxed, unmarked and fresh. When Jerry eased himself up from his stool, both fighters again stared at each other, but this time with something approaching respect. The bell sounded and they both met centre ring. At first, it looked as though they had come together to finally slug it out, but again Ali opted to hop and skip around his opponent, leaving Jerry the only option of trudging along after him. The speedy Ali was again the first to land, as he zipped in a quick left to Jerry's head, with his opponent countering with his own left jab, but falling inches short once more.

Ali's preparations had been daily roadwork and up to this point, it was paying off handsomely as he barely stood still for more than a couple of seconds. Roadwork had also been a major part of Jerry's preparations, claiming he had covered over 100 miles while in training, but the leg exercises he had completed were still not making him fast enough to catch his opponent. Quarry though, didn't only have to catch up with Ali, he had to also get him to stand still long enough to get hit; and it just wasn't happening regularly enough.

The constant movement of Ali looked good and much of the crowd liked what they were seeing, but the 'dancing steps' caused Bundini to change his war-cry a touch, shouting out from the corner, 'Stick him while you're dancin' champ!' Ali kept moving backwards though and was momentarily pinned just above Bundini. Both fighters connected with stinging left hooks and it was a good exchange, but again, when Jerry seemed set to capitalize on his success, his opponent had already moved out of harm's way. 'Out of distance all night long!' shouted a jubilant Bundini. Ali was certainly moving fast, but he seemed to be heeding Bundini's shouts, as his jabs started to shoot out with more authority behind them and his clenched left glove rattled the features of his fiery and gutsy opponent.

Quarry, now looked slightly dejected, swung two hooks that missed again, but the momentum pushed Ali back onto the ropes where Jerry dug another sledgehammer left hook deep into Ali's ribs. The punch caused a few groans and squeals in the audience, but Ali quickly quelled the murmers of apprehension as he grabbed his opponent around his head with both hands to nullify all of Jerry's work. The hold forced them both into a clinch, where Ali held on until the referee broke them up. The 'hold and break' technique allowed Ali time to gain a measurable distance between himself and his opponent and to get on his bike again. His movement was covered by that persistent super-fast jab, now ramming into the face of Jerry with more regularity and accuracy.

By mid-round, Ali's constant whipping, slashing and stabbing punches made the red blotch above Jerry's left eye begin trickling blood. It may have been the feel of that warm claret running down his left cheek that spurred Jerry on to suddenly unleash an impressive barrage of lefts and rights that forced Ali on the defensive. The punching combination pushed Ali back against a ring post, but just when it looked like Jerry would get some punching momentum going, his efforts were thwarted again, as Ali clamped himself on to Jerry.

When they separated, blood was seen dripping down the side of Jerry's face from a slash above his left eye. Although the increased claret didn't seem to deter Jerry, the fast punches that came his way now became relentless, each one landing on or near his ripped skin. The former champion tore into him with sizzling speed and accuracy.

Ali, an instinctive 'headhunter' whose style almost always ignored punches to the body, wasn't going to change his methods now. He unleashed a solid right that caught his opponent flush and caused Jerry's arms to drop momentarily. The crowd sensed the fight's ending as blood spilled down Jerry's body onto the ring canvas. Even those in the far-off $15 balcony seats could see the blood smearing Jerry's torso and on his shorts. As the cheers rang out throughout the auditorium, Ali reversed his sometimes retreating movements and came forward looking to deliver a solid punching attack that would finalize the night's action.

A now wounded Quarry was forced to back up against the ropes, adopting a defensive stance, while Ali moved in throwing and connecting another left and right to Quarry's head. The ramrod punches forced Jerry to instinctively go on the attack, in an attempt to punch his way off the ropes and out of trouble. Both fighters flailed away with powerful shots.

Jerry was certainly courageous, but the flying leather was coming from all angles and turning his face into a crimson mask. Seconds before the round's end, both fighters fell into a clinch again and when they parted, Ali stood back, looking as though he was inspecting the damage he had inflicted. What he saw was an injury that cut deep, almost to the bone and he must have sensed the battle was nearing its end.

As the bell to end the round sounded, Jerry turned and walked head bowed back to his corner, with blood streaming down his face. When he slumped dejectedly on his stool, referee Tony Perez followed him back and stood over the corner as his seconds worked feverishly, attempting to stem the blood flow. When the claret was wiped, Teddy Bentham could see the severity of the wound and called for the fight to be stopped.

Initially, there was some confusion, as ringside doctors would normally be called, which Perez began to do, but in the melee and as Jerry pulled himself away from Bentham in an apparent attempt to continue, Perez had already signalled the fight's end.

Jerry, blood still streaming, trudged over to centre ring to embrace the victor. Ali offered his commiserations and a few words of encouragement. Ali's shorts were also blotched with Jerry's blood as a jubilant Drew 'Bundini' Brown entered the ring, raising an arm in a victory salute, while his other arm was wrapped around the sweating shoulders of Ali. The former champion also looked relieved that his first return fight was behind him. On his fight record, defeating the number one heavyweight contender in only nine minutes was more than impressive.

Despite there being four doctors assigned to the fight, it was a fifth doctor who was first to inspect Jerry's facial injury. This was Ferdie Pacheco, Ali's own doctor, who was already inside the ring.

While it was blood and tears in the Quarry corner, it was jubilation in the other, with Angelo Dundee, Luis Sarria, artist LeRoy Neiman, Jesse Jackson and Leroy Johnson surrounding Ali, all there to offer their congratulations. When the laces were cut from Ali's gloves and removed, the words Angelo had penned inside one of them prior to the fight start were revealed: 'round 3'.

Those bloodied red gloves of Ali's had instantly become a special piece of sporting memorabilia and they were handed over to the man who helped make the whole occasion possible, Leroy Johnson. A keepsake that many say he still has to this day. Leroy seems too smart not to have tucked them away somewhere.

The PA system announced Ali as a third-round winner, the same round his brother won in earlier in the evening. Both brothers were still undefeated and both would go on to share the same bill in their next couple of fights. (On the night Ali would suffer his first pro loss against Frazier on points in 1971, his brother would also lose for the first time, again by a points decision, to future British and Commonwealth champ, Danny McAlinden.)

After the Quarry fight, the ex-champ's win stretched his fight record to an impressive 30 fights, 0 losses, 0 draws, which now included 24 stoppages or knockout wins. Jerry's pro record now read 46 fights, 37 wins, 5 losses and 4 draws.

While still in the ring, Ali praised his opponent, saying he was 'tricky' and that Jerry had a hard left hook, but said he came well prepared, as a couple of his sparring partners had similar styles to Jerry, so he was able to make his opponent's best weapon, the left hook, mostly ineffective.

Ali looked unmarked, but reiterated what he had said during the build-up to the fight, that he believed he was a much better fighter now than before his exile years as he was more mature and stronger. He admitted being hurt once in the fight by a body punch in the second round, but said his conditioning would have carried him through the full 15 rounds if necessary. He said he was disappointed that the fight ended by a cut in only the third round, as he would have liked more 'work' and declared that he needed more rounds under his belt to reestablish himself as champion. Ali was also quick to point out that he had not only beaten Quarry quicker than Frazier, but that Joe had received more punishing shots than he did, as Quarry could hardly land a clean punch on him.

Frazier's seventh-round stoppage over Quarry came after both fighters were involved in that 'fight of the year' war, while Ali's quick reflexes and gazelle-like movements prevented an all-out slugging match.

Afterwards, referee Tony Perez confirmed that it was he and not Teddy Bentham who stopped the fight. Perez also verified that he did call a doctor into the ring to inspect the cut, but he stopped it before one of the four doctors managed to climb through the ropes. Perez's and the two judges' scorecards had Ali winning each of the three rounds.

On this night, it was supposed to be Joe Frazier standing in the opposite corner to Ali, not Jerry Quarry – if that had happened, how would have Ali coped? Would his conditioning at that point in time been enough to handle 'the Smoke'?

It could be argued that this fight came down to right hands. In the first round, Ali unleashed a barrage of straight rights and in the second round, it was the *absence* of Quarry's right hand that was most evident. In the third and final round, it was the effective use of Ali's right hand again that helped cause the swelling above Jerry's left eye, which signalled the beginning of the end for his gallant opponent. After the ring interviews, Ali had a harder time trying to get back to the sanctuary of his dressing room than he had in the previous nine minutes of boxing.

Jerry slumped dejectedly on a chair in his room in his now heavily bloodstained blue satin trunks, while eleven zig-zag stitches were inserted above his eye. The cut was long and deep. While the fighter's family and friends consoled him, there was mention that the wound was caused by Ali's head, but Quarry made it clear to everyone that it was Ali's right hand, not head, that tore his skin. Teddy Bentham said the severity of the injury meant a long rest for Jerry, which probaby came as a welcome relief; Quarry talked of finally getting the opportunity of spending more time with his family and not in another training camp.

Jerry said he had first pushed past Teddy Bentham before the start of the fourth as he wanted to continue fighting, but once he felt the blood running, he realized the decision to stop the bout was the right one. Jerry said he went up to Ali in centre ring to tell him he was a good fighter. Later, Bundini Brown walked into Jerry's dressing room to offer a few words of encouragement and a brief reminder that Jerry would be returning home with his health intact and a healthy pay packet to boot. Only minutes before, Bundini had been yelling from ringside for Ali to 'lower the boom' on Jerry, but now, in a mark of respect, planted a kiss on the stubbly chin of the 'Bellflower Belter'.

Quarry spoke of Ali's speed, but said his opponent's punches lacked power and he was never hurt during the fight. He was just disappointed that the bout ended so early and on a cut. According to Quarry, the fight was going as planned and it would have been a different result had the fight moved into the latter rounds, as his body punches would have eventually had the desired effect.

There is another story about the cut. Colourful fight character Max Yeargain had promoted fights in his home city and had even tried to secure the telecast rights of the Ali v Quarry fight. Max was a friend of Jerry's ex-manager/trainer, Johnny Flores and he got to know Jerry in his early fighting days, even promoting a couple of his early pro fights. He would sometimes supply fighters with a 'magic potion' that had been very successful in closing large wounds. Max, later told his story to the *St Louis Post-Dispatch* about how he came about his 'secret formula' during his time in a Navy hospital during the Second World War. The mixture was used to close wounds caused by shell blasts and the like. In the article, Max claimed that Quarry's father wanted some of the mix made up for the Ali fight, but the rift between Quarry and Johnny Flores made him decide not to send any. Of course, it will never be known if his 'secret formula' would have closed the deep cut Jerry suffered, but his coagulant had allegedly closed larger wounds. In the same interview, Max reeled off names of fighters who swore by it, one who ended up having 23 stitches in his face but still managed to finish his bout. Jerry suffered half as many stitches.

Ali almost inevitably mentioned Frazier would be an easier target than the ducking, weaving, counter-punching style of 'tricky' Quarry. He was surrounded by well-wishers, fans and a horde of pressmen, all trying in the chaos for their own moment with the fighter. The newshounds wanted a memorable quote for the next day's tabloids, but they got something more unusual when the victor held up his painting showing how he thought the fight would turn out. Considering the painted predictions and Dundee's scribble inside Ali's glove, it was little surprise that Ali told the press the bout went just the way he thought it would.

Amidst the chaos, the Rev. Ralph Abernathy and the widow of Dr Martin Luther King Jr, Mrs Coretta King, presented Ali with the 'Martin Luther King medallion'. As Rev. Abernathy handed Ali the medallion, they spoke of how Ali was a great example of 'soul power' and how they thought he was not only a champion of boxing, but also justice and peace. Afterwards, Ali was surrounded by police as he was escorted through the crowds away from the press area. While all this was going on, Angelo Dundee was still describing his fighter's performance as 'sensational' and 'terrific' while Diana Ross said Ali had simply looked 'beautiful'.

Back in East Stroudsburg, Pennsylvania, the man both winner and loser wanted to fight, Joe Frazier, slept through the whole thing. It was early to bed and early to rise every day for the 'Smoke', as he was in training for his own upcoming fight against world light-heavyweight champion Bob Foster in only a few weeks' time, on 18 November.

Back in Ali's Overbrook home in Philly, the last thing his 21-year-old wife got that night was sleep. Moments after her husband's arm was raised in victory, Belinda and an on-site bodyguard received the first of ten threatening phone calls. The last said a bomb would go off at their home at 1 a.m. Police and firemen were immediately called and the house was thoroughly searched, including the roof and outer grounds, but no devices were found. The family moved to alternative accommodation for the rest of the night. It was also later reported in *The Baltimore*

Sun that police received three telephone bomb threats in Atlanta that night, presumably about the city arena.

With Ali back, the Frazier camp was now itching to get Joe and Ali in the ring together. Yank Durham wanted the fight as early as possible and talked of a February 1971 date for the two to meet in potentially the biggest money-spinning fight of all time. Yank commented that he figured Ali would eventually slice open the skin of Quarry, but admitted he didn't expect the cut to come so early. However, he said that the 'hit-and-run' style, which worked almost to perfection against Quarry, would be no good when his fighter climbed through the ropes. Yank proclaimed that Joe wouldn't allow Ali to run around, as he believed Jerry had, but would force him to, which was different. He firmly believed Joe would eventually cut Ali down and stop or KO him.

In the following month's *Ring* ratings (week ending 9 November 1970) Ali replaced Quarry as number one contender and Quarry slipped down to number four. The victor also picked up the *Ring* fighter of the month award.

Oscar Bonavena, who had reportedly already signed to meet the winner, now followed Ali in both the *Ring and Boxing Illustrated* ratings. Oscar predicted more doom for the returning champion and declared he had all the tools to defeat Ali when they met. The tough boxer from Buenos Aries, who was due to fight three days after the Ali v Quarry bout against Luis Pires, proclaimed his 'warrior blood' and brutal strength would overcome the fast-moving style of the former champion. Both Ali and Dundee though, denied all the press rumours that he was going to meet Bonavena next.

Madison Square Garden boxing director Harry Markson was quick to say they were going to do everything they could to bring the 'big one' (Ali v Frazier) to New York. This wouldn't have sat too well with the executives of House of Sports Inc. Their initial and ultimate goal was to not only bring Ali to Atlanta, but to bring Joe Frazier along with him. They still aimed to do this, but now the big players were in the game, running alongside them.

In the initial stages of obtaining Ali a licence, both House of Sports Inc and Sports Action Inc held all the aces and it was surprising that Ali had not been tied into a three- or four-fight deal. He had nowhere else to go.

The kaleidoscope of people that had been inside the arena rolled out onto the streets of Atlanta and the after-fight parties began, with the main one taking place at the Regency-Hyatt House hotel. The man responsible for all the joyous mayhem, Ali himself, only stayed around the wild scene for a few hours before returning to the countryside cabin. The main 'insiders' party took place on the top floor of the hotel. Parties were swinging on the lower floors too. This was much more than an after-fight party, it was more akin to a new Millennium celebration. The jubilation found in the Hyatt that night wasn't only about the rebirth of a fighting hero, it was also a celebration and mass gathering of African Americans who had hit the big time. Inside the lobby, the sound of champagne corks popping were not confined to the unusual bar that resembled a carousel suspended from the roof by a steel cable, it echoed upwards, past each level towards the epicentre of fun on the top floor.

In Atlanta that night though, there were others outside the protected confines of the Regency-Hyatt who planned on getting a slice of the action. Their objective was to emulate both Ali and Quarry on their fight night; they were hoping to be much richer the day after.

15

THE LUCKY ONES LOST
THEIR INVITE

Remember the party on Handy Drive in Collier Heights – the one that went on all weekend in a house owned by 'Chicken Man' Williams? It was later reported that he shared the property with his girlfriend, Barbara Smith, and the culmination of the party was now, Monday night. It was not only 'Tobe's' birthday, which had been organized by 'Frank' and 'Fireball', but also the night when the invited high rollers handed tickets at the fight would arrive to join in the birthday celebrations with some high-stakes gambling.

It was later reported in the *Atlanta Constitution* that, earlier that weekend, one guy arrived at the temporary gambling den set up in the basement of the property with $16,000 in cash and lost the lot. The financial setback didn't deter him; he was back again on Monday night to try his luck once more.

Before ten that Monday evening, as the boxing preliminaries inside the city arena ended, 'Chicken Man's' girlfriend had helped two of her friends prepare food for the potential avalanche of guests. She planned to meet her boyfriend at the fight, presumably just in time for the start of the main event. However, the evening's plans went awry after a knock at the door. When a fellow party guest opened it, there were three men standing outside and all were invited in, presumed to be just some more arriving guests. As they headed inside, from one of the new arrivals' coats came a handgun.

One of the men brought out a walkie-talkie, and after a few quiet words into the device more armed – and this time masked – villains entered. They all carried sawn-off shotguns and they quickly started shouting orders. There were between five and eight robbers in total, and all but one ended up with their faces covered with ski masks. The sawn-off shotguns quickly got people's attention, and the men took control of the house.

Most of the party people already there were marched down into the large basement, some were then ordered to disrobe and all had to throw their valuables into the centre of the room. They were then forced to lie face-down on the basement floor.

As the majority of the invitees wouldn't arrive until after 12 a.m., the bandits had plenty of time to get things ready. A terrified Barbara Smith was ordered to stand at the entrance door and to provide a smiling welcome to each new guest, as the masked men took up their positions. It was believed one bandit remained unmasked, but still concealed a gun, as he stood alongside Barbara Smith. All the crooks kept in contact with each other by walkie-talkies.

One of the few guests who was allowed to remain upstairs and clothed had one of the robber's sawn-offs pressed to his back; he and the few others were there to fool the newcomers that all was well. The respectable neighbourhood helped to put people at ease. Saying that, many of the engraved invitation holders were believed by police to be out-of-town criminals. Not all party guests were big-time gangsters or rich businessmen, however. One was a cop from New York!

As midnight approached, the fancy autos started rolling up outside the red brick house. As the bejeweled guests approached the front door, each one was greeted by their smiling hostess, Barbara Smith. Three-quarters were men, though a person's gender didn't change the disciplined procedure. As each person stepped through the door, the bandit standing inside quickly unveiled his shooter to encourage them to move further inside. From there, they were forced down to the 'room of doom' – deep down into the basement.

One of the most reliable witnesses who was fleeced was that New York cop, who had travelled to Atlanta to see the fight. Once past the first gunman he saw other masked men in the room with shotguns and when he was led down into the basement he saw more. He was ordered to strip off his clothes, while at the same time he was stripped of his valuables. He was then told to lie face-down on the floor, and told what would happen if he dared look up. He lost $485 in cash, a $5,600 diamond ring, a $175 watch and his police badge. Apparently, a couple of guests received the butt of a 12-gauge upside their heads when they foolishly attempted to turn their heads up from the floor. The same head-cracking technique was also used for any guests that were a touch slow in making their way down the basement steps.

The bandits reportedly used brooms to stack everything of value into piles, then the stash was piled into distinctive coloured and patterned pillow cases. When 'Chicken Man' finally arrived at his loaned-out home/gambling den, he was also apparently ordered to go through the same routine and was relived of $971. The heist was carried out with precision, any visiting racketeers and gangsters receiving the same treatment as the New York cop.

The calibre of some of the gangsters that attended the fight and who police believe later turned up at the party was not the type that usually suffered robbery; certainly they were not the type to report losses to the police. At that moment they were just hoping to get out of the basement alive.

The only problem the looters eventually had was that the basement space where they were storing their semi-naked victims was not large enough. As soon as rolls of cash and small mountains of jewelry had been swept up and 'bagged', more frightened faces were led down into the basement. As the piles of valuables and discarded clothing became bigger, so did the mass of terrified flesh. The basement bandits were forced eventually to improvise, and they did this by ordering each freshly disrobed person to lay on top of someone that had already been stripped and fleeced. This wasn't some kind of comedy-caper, but despite the terror tactics attached to the heist, you have to admit there was an element of humour in the way the cocky crooks improvised their working routine to gain maximum reward.

It was said the robbers' work took about four hours, but it was also believed that the looting would maybe have gone on longer if there had been any more available space left to stack the bodies. Estimates as to the number of people laid flat and stacked up in the basement ranged anywhere between 80 and 200. The wide range is the result of the reluctance of some victims to talk to the police.

Some time after 2 a.m., with their pillow cases stuffed, a voice came over the walkie-talkies that instructed the robbers it was time to leave. All the basement bandits scrambled out of the house, but not before pulling masks over Barbara Smith and two of her girlfriends' faces and taking them as hostages. As the fleeing felons legged it up the street, one of the villains released one of the hooded girls as he saw the getaway cars moving off. He obviously didn't want to miss his ride; he also flung a holdall and a sawn-off into a wooded area near the house. Once he reached the open door of the car, he scrambled inside; the cars were last seen disappearing into the misty October morning along with Barbara Smith and one of her pals inside. The girls couldn't see where they were going, or who talked to them. Both petrified girls were released having been driven around the streets of Atlanta for a few hours. They were let out of the car unharmed and even given a few dollars for a cab!

Back in the basement, it was likely no one moved for fear one of the gunslingers might just be hanging around. Eventually they started to untangle themselves, along with the pile of discarded clothing on the floor.

It goes without saying that any big-time villains or racketeers who were in the basement didn't take too kindly to the experience. The robbery would have hurt their pockets and their street cred. Feelings obviously ran high and it was said 'Chicken Man' was initially in the frame. It was in his house that they had all been robbed and it was his girlfriend who disappeared with all their moolah.

However, for many of the unsmiling victims, this wasn't the time or place to begin their 'investigations'; that would take place later. Police had been called and the last thing some needed or wanted was a chat with detectives from the Atlanta Police Department. It was likely many made a quicker getaway from Handy Drive than the robbers did, with some returning to their hotels and others going straight back to their home city.

When police arrived, there were apparently 60 people still inside the property and all were visibly shaken, but almost everyone remained tight-lipped. Almost everyone robbed was from the black community, and out of all the people left inside only five made formal statements.

Was gangster Frank Lucas at the party? So far as I know, he never said. But he was certainly at Madison Square Garden on 8 March 1971 for Frazier v Ali. Again, the rich and famous turned up and mingled alongside gangsters, pimps and villains, some of whom had attended the Ali v Quarry fight in Atlanta. Only at the later fight, some cops that mingled among the spectators were not there to quell trouble or keep order; they were working on a specially assigned mission. Each undercover detective was there to find out how some of those settling into their expensive ringside seats had come by so much wealth. One guy who caught their eye was even decked out in a $120,000 Chinchilla coat and hat. That was Frank, who claimed he normally kept a low profile. His wearing one of the most expensive coats money could buy to the richest fight in history was the start of justice catching up with the 'American gangster'.

Fellow big-time villain Pee Wee Kirkland was interviewed about the Handy Drive 'party' by David Davis for the *Atlanta* magazine in 2005. Pee Wee denied being at that particular shindig, saying he was at the one back at the hotel. I assume he meant the one at the Regency-Hyatt.

In the first few hours after the armed heist, the only solid thing police had was that the house owner was Gordon Williams and he shared it with his girlfriend Barbara Smith. At the crime scene, Detective W. H. Byrd spoke to 'Chicken Man', who promised to come down to police headquarters and tell them everything he knew. However, at that point his girlfriend was still missing and Williams temporarily dropped off the radar. Police soon became aware that this wasn't a small-time holdup.

16

ROBBERY AND FIGHT AFTERMATH

As the fog in the Atlanta skies cleared on the morning of 27 October, 1970, there must have been many a savage hangover. Maybe some heads were thumping more than others; Quarry's for one. However, the stitches and bruises didn't stop him reliving the fight at a 10 a.m. press conference. Quarry's version of events was at odds with what most had witnessed. He said that he didn't lose to a superior fighter and that if he hadn't been cut he would have stopped his opponent in the later rounds. Jerry declared that his previous night's opponent wasn't nearly as fast as he boasted, and claimed not to have been seriously hurt at any stage. As he talked, he kept touching the damage above his eye. He said it was perhaps the nastiest cut he had ever seen in boxing.

As for fighting Joe Frazier, Jerry declared that the ex-champion's chances were 'zero'; six rounds would be enough time for Joe to finish the job. Jerry's father Jack backed up his son's words and said Frazier would provide Ali with pressure he had never experienced before and would eventually catch up with Ali and knock him out.

Jerry's most successful round in the short fight was the second and he said he had talked to his opponent during that session, informing Ali that his punches were not hurting. The evidence of his good showing in that round was perhaps enough for him to proclaim that his best rounds were still in front of him, while Ali's speed would have slowly diminished.

He also mentioned that at one point he missed Ali's kisser by a fraction of an inch, and that if that punch had landed the cut wouldn't have been an issue.

Up to that point, Quarry became the fourth losing pro opponent Ali and Frazier had in common. One was Billy Daniels, who was handed his first ever defeat by Ali/Clay back in 1962 with a seventh-round stoppage, and four years later he didn't come out for the seventh against Frazier. Doug Jones lasted the 10-round distance with Ali/Clay back in 1963, but again four years later was cut down unmercifully by Frazier in six rounds. George Chuvalo lasted 15 with Ali in 1966, but was stopped by the 'Smoke' in four only one year later in 1967. Jerry lasted more than double the rounds with Frazier than he did with Ali, with both losses coming through severe eye damage. Fight reports tell us Jerry also received minor eye cuts in the Foster, Brassell and George 'Scrap Iron' Johnson bouts earlier in 1970. Winning fights they may have been, but the chances were that he would cut again when faced with the type of punches Ali was known to deliver.

One other notable thing from after the fight, apart from the robbery of course, was how little was made in the press headlines of Jerry Quarry approaching future bouts as a 'Great White Hope'. He reverted back to being 'Irish' Jerry Quarry or the 'Bellflower Belter' and the 'white hope' press line faded away.

I don't think I ever heard of another white heavyweight fighter being seriously cast as a 'White Hope' until another Jerry came along 12 years later. That was Gerry Cooney, prior to his losing

WBC title fight against the 'Easton Assassin' Larry Holmes in 1982.

Back to the day after the fight in 1970, inside the main fight headquarters at the Regency-Hyatt House Hotel, promoters began to receive the financial numbers from around the country and world. It seemed to be a huge financial success. Across America and Canada, the cinemas filled roughly 500,000 seats. The *Atlanta Constitution* reported that the closed-circuit numbers had been the biggest in history, bringing in an incredible $3,490,000. The arena had also done extremely well, drawing a live gate of $206,450. This was reported to be a dollar record for the old auditorium. The hire of the arena was a mere $500, but according to a report in the *Atlanta Constitution*, attached to that figure was also a small percentage taken by the city from the gross takings. The old Sports Arena, where the fight had been piped on to a large screen in front of approximately 1,800 fans, had also done extremely well. Both the auditorium and arena had similar arrangements, whereby the city took a small percentage cut from the gross revenues.

With the $50,000 already handed over on the night of the fight and the percentage cut from the auditorium and Sports Arena, Leroy Johnson had been correct when he said that the city would greatly benefit from the fight.

In New York's Madison Square Garden, a crowd of almost 19,000 paid between $7 and $15 to watch the fight by satellite. It was shown on the same giant four-sided screen that projected images of Jack Dempsey's fights before the Foster v Quarry fight in June. The take for the CCTV screening of the Ali v Quarry fight was reported to be a staggering $201,000.

In Ali's home city of Louisville, over in Kentucky, promoter Bill King had the fight piped into the location of Ali/Clay's first professional fight, the Freedom Hall. The show drew about $33,000, but most of the monies had to be refunded as problems with the satellite connection meant the picture didn't get up on the giant screen until the blood was already dripping on the canvas in the third round. A similar thing happened at the satellite screening in Santa Barbara, when 1,400 patrons turned up, only to watch a blank screen and listen to the commentary. However, most of the satellite screenings went ahead without a hitch. No fewer than 14,000 fans turned up at the Inglewood Forum in Los Angeles and in Boston 11,936 fans turned up at the Boston Garden, paying a gross gate of $75,175. This was only one of three locations that a promoter put on in New England, with the four shows attracting 18,736 fans, paying a grand total of $107,675.

Nine thousand one hundred and three fans had turned out at the Olympia in Detroit, Michigan, to watch colour pictures beamed live. Most there were Ali fans and whooped with delight, even when the former champion missed with a punch. It was the same story in Honolulu, where 5,200 fans turned up at the Honolulu International Center.

The international interest stretched to far-off places such as Bangkok, where Premier Thanom Kittikachorn along with cabinet ministers watched the live telecast. In Russia, where millions of people got to see the fight both live and free, the official agency, Tass, attempted to turn Ali's win into a defeat for an American system that illegally confiscated his world title.

The fight went out live in Europe, Asia, Australia, Africa and South America, with fans in the United Kingdom, getting to watch the fight free, but on Tuesday night on BBC1 at 9.20 p.m. For fans who missed it, the bout was repeated a few days later on the then regular Saturday daytime sports show, *Grandstand*.

For the general populace of America who didn't buy a cinema ticket, they would get to see the fight on the same day as the repeat showing in the UK. ABC TV program, *Wide World of Sports*, screened the bout on Saturday 31 October. The huge global interest and turn-out meant Ali himself pulled in roughly $1 million, while Jerry earned about half that amount, with some sources reporting his final take as between $338,000–400,000.

One man who maybe didn't contribute to the global viewing figures was Lester Maddox. When contacted at the governor's mansion, he said he didn't want to make any comment, apart from that he was aware of who won. He was probably more concerned about the upcoming elections, as the statewide poll for the new state governor and lieutenant governor would be held only one week later. Lester Maddox faced Frank Miller for the position of lieutenant governor and Jimmy Carter was up against Republican Hal Suit. Carter would become the new state governor and Lester Maddox would become lieutenant governor.

A couple of days after the fight some of the press were still found clattering away at their typewriters in the press suite in the Hyatt and were probably more interested in hearing stories emerging about the after-fight robbery than the state governor's election hopes. News of the brazen robbery had already been blasted through local TV and radio stations, with the *Atlanta Constitution* splashing the story on the front page.

This particular news story wasn't going to be confined to local interest. Newspapers around the country were not far behind in wanting to report and know about every detail of the big robbery after the big fight. Even in Jerry's home state, *The Daily Report* (Ontario, California) had the robbery story on the front page. The 27 October story told of how fight fans were handed invitations on the day of the fight only to be robbed afterwards of up to $100,000 in cash and jewelry.

On the east coast, in New York, *The Post-Standard* had a similar front page headline in their 28 October issue. Of course, Ali's big winning return hit the front pages of the newspapers too, but the story now shared space with accounts of what happened afterwards. City Mayor Sam Massell, who earlier proclaimed that the 'eyes of the world' would be focused on Atlanta's weekend sporting spectacular, wasn't far wrong, but he wouldn't have guessed the extravaganza would come with such a sting in the tail.

As each day passed, the amount thought stolen became larger. A few days after the heist, the *Atlanta Constitution* along with practically every newspaper in the country jacked up the estimate to $200,000 and future estimates only went in one direction – up. They were more or less bound to increase when stories reached the ears of detectives about who attended the party. Big-time hoods from California, Washington, New York, Philadelphia, Chicago, Los Angeles and Detroit had all allegedly turned up on Handy Drive after the fight. One guy apparently lost $40,000 in cash and jewelry and another four 'guests' lost a total of $78,000 – but none filed their losses with the police.

One of the detectives assigned to the case was the man who had been head of Ali's security in the run-up to the fight, Lieutenant J. D. Hudson; another was Lieutenant Joe Amos. Both would find themselves with the difficult task of getting people to come forward and much of the information came anonymously. However, it wasn't long before they started finding out more about who was at the party. They believed that saying 'rich' gangsters attended was an understatement – super-rich was more like it. Later, Lieutenant Hudson famously commented that if there was such a thing as the Black Mafia – then the Black Mafia had been robbed in Atlanta that Monday night.

Despite the disappearance and/or silence of most witnesses, the investigation still moved at a brisk pace. The first evidence police found was the holdall and sawn-off shotgun discarded by one of the looters. Inside the bag, among other items, was a walkie-talkie and a couple of those distinctive coloured pillow cases.

Fellow detectives working on the case, Lieutenant J. R. Shattles and detective W. H. Byrd, who had been expecting the owner of the property, Gordon Williams to attend the police headquarters on Tuesday, were left disappointed. So the APB went out for 'Chicken Man', his girlfriend, and the owner of the 'modified' shotgun found alongside the discarded holdall. It wasn't long before all three turned up.

Two days after the fight and robbery, on Wednesday 28 October, 'Chicken Man' and Barbara Smith, accompanied by their attorney, attended the police headquarters to make a formal statement. Williams' simple explanation about not showing up at the appointed time was that he was 'scared to death'. He said he and his girlfriend were terrified victims, not perpetrators, and he had left his cellar much poorer than when he went in. Barbara Smith described how the armed masked men ransacked the house. After being forced to greet the guests and after the robbers were finished with their night's work, she and another girl were driven around the streets of Atlanta until they were released at about 6 a.m.

'Chicken Man' of course had a good alibi, as he was ringside at the time the villains invaded the property and he was seen by detective J. D. Hudson. But what about the mysterious characters that hosted the party, 'Fireball' and 'Frank'? Williams said that he only knew them by those names and had met them in New York a few weeks previously. According to a report in the *Atlanta Constitution*, police soon discovered that both Frank and 'Fireball' were also robbed, along with birthday boy 'Tobe' and all were dismissed as possible suspects. Police would also eventually get to know Frank's second name – even though it was never publicly revealed.

Lieutenant Hudson was already aware of the type of crime 'Chicken Man' had been involved in over the years and it certainly didn't include robbing dangerous gangsters. Police ended up believing his story, even to the point of going public about his non-involvement. It seemed like a sensible move, because some of those underworld figures believed to have been fleeced had a deadly way of solving their outstanding cases themselves. 'Chicken Man' would have known the street reputations of some of those 'villain-victims', and how many had a way of turning a possible suspect into a definite target.

On the same day it wasn't only those robbed who had money troubles. As if getting part of his face torn open wasn't bad enough, Jerry Quarry was hit by news that his former manager, Johnny Flores, was now attempting to muscle in on earnings from the fight. Flores claimed he was still co-manager of Quarry and was entitled to a share of the fighter's purse and TV monies. Action was filed in the Fulton County Circuit court in Georgia. A state arbitrator in Los Angeles eventually ruled in August 1971 on the side of Flores. Jerry's attorney, Paul Caruso, stated at the time that they planned to take the case to the Supreme Court. (It is not known what transpired after the LA ruling.)

Jerry already talked about settling the dispute he had with the California State Athletic Commission; the fine that was meant to be paid by 30 September had not been settled and a suspension had been re-imposed. Now he said he was willing to pay the $1,000 penalty.

While Quarry pondered handing the money over, cops had traced the discarded shotgun from the crime scene all the way back to a city pawn shop. They found the gun had been previously sold on but on the day of purchase, identification that was used for the firearm transaction had been copied and retained by the pawnbroker. The name staring back at the detectives from the paperwork was Houston Jimmy Hammonds.

According to a report in *The Town Talk* (1/11/70, Alexandria, Louisiana) two people had arrived at the pawn shop to purchase weapons. The one that bought the shotgun ended up in a scuffle as he tried unsuccessfully to snatch back the paperwork from the pawnbroker.

On Friday 30 October, 27-year-old Hammonds was arrested and held in custody. His story evolved: first, he had being 'tricked' into buying the gun for someone else, then he had received a few dollars for doing so. He also claimed not to know the name of the man he carried out the purchase for, but later identified a person from police photo mug shots, James Henry Hall. Police would later discover that Hall had also bought some walkie-talkies and another weapon from various other city shops, all of which were purchased on the day of the fight.

Later, journalist Margaret Shannon wrote an in-depth account of the police investigation into the robbery in the *Atlanta Journal and Constitution Mag*. She explained how the apartment where Hall lived was eventually traced, but when detectives entered his residence, they found that he had made a sudden departure. Half-eaten food left on the table and a closet full of clothes suggested it. Hall himself was nowhere to be found, but a mass of evidence was left behind. The evidence they found also revealed the identity of another suspect. His name was McKinley Rogers, but of course he was also nowhere to be found. Although detectives traced names and evidence, they still didn't know how much was actually stolen or how many people took part in the robbery.

Less than a month after the robbery, on 17 November 1970, three people out of the possible five to eight robbers suggested by the witnesses were indicted on charges of armed robbery. They were McKinley Rogers Jr, James Henry Hall and Houston Jimmy Hammonds. Only Hammonds was in custody while the others were still on the loose. Eventually, only six victims out of a possible couple of hundred came forward to the police and out of those six named in the case, one was Gordon 'Chicken Man' Williams and another a man who said he lost his shoes, twenty dollars and the keys to his car! Soon after the court case, newspapers around the country were talking of a likely $500,000 haul.

Lieutenants Hudson and Joe Amos said they were still looking for a possible five other gang members, and gave dire warnings to all those still on the loose, especially to Rogers and Hall. Now that their names were in the public domain, much of the 'detective work' any of those robbed had been undertaking themselves had been completed for them. It was one thing being hunted by police, but another been hunted by police and dangerous gangsters at the same time. Those fleeced would have known there were more than three robbers involved. Sometimes when there was an unexplained underworld execution, it was linked to the robbery in Atlanta. For all the cops knew, the robbers could already be dead, but if Rogers and Hall were still alive, their identity was printed in practically every newspaper in the land. It was only a matter of time. As the months past, the heist figure grew to $1 million.

If Hammonds told the truth and he only bought the shotgun for someone else, none of the bandits had actually been caught. The loot had still not been recovered, and no one knew how much of it there was because the victims didn't or couldn't declare their losses. A couple of witnesses, although their faces were turned to the basement floor on the night of the robbery, were convinced one of the bandits was a woman. Maybe this was one of those crimes that the mean streets and not diligent detective work would solve.

Seven months after the crime took place, things came to a head. At 12.35 a.m. on 8 May 1971, on a darkened street in the Bronx, 25-year-old James Henry Hall, 32-year-old McKinley Rogers and another guy called Donald Philips from Brunswick, Georgia, were lounging in a stolen Cadillac. Two men approached the stationary vehicle. Those inside had guns, so maybe they were expecting trouble. Perhaps though, there was just a tap at the car's window and someone attempted to make some small talk.

If any chit-chat took place, it was quickly interrupted by the crackling sound of gun-fire. The men outside the car carried shooters themselves and popped some lead into the car's interior hitting all three men inside. After a few seconds, the noise of gunfire ceased and was replaced by the sound of shoe leather hitting the street as they fled. The car that they were so quick to get away from was left riddled with bullet holes and three dead bodies were slumped inside.

The killings weren't motivated by robbery, as one of those lying dead had hundreds of dollars in his pockets. Two guns were also found inside the vehicle. According to a report in the *New York Times,* the three deceased men all carried false identities. Police believed Hall was the 'mastermind' behind the operation, while many from the criminal world had their own theories. Some thought those unfortunate souls murdered in the car were merely working for a bigger crime figure or syndicate.

There were and still are, many intriguing stories attached to that Handy Drive robbery and the subsequent killings. In the underworld, there were never going to be many people who would spill the beans. The police themselves believed they went as far as they could with the physical evidence they had managed to obtain at the time. What is known is that at first, detectives received anonymous calls about who was at the party. Over time, those anonymous callers changed their tune. Lt Hudson later said that when they believed there was no one else alive to arrest, there was nothing left to investigate, so the Handy Drive Robbery case was closed.

What became of the owner of the property, the man some originally suspected as being involved, Gordon Williams? Five months after the fight and heist, on 2 March 1971, the *Atlanta Constitution* reported that 'Chicken Man' had been involved in a police chase along the wet roads of Fulton County. He touched speeds of over 100 mph, while at the same time throwing little bags that contained white powder out the windows, until the chase was eventually brought to a halt.

A while later, 'Chicken Man' received a seven-year sentence and a $4,000 fine at a court in Fulton County for possession of cocaine and marijuana. It is not known if Williams appealed.

'Chicken Man' would eventually mend his ways and become the Rev. Gordon Williams, Pastor at the Salem Baptist Church in Georgia.

17

THE WAR ENDS,
THE FIGHTS CONTINUE

Only a couple of days after his victory, Ali was back home in Philadelphia, hearing first-hand about the telephone bomb threat shortly after his victory. Three days after the fight, Ali, his wife Belinda and two-year-old daughter, Maryum, turned up at the ABC-TV studios in New York. Ali was there to take part in a pre-recorded *Wide World of Sports* to be screened on Saturday, showing Monday's night's fight.

Surprisingly, it would be Ali's 'fight' with Marciano, not his *real* encounter with Quarry, which was the most watched *Wide World of Sports* show of 1970. During the taping of the October 1970 show, broadcaster Howard Cosell analyzed the fight with Quarry and discussed Ali's ring future. The fighter said he was already in training for his next bout, which, after all the Frazier fever, was going to be against Oscar Bonavena. The fight itself wouldn't be formally announced for another week, and would take place on 7 December 1970. The Argentinian provided himself with a good workout to stay in trim for his December fight when, on the same day Ali and his family were in the TV studios, he stopped Luis Pires in the fourth round at Luna Park stadium in Buenos Aires.

Frazier would also get a mention in the ABC-TV interview, but Joe was still tucked up in his training camp at Vacation Valley Club Lodge in East Stroudsburg preparing for Bob Foster. Ali would get to see the title bout between Frazier and Foster, when it took place on 18 November, but not in the fight arena itself, back in the same place that his bout with Quarry had been held, inside the Atlanta Municipal Auditorium.

House of Sports Inc were involved in organizing the CCTV screening for the city and it would come as a double-header, as both Frazier's fight from Detroit and George Foreman's bout against Boone Kirkman from New York were shown. Fans in the UK would also get to see both fights a few days later. Both fights from the two cities were screened live in various other venues across America. Ali sat among some 700-1,000 boxing fans for the double-fight night, which was a short one. The 24 by 18ft screen showed Foreman battering Kirkman to a two-round stoppage and Frazier stop his own opponent with a left hook, also in the second. The wins stretched Foreman's record to 24–0, while the heavyweight champion's record reached 26 wins without defeat.

Ali couldn't resist. As the victorious Joe Frazier was seen on the giant screen being interviewed in the ring after his win, Ali started shouting out about wanting to fight him. By all accounts, he was so worked up, throwing jabs and hooks, that he was sweating almost as much as Frazier under the hot ring lights over in Detroit. He called out that Frazier had only 'whupped' a light-heavy and Joe owed him three years back pay!

The show ended when his travelling companion Bundini Brown eventually restrained him from going the full 15 rounds with himself. The sparse turnout in the 5,000-capacity city auditorium and also over in the Cobo Hall back in Detroit (6,300 fans turned up in the 12,500-capacity venue, compared to the 9,103 fans that showed up at the Detroit Olympia for the CCTV screening of the Quarry fight) also didn't go unnoticed by the former champion: the disappointing turnout was 'proof' that it was Ali and not Joe Frazier who was the *real* champion and the 'greatest draw' in boxing.

Nevertheless, with Ali and Frazier both winning their respective bouts and with Ali already signed up for his next fight, the future looked bright for the two heavyweight superstars. If the former champion was successful against Bonavena, the epic meeting between the two undefeated heavyweight champions would likely take place the following year. At that time, Leroy Johnson was still optimistic of not only bringing that big fight to Atlanta, but maybe other big fights in the future. However, things were changing fast not only in Atlanta, but the world of boxing.

Ali went on to win his December bout against Bonavena at Madison Square Garden, with 4,000 fans in Atlanta watching the bout by way of CCTV back inside the city auditorium. Only days after Ali's win over Bonavena, he was granted a licence to box in the very state his troubles began back in 1967, Texas.

Houston-based 'Astrodome Championship Enterprises' talked confidently about putting the Ali v Frazier fight on at the 60,000-seat Astrodome, where Ali defended his title against Cleveland Williams in 1966 and Ernie Terrell in 1967. The fights drew an impressive combined audience of 72,781 fans and a combined gate of $861,435. This, together with a favourable tax situation in the state, meant promoters in Houston were now optimistic about bringing the fight to their city.

According to *Jet Magazine* (January 1971), Leroy Johnson along with a group of others wanted to apply for a permit in Houston to promote the Ali v Frazier fight – but it is not known if that group was linked to 'Astrodome Championship Enterprises'.

One likely reason why Leroy was willing to move his efforts from Atlanta to Houston was that Atlanta was looking more problematic. The potential difficulties wouldn't come from rival boxing promoters, but politicians.

In January 1971, the same month that Lester Maddox moved office to become lieutenant governor, being replaced by Jimmy Carter as state governor, a Bill was raised in the Senate to create a state athletic commission. No problem with that you may think, but one of the reasons given for the Bill was that the state of Georgia had no control over professional athletics (including professional boxing) and was in need of some. Guess who was proposed for the state athletic commission committee? Lester Garfield Maddox. The makeup of the new commission was initially proposed to be 10 members, including, among others, the state governor, Jimmy Carter, the lieutenant governor, Lester Maddox, the Attorney-General, the Secretary of State and the Speaker of the House.

Leroy Johnson claimed it had only been raised to stop a future Ali fight taking place in Georgia. Those opposed to the bill even started calling it the 'anti-Ali-bill', but despite objections, it was passed through the Senate on a vote of 36-8.

However, there had been some adjustments after questions had been raised about the political make-up of the committee, with the governor, lieutenant governor and House speaker only appointing suitable individuals for a seven-man committee. The bill was then passed to state governor Jimmy Carter for him to sign into law, but on Friday 19 March 1971 it was announced that Carter had vetoed! (Today, Georgia has a state athletic commission, called the 'Georgia Athletic and Entertainment Commission', which is made up of five members, each member appointed by the state governor.)

Anyway, back to 1971 and on Monday evening, 8 March, Atlanta still got to see the Ali v Frazier 'super-fight', but it only arrived by way of satellite TV. The fight was seen at a packed City Auditorium, inside the Sports Arena, and the Dinkler Plaza Hotel. The fight attracted 8,375 fans, who shelled out either $10 or $15 for a seat.

One can only imagine the astronomical figures that would have been amassed in Atlanta if the 'battle of champions' had taken place there. However, it wasn't meant to be and Atlanta, indeed Georgia, would never host another Ali fight, However, Ali would still return to Atlanta for charity boxing exhibitions, etc.

For Leroy Johnson, if putting on an Ali fight in Atlanta proved impossible, there didn't appear anything to stop him creating a movie about the bizarre robbery that had taken place after the fight. *Jet Magazine* (November 1971) reported that Leroy had teamed up with two others and formed a company called JWJ Productions Inc to do just that.

By the following year, a screenplay had apparently been written by William Diehl, a director and producer. They hoped to release *The Party After The Fight* by the end of 1972. And just like in the real robbery, with those from the Atlanta police department searching for the villains having their leads run dry, mine also ran dry; if *The Party After The Fight* ever went into production I couldn't find it.

It's not known if the man that took part in 'the fight before the party', Jerry Quarry, attended or even watched the Ali v Frazier fight in New York, but what is known is that despite his defeat in Atlanta, he eventually resumed his fighting career a few months after. In a touch over five weeks, Jerry took part in two 10-round winning fights, the first against Dick Gosha in June 1971 and then a return bout against Tony Doyle, that took place at the Playboy Club Hotel, in Wisconsin on 24 July

Somewhat surprisingly, not long after the Doyle win, an Ali v Quarry II fight was mooted for September or October of that same year, with various promoters talking of staging the bout in arenas that ranged from the Astrodome in Houston to the Dodgers Stadium in LA. Another promoter wanted the fight to take place in Canada, but all proposals failed to materialize.

Ali ended up beating Buster Mathis over 12 rounds inside the Astrodome in November 1971, while in the same month, Jerry travelled to the UK and tackled the then recently crowned British, Empire and European heavyweight champion, Jack Bodell. Southpaw Jack, who was once employed as a sparring partner for Ali before his fight against Karl Mildenberger back in 1966, was a big fella and had a notoriously awkward boxing style. He had just recently scored a huge upset, beating 'Golden Boy' Joe Bugner in September and took along with his win all of Joe's titles.

Jerry met Jack at the Empire Pool, Wembley, in London on 16 November 1971 and it appeared Jerry fathomed out Jack's awkward style rather quickly; he flattened Bodell in only 64 seconds of the first round and his devastatingly quick win earned Jerry the *Ring* magazine 'Fighter of the month' award.

The exciting Quarry was brought back to the same London venue the following year, this time in his sixth comeback fight, when he beat fellow American Larry Middleton on a close points decision. That bout took place one month before Jerry finally fought Ali again. Their second encounter took place in Las Vegas in June 1972 and Jerry was paid a reported guaranteed $175,000 for the fight.

The fight night was promoted as the 'Soul Brothers versus the Quarry Brothers', with Jerry facing Ali for the North American Boxing Federation (NABF) title and his younger brother Mike going on first against the destructive power-punching of defending world light-heavyweight champion Bob Foster. Mike held a highly impressive record at the time, with 35 straight wins and not one defeat. He well deserved his shot at the undisputed title. (Bob Foster became undisputed champion again earlier that year, when he reclaimed the WBA title and added it to his WBC crown after stopping WBA champ Vicente Rondon in the second. The WBA had previously withdrawn their recognition of Foster as champion a few weeks after his bout with Frazier in 1970.) Mike was knocked out in the fourth. The sight of his younger brother lying flat on the canvas unconscious didn't help Jerry when it was his turn to climb up the same ring steps to face a now imperious Ali. Mike eventually recovered and got up from the canvas, but it was a sickening knockout.

In the Ali v Quarry II bout, after only a few seconds of the first round, Jerry lifted the then 216½lb Ali clean off his feet as though attempting to throw his heavyweight rival out over the top ropes. Maybe he should have tried it. Ali stopped him in a one-sided fight in the seventh round. Ali looked almost unbeatable that night, with his silky skills well honed. After the defeat, even Jerry believed Ali would defeat Frazier in a return fight.

That second Quarry fight had been the former champion's ninth since his initial return in Atlanta. It was hardly surprising that he was found to be extra-quick by 1972, after fighting Jerry Quarry, Oscar Bonavena and Joe Frazier all in a six-month period between October 1970 and March 1971.

They say the 1970s was the golden era of heavyweight boxing – no wonder when fans were treated to fights like those mentioned. George Foreman was at the Ali v Quarry II bout. George, then 23 years old, was still seven months away from putting Joe Frazier away and only one month past scoring his 36th straight win, (33 KOs) knocking out Miguel Angel Paez in 2:29 of the second.

Three years after the Ali v Quarry II fight, Ali stated that he wanted 'seriously' to fight both Joe Frazier and George Foreman on the same night. Minutes after his second bout with Quarry, it may have looked to many high up in the bleachers that he was about to fight Quarry and Foreman on the same night. Shortly after the battered and demoralized Quarry was led back to his corner, Foreman was seen walking towards ringside and when Ali spotted him approaching, he put on a show of wanting to jump over the ropes and take on the undefeated KO puncher there and then. It was all entertaining theatrics of course and where else better to do it than Las Vegas.

Despite another devastating loss to Ali, which sent the then 27-year-old Jerry into a temporary retirement, it wasn't long before he dusted his gloves off again and resumed his boxing career the following year; 1973 would be one of his best too, with five straight victories including four by the short route and three at Madison Square Garden.

After stopping Randy Neumann in the seventh round in January, Jerry was pitched in with undefeated ranking contender Ron Lyle in February (both fights held in the Garden).

Lyle stood 6ft 3in and was another heavily muscled, undefeated and fearsome fighter, who was causing carnage in the heavyweight division, with a faultless ring record of 19 fights, 19 wins, including 17 knockouts. Again, Jerry was outweighed, this time by 19lbs, but Lyle's reputation and size difference didn't deter Jerry from handing Lyle his first ever defeat as a pro, smashing out a unanimous points decision win over 12 rounds.

Jerry then crammed in another two stoppage wins, one of which was against his old rival Tony Doyle (their third and last fight took place on the undercard of Muhammad Ali's return bout against Ken Norton), before he returned to Madison Square Garden in December to score another stunning victory. His win also came with the trio of greats, Ali, Foreman and Frazier, all sat ringside to witness his action-packed performance.

This time, Jerry went in against Earnie 'KO' Shavers, who was the same guy who had stopped Ali's sparring partner Johnny Hudgins back in 1970. Earnie had been catapulted into title contention by virtue of a long string of knockout victories that included a crunching one round knockout win over Jimmy Ellis in his previous fight. (Remember Ellis had defeated Quarry.)

Shavers flattened Ellis in only 2:39 of the first round, again in the same arena, Madison Square Garden, six months previously in June 1973. Shavers' record then stood at 47 fights, 45 wins (44 by KO) and only 2 defeats.

So Earnie was the man that beat the man (Ellis) who beat the man (Quarry). On paper, going into his 48th fight, it looked like it would be another 'KO' win', for Shavers, but when the leather started flying, it was 'The black Destroyer', Shavers, who had to pick himself off the canvas after Jerry Quarry's fast and early onslaught. The fight lasted 2:21 of the first round, after referee Arthur Mercante stopped the fight soon after the knockdown.

Unfortunately, this was Jerry's last great win and the end of big-time boxing was just around the corner. In the next two years, he would fight in Madison Square Garden two more times, losing to Joe Frazier in 1974 in five rounds and in the same round to Ken Norton the following year in 1975. To say they were two devastating defeats was an understatement, as both Joe and Ken landed some crunching blows on the game and gutsy Quarry. Over the next 17 years, Jerry would fight professionally four more times, winning three of those contests. His fighting days finally came to an end after he lost to Ron Cranmer on 30 October 1992 at the Holiday Inn trade center in Aurora, Colorado. Jerry was then aged 47 years old and he finished with a career record of 66 bouts, 53 wins (32 KOs), 9 losses and 4 draws.

Over his turbulent and exciting career, Jerry may have looked back at Atlanta as just another venue. For Ali though, the city of their first encounter would not only be the place where he reignited his boxing career, but also a city that would intertwine with his life and be forever linked to his legacy. Atlanta was the beginning of a marvellous period for Ali. His return to the ring was astonishing, revolutionary.

Budd Schulberg wrote a fine book about Ali called *Loser and Still Champion* and that title summed Ali's life up for the next few years, after losing to Frazier in 1971. Ali may have been defeated by a points decision, but the fight itself was a truly remarkable spectacle and one of boxing's and indeed sport's greatest occasions. By the time the fight ended, both fighters had brutalized each other. After Ali took out of the ring a defeat and a grotesquely swollen jaw, many thought he wouldn't fight again. That was arguably the biggest misjudgement of a fighter in the history of the game.

Months after losing to Joe, in June 1971, his draft case was overturned in the Supreme Court and he was vindicated for his stand against taking part in the Vietnam War. Some believe this was his greatest triumph. It was also at the end of this month that the existing laws on draft were meant to expire, but they were eventually extended until January 1973. That same month undefeated George Foreman became world heavyweight champion when he destroyed Joe Frazier in two brutal rounds in Kingston, Jamaica. A couple of months later, Ali lost a points decision to ex-marine, Ken Norton, but reversed the loss later that same year and also gained a revenge win over Joe Frazier four months later, in January 1974.

This meant although he wasn't now world champion, Ali still held a win over every fighter he had previously fought and many believed this was the opportune time for the former champion to retire, to keep his record intact rather than continue and face the destructive fists of new champion George Foreman.

Most 'boxing experts' told us that Ali would not only lose if he proceeded to fight Foreman, but would likely get seriously hurt. The majority of boxing fans sided with the 'experts'.

Of course, Ali didn't retire and nine months after gaining that revenge win over Joe Frazier, Ali and Foreman were found in the heart of Africa in a $10 million showdown.

As the world knows, just before the break of dawn on Wednesday 30 October 1974, inside the Stade du 20 Mai

Stadium in front of 60,000 fans in Kinshasa, Zaire, Ali won by a spectacular knockout in the eighth round. As an exhausted Foreman lay on the canvas, looking out into the black African sky wondering what had happened, a victorious Ali not only became king of boxing, but almost king of the world, as his startling victory pushed him onto yet another level of world popularity. At 32 years old, he was at his peak and he became arguably the most recognized person on the planet, as the charismatic champion's appeal crossed all racial and national barriers.

Only three months after regaining the World Heavyweight title, on Tuesday, 21 January 1975, Ali returned to the place where his boxing life had been reignited, Atlanta, Georgia. He turned up for a money-raising boxing exhibition where 8,000 people attended and paid $3 a head to watch Ali going three exhibition rounds with a local guy and one fun round with the then Atlanta mayor, Maynard Jackson. The 'guest referee' for the Ali v Mayor bout was state Senator Julian Bond and after the mayor 'decked' the new champion twice in the first, the fun bout was declared a draw.

One month later, on 25 February 1975, the leader of the Nation of Islam and Ali's spiritual leader and teacher, Elijah Muhammad, died in Chicago. His passing coincided with the 11th anniversary of when Ali/Clay first shocked the world to become the king of the heavyweights back on 25 February 1964. Two months after the death of Elijah Muhammad, the war in Vietnam came to an end after the takeover of Saigon by North Vietnamese troops.

For Ali, as regards his career, the year of 1975 was not only successful, but extremely prosperous, defending the world title four times, defeating Chuck Wepner, Ron Lyle, Joe Bugner and Joe Frazier. For the Frazier fight alone, he was reported to have received a $6 million purse and it was the same staggering amount one year later when he defended his title against Ken Norton in 1976.

Not long after that fight, Ali was again found in Atlanta, to film scenes for the movie based on his life, *The Greatest* – and to repeat something he said shortly after the Norton fight, that he was definitely going to retire.

While actor Ali was in Atlanta, he heard about a hotel that Leroy Johnson and six other businessmen purchased the previous year going through financial difficulties. The Atlanta Internationale had 425 rooms and they needed them filled with paying guests. The first thing Ali did to help was to move himself, the cast and all the film crew out of the hotel they were staying in, over to the Internationale. Then, while there, on 1 December 1976, he held a press conference, promoting the complex and saying he would help support it in some way.

A Sports Hall of Fame was also said to be going to be based inside the Internationale, with Ali stating he would donate some of his gloves and trunks he had worn in some of his major fights. Baseball star Hank Aaron was also there to help promote the venture. During the press conference, Ali spoke about the movie, *The Greatest,* which would be released the following year and repeated his statement of never wanting to enter a boxing ring again.

However, by the time he arrived in my home city of Newcastle Upon Tyne in the UK in July 1977, Ali had not only changed his mind about retiring, but he had already taken part in another 15-round championship fight. That been his ninth title defence after beating Foreman and his 56th paid bout, against Alfredo Evangelista, in May 1977. Not only that, he had another fight in the pipeline against the same boxer Quarry beat four years previously, Earnie Shavers.

It was a coincidental meeting in my home city that would result in Ali cementing his ties with Atlanta even further. Ali and his family had travelled from their home in Chicago all the way over to Newcastle in the UK for a few summer days to help raise funds for local boys clubs. On the champion's first day in the city on 14 July 1977, he found out by chance that Newcastle had been chosen as the first city in the world to take part in an 'International friendship scheme' – with Atlanta, Georgia. The 'Friendship Force' was the brainchild of fellow Atlanta man, Wayne Smith, but was unveiled by the ex-governor of Georgia and the then recently elected US President, Jimmy Carter.

The US contingent of 381 persons were on their last full day in Newcastle, while it was Ali's first. When he heard about the US/UK international friendship program, he took time out of his already hectic schedule to make a surprise visit to the city civic center to meet all those involved. Ali was so taken by Wayne's program that he eventually became actively involved, becoming one of the international friendship force ambassadors.

After Ali's visit to Newcastle, he returned to America to face the 'sledgehammer' fists of Earnie Shavers. Ali was four months shy of 36 years old. The fight went ahead inside Madison Square Garden on 29 September 1977 and although Ali won by a points decision, it had been another brutal fight. The champion was seen to be rocked on more than a couple of occasions during the 15-round slugging match, but he somehow survived those moments and hung on to his title, securing a points win. Afterwards, Ali looked exhausted and it was clear to many it was now time for him to say goodbye to the fight game.

Two weeks later, he was back inside a boxing ring, but this time for a charity exhibition in Atlanta. This time it was to raise money for the scheme that had captured his interest back in Newcastle in the UK. Three thousand fans turned up at The Omni Coliseum to see the heavyweight champion of the world go through his paces. One of the ticket holders that night was even picked out to go the last round with Ali, with former WBA champion and regular sparring partner Jimmy Ellis going the first three. Ali's link with the 'Atlanta Friendship Force' would never break; he attended the 20th anniversary of the program and it all came about by that chance meeting in faraway 'Geordie Land' back in 1977.

In Ali's boxing life though, after his real life 'Rocky' encounter with Shavers, things started to change for the champion boxer. His career would last another four years and in those years, he would take part in four fights, losing three of those contests. This would include losing the title and regaining the WBA version of it against former Olympic champion, Leon Spinks, in 1978.

During his inactive and 'final' retirement year of 1979, the President of Afro-American Services Inc, Lloyd Von Blaine proposed that Ali might take an interest in the idea of running for the US Senate. It's not known if Ali ever responded to Von Blaine, but Ali was already in the 'Senate' that year. American TV viewers watched him on NBC-TV portraying someone who reached the US Senate, but during the period after the Civil War. Ali played an ex-slave called Gideon Jackson, who educated himself and overcame struggles with the Ku Klux Klan and landowners in the South. The drama was called *Freedom Road* and starred Kris Kristofferson.

Ali put his retirement in writing to the WBA and had taken part in a world-wide farewell exhibition tour for his fans. His WBA title became the possession of new champion John Tate, who was a 1976 Olympian and was undefeated at the time. Tate won the title after picking up a 15-round points win over South African Gerrie Coetzee in front of 81,000 fans in the Loftus Versfeld Stadium in Pretoria. He also picked up a $27,000 gold belt along with a reported $400,000 purse.

At the start of the second year of Ali's 'retirement' in 1980, he was involved in a political mission on behalf of US President, Jimmy Carter, following the Soviet Union's invasion of Afghanistan in 1979. Carter decided the US should boycott the 1980 Moscow Olympics and sent Ali off to lobby various

African countries. Ali was tremendously popular in Africa and the international mission might have suited him at that time, but it didn't turn out the way Carter might have wished. After the ex-champion heard the Africans' side of the story, convincing them to boycott was no longer his priority.

Ali returned to America and unbelievably, it wasn't long before newspaper stories emerged of another Ali comeback. By this time, he was 38 years old and the fighter that was eventually lined up to meet him was the WBC champion, the 'Easton Assassin' Larry Holmes. Larry was not only seven years Ali's junior, but he had defended his world title seven times since Ali's last fight. Ali was stopped in his corner after 10 one-sided rounds in Las Vegas on 2 October.

Ali's final loss was to Trevor Berbick in December 1981. The 1980s began with increasing concerns and rumours about Ali's health. He also somehow involved himself in a string of business deals where some just didn't work out the way they should. The most famous was the time his name was attached to a company called MAPS (Muhammad Ali Professional Sports). A man who called himself Harold Smith convinced Ali to allow his sports company to use his name in first promoting athletics, then professional boxing.

There was no shortage of money either, promoting bouts that featured, among others, Thomas 'Hit Man' Hearns and Matthew Saad Muhammad. The fighters on the promotions were earning small fortunes, so much so that even the top promoters at that time were getting a touch concerned about being knocked off their perches. It all came crashing down in 1981, prior to MAPS' hopeful promotion of a Ken Norton/Gerry Cooney matchup. 'Harold Smith', real name Ross Fields, was found to have a long history of leaving bad cheques across various states. The money used for his fight enterprises was embezzled from Wells Fargo bank. The embezzlement was made possible through a computer scam and inside help. Anyway, by the time the bank became aware of the fraud, they were out some $21 million and initially Ross/Harold was nowhere to be found. The former champ knew nothing of the embezzlement of course, but it was his name that was attached to it.

In 1982, Smith/Fields was sentenced to 10 years. That scam and the endless press stories that followed still didn't stop Ali trying to come to the aid of Atlanta during one of its darkest periods. In the same month that the Norton v Cooney fight eventually went ahead in May 1981, but obviously under a different promotional banner, Ali pledged $400,000 of his own money to help catch a serial killer in the city.

At the time, Ali was in Atlanta for another money raiser, this time for the Cerebral Palsy Foundation and he was shocked to hear about the murders that had taken place. His financial pledge would be added to the $100,000 reward fund. The killer had been on the rampage in Atlanta since 1979 and there had been at least 28 African American adults, teenagers and children murdered. One month after Ali's financial pledge, the case was cracked and suspect Wayne Williams was arrested on 21 June 1981.

The health stories were getting worse. When the former champ was found back in Atlanta in July 1982 doing some promotional work for another company, the stories about his slow movement and quiet speech overshadowed the purpose of his visit.

In the UK, I remember especially a picture of a tired-looking Ali on the front page of the national tabloid called *The Daily Star*. A reporter had visited Ali's LA home and wrote a feature story that stretched over a few days back in July 1983. Readers were informed about the ex-champion's health and how everybody should be concerned about him, all the way from the then US President, Ronald Reagan, down to his everyday fans. The story sent shock waves through his army of his admirers in the UK.

It was around this point that I started writing to the champ, saying that although he didn't know me, I was one of his millions of fans thinking about him and hoped he would be OK.

The following year in September 1984, practically every newspaper in the world told us that the former champion had just been released from hospital and that he had been diagnosed with Parkinson's Syndrome. The news of the diagnosis sent more reverberations around the world and it was scary as some press stories painted a bleak future for Ali. All the cheers and plaudits he had received over the years changed to deep concern and thoughts about where the ex-fighter's life was headed.

It came to pass though, that my personal fears were alleviated when only one month after that hospital story broke around the world Ali telephoned my home in Newcastle and invited me for one week's stay at his home in Los Angeles. The times I experienced with him were fabulous, but those remarkable tales and what they led onto are for another time.

When I returned home, I believed that some of the press reports that I had read about his ill health had been exaggerated, as he was as funny and as sharp as ever during the times I was fortunate enough to be with him, despite the medical diagnoses.

During those times in the 1980s though, it did seem Ali went through a transition period, a time when he was searching for something else to replace his former life as a famous fighter. He was seen at many of the big fights of the day, usually at Don King's promotions, promoting various products, from shoe polish to chocolate bars. During that 1982 visit in Atlanta, he was there endorsing something that would apparently reduce power consumption in people's homes.

I am sure the ex-champ enjoyed his times doing those things, but for me and millions of his fans we felt he deserved something bigger, something that fitted in with his hard-earned reputaton – something that represented his lifetime of struggles, successes, beliefs and values.

In 1986, Ali turned up in London along with Don King and WBA heavyweight Champion, Tim Witherspoon. Tim was in town to defend his title against Briton's Frank Bruno at Wembley Stadium and the match was billed as the fight of the decade in the UK. Ali was also in London to complete a commercial at Fulham Film studios. The product he endorsed that time was powdered milk destined for the Middle Eastern market called *Primo* and the filming took about a week to complete.

By the time Tim Witherspoon turned up in London, Tim had already won and lost the WBC heavyweight title back in 1984, but by the turn of 1986, he found himself crowned as WBA heavyweight champion after he beat Tony Tubbs by a points decision on another Don King promotion. That fight took place inside The Omni in Atlanta on 17 January 1986, the same venue where Ali carried out his boxing exhibitions in aid of the 'Friendship Force' nine years previously. The WBA title fight also just happened to be the first major heavyweight fight in the city since Ali beat Quarry 16 years previously. Ali was sat ringside among the reported 6,000 fans and watched his two pals battle it out for a title he once owned on the night of his 44th birthday.

On the evening of 19 July 1986 at Wembley Stadium, Tim Witherspoon successfully defended his title for the first time against Frank Bruno in a battle of 11 brutal rounds, with both fighters exchanging sledgehammer blows.

Ali allowed me and my friend Ian Parsons to be his sidekicks that night, being picked up in a motorcade of limos at the Grosvenor House Hotel on Park Lane and walking out onto to the famous Wembley turf alongside him. It was amazing to think that the last time Ali walked out to a fight at the stadium was to one of his own, when he fought Henry Cooper back in 1963. It was another memorable experience for me; but what Muhammad, Ian or myself could never guessed, was that 10 years to the day on 19 July 1996, something remarkable would happen. Ali would walk out into another open-air stadium, in Atlanta of all places, and the occasion would become one of the most memorable moments in sporting history.

18

RETURN TO ATLANTA – THE GREATEST COMEBACK OF ALL

Atlanta had changed much over the years. The 'beacon of the south' had seen its population decrease from 496,973 in 1970 to 394,017 in 1990. Over the same period, the black, or African-American population increased from 51.3% in 1970 to 67.1% in 1990.

After the end of Sam Massell's term in office in 1973, the first African American mayor in Atlanta, Maynard Jackson, was elected and his term in office began in 1974. During the new mayor's term, something called 'Affirmative Action' was increased, designed to bring about a fairer racial balance in jobs and opportunities throughout the city.

As we know, Jimmy Carter, had gone on to become the 39th President of the United States in 1977 and on the very first day after his inauguration, Carter pardoned all those in the country that had evaded the draft during the Vietnam War.

Lester Garfield Maddox, aged 75 in 1990, after a long spell away from political life returned in a campaign to become state governor again. His bid was unsuccessful, as the race for governor that year was won by Zell Miller, with his term in office starting in January 1991. Surprisingly, Zell had succeeded Lester Maddox as lieutenant governor as long ago as 1975 and remained in office all the way to the beginning of his term as state governor. By 1996, Zell Miller was still state governor, and his term in office that year coincided with the 1996 Olympics in Atlanta. Although the choice of the southern city for the Olympics was decided years previously, Zell, along with others, including the city Mayor at the time, Bill Campbell and previous mayors Andrew Young and Maynard Jackson, were all instrumental in bringing the games to Atlanta.

Despite the costs and again, some protests, Atlanta still promoted itself as 'a city too busy to hate' and wanted to showcase itself as a place that had overcome a past of racial division. The 1996 Olympic Games was a marvellous opportunity to do just that.

By 1996, Muhammad Ali had also changed much. The fast talking and even faster fists had been replaced with trembling hands and quietness. It had been 12 years since he was first diagnosed with Parkinson's Syndrome, but despite his ailment, his mind remained as sharp as ever.

Ask those who were around the former champion at that time and they will tell you that his wit and humour remained the same throughout and despite his sometimes enforced silence, many said the 'quiet Ali' had more impact on people than the Louisville Lip ever had. Ali had moved away from the Nation of Islam and aligned himself to a more orthodox form of the Muslim religion and by 1996, he spread the word of Islam wherever he travelled.

Ali also came with a different message in the 1990s than the 1960s and 1970s – it was no longer about him being the 'greatest', but about how everyone could be the greatest in their own right if they possessed a dream and the burning desire to follow it.

The opening ceremony of the Atlanta Olympics took place at the new $209 million Centennial Olympic stadium on the night of 19 July 1996. On that special evening and to the surprise of the 85,600 in attendance, Atlanta boxer and 1984 Olympic bronze medallist Evander Holyfield emerged from a huge circular structure in the centre of the stadium holding aloft the Olympic torch. The former heavyweight champion of the world made his way onto the running track, where he was joined by 1992 Olympic gold 100-metre hurdler Voula Patoulidou. They both jogged along the track to be met by former quadruple Olympic gold medal winner, swimmer Janet Evans. The flaming torch was then passed to Janet who carried the torch the final few hundred yards to the north end of the stadium. She then jogged up a ramp onto a high podium and stood ready to hand the torch to the person who would light the giant Olympic Centennial beacon to start the games.

The identity of the person chosen had been a closely guarded secret, so secret in fact that some said that the man who officially opened the Games, US President Bill Clinton, didn't even know who it would be on the night. Even 22 years on, for just about everyone in the world, I don't have to give a spoiler alert.

I watched the ceremony on TV back home in Newcastle, and when the moment came for the mystery person to be revealed, I thought I vaguely recognized the middle-aged gentleman walking out of the shadows onto the podium. At first, the tens of thousands in attendance also seemed unsure of who he was. Then, the powerful spotlights hit him as he walked out with an unlit torch.

The initial reaction of the thousands of people in the stadium was to break into applause and then start chanting, '*Ah-Lee, Ah-Lee, Ah-Lee, Ah-Lee*' and the sound of Ali's old war cry reverberated around the gigantic stadium. Ali, showing the effects of his debilitating condition, had his shaking hands almost singed by the flame, but he held on determinedly. His torch lit a combustible rocket-ball that immediately shot up high above the stadium canopy to light the gigantic Centennial Torch.

As I sat at home over 4,000 miles away I nearly fell off my chair when I first realized it was Ali walking out onto the podium. I always knew he loved shocking people, but this surprise was unforgettable. It also hit me that Ali's worldwide Olympic introduction took place in the same city where he was reintroduced to the boxing world back in 1970. It was rather fitting I thought that Celine Dion's powerful song *Power of the Dream* was chosen to open the Games – a song that encapsulates the spirit of both Ali and the Olympics. One person who may have been inspired by those values was Wladimir Klitschko, who represented the Ukraine at the Games, won gold at super-heavyweight and went on to win his first heavyweight championship four years later. It was certainly a memorable year for Atlanta and the people of that city, but it was also for the man known as the 'Greatest'. Ali's iconic Olympic moment would forever link his name to the soul of Atlanta.

Of course, since his retirement in 1981, Ali was always popular and he would have remained so without his Olympic appearance, but his shining moment in 1996 went further, touching the hearts of people who never watched a fight in their lives. After that appearance, Ali would pick up every accolade and award imaginable. He was presented with the Presidential Medal of Freedom in the White House, ranking him forever among other sporting greats such as Jesse Owens and Michael Jordan. He was acclaimed as the BBC Sports Personality of the Century in the UK – the list was endless. In the commercial world, it was 'blue chip' all the way as he was courted by companies that not only paid top dollar, but also promoted some of his inner principles and values, such as in the Addidas 'impossible is nothing' commercial in 2004.

Ali's legacy is now intact. During his boxing career, he was regularly heard shouting out 'the Greatest!' By the time he lit the Olympic torch in Atlanta, he very rarely used the tag. He didn't need to as people around the globe were greeting him with those same words.

19

THE BELL TOLLS

Everyone's life has a beginning and end. There are no exceptions. Even for Jerry Quarry and Muhammad Ali, the 'greatest' of my boyhood heroes, all must end.

Jerry Quarry's final years were cruel and his life ended prematurely. In the same year he was inducted into the boxing Hall of Fame in Los Angeles in 1995, he was diagnosed as suffering from Dementia Pugilistica, a subtype of Chronic Traumatic Encephalopathy (CTE).

He was cared for by his loving family, but when he was admitted into hospital near the end of December 1998, suffering flu/cold-like symptoms, he was soon diagnosed with pneumonia. The fighter remained in the Twin Cities Community Hospital, in Templeton, California, as his condition worsened. Three days into the New Year of 1999, Jerry passed away and the loss sent his loving family and the boxing world into mourning. The 'Bellflower Belter', or 'Irish' Jerry Quarry died at the age of 53.

His brother Mike, who helped Jerry prepare not just for the Ali bout in 1970 fight but many others, also ended up following a similar path. He eventually suffered from dementia in his final years and passed away at 55 on 11 June 2006. The frightening and shocking knockout loss he suffered at the hands of Bob Foster on the Ali v Quarry II bill in 1972 was his first and only shot at the world light-heavyweight title. I still remember that bout and it looked like Mike was never going to get up off the canvas. Mercifully he did, but the knockout was the type of loss that would end most boxers' careers, but as the brothers would say, 'there is no quit in Quarry.' It wasn't long before he was boxing again. Mike would go on to have another 45 fights after the Foster loss, eventually capturing the light-heavyweight California State title in 1973 and the light-heavyweight Texas State title in 1975. Mike Wayne Quarry would end his career with a ring record of 81 fights, 62 wins, 13 losses, including 6 draws, cramming all these professional bouts in between the years 1969 to 1982.

Who on this planet did not hear and register the sad news that Muhammad Ali passed away on 3 June 2016? I became aware of Muhammad's passing a short while after I received a phone call from a news agency asking if I 'wanted to talk about Ali'. He obviously assumed that I already knew about Ali's death, but I didn't. I told the newshound I really didn't want to comment about Ali and that it was best that only his family did so and quietly replaced the receiver.

I sat in stunned silence, as memories and thoughts flooded my mind of the man who had been exceptionally kind to me and allowed me to achieve my ultimate boyhood dream of hanging out with the greatest. Memories of him driving me through Hollywood in his Stutz Bearcat sports car. Memories of arriving in various eateries in LA along with his wisecracking assistant Abdel Kader and causing mayhem and excitement wherever he went. Memories of him showing me the sequinned robe he received from Elvis Presley in Las Vegas in 1973. Memories of being alongside him for 10 days during his trip to London in 1986 and also him letting me tag along with him on some of the book signing tours over the years. Then there was one overarching memory: the smiles and joy he brought to everyone he met. I always loved the effect he had on people and couldn't think of anyone else on the planet who evinced that type of affection or attention from everyday folk.

I needed to to go to his funeral, which was planned for 10 June in his hometown in Louisville, Kentucky. In Louisville, on 9 June, there was a Muslim ceremony held for him at the Freedom Hall on the outskirts of the city. How appropriate it was that Ali should be brought here – the place where his boxing journey began back in 1960. Inside, I sat to the side but at the front and watched the outpouring of love and grief as the coffin was brought into the hall. For a few brief moments, Jesse Jackson sat down in the seat next to me. Of course, that wasn't the place or time to talk to him about his times with Ali, but I couldn't help but wonder about the memories he must have had, including of course those of Atlanta in 1970. Don King, Louis Farrakhan and 'Sugar' Ray Leonard also attended.

The next day, a funeral procession of black limos rode through the streets of his hometown, stopping at the small house where he and his brother Rahaman were raised on 3302 Grand Avenue. The funeral procession also stopped opposite the Ali Center in Downtown Louisville. The motorcade of vehicles eventually arrived at the Cave Hill Cemetery where after a short ceremony, the champ was finally laid to rest.

Afterwards, there was another service at the KFC Yum Center where everyone was welcome. People poured in, from locals to boxing champs, Mike Tyson and Lennox Lewis and former US President, Bill Clinton. The service was beamed around the world.

The next day, I was fortunate to meet up with Rahaman and wife Caroline at the refurbished childhood home at 3302 Grand Avenue. To my delight, Ali's daughters May May (Maryum) and

Hana also turned up. I had a lot to thank Hana for as it was with her help, along with film maker Tina Gharvi, that I met Muhammad Ali in private for the very last time. This was at a 70th birthday party at the MGM hotel in Las Vegas in February 2012. We met up with Muhammad in his luxury villa apartment where he stayed during his time in Vegas. Rahaman and wife Caroline had already invited me to Ali's other 70th birthday party earlier in January, which was held inside the Ali center in Louisville. If the Queen can have two birthdays, Ali can have two birthday parties. On that January evening, Lennox Lewis was there and so was Ali's pal Howard Bingham. Ninety-year-old Angelo Dundee didn't want to miss the party either and flew in from Florida. I was thrilled to catch a few words with Angelo after the celebration finished, but I was shocked when only a couple of weeks later, on 1 February 2012, Angelo, the man who was so instrumental in Ali's career, passed away in Tampa.

The day after the funeral, outside his old home, there were still flowers lying on the grass from the thousands that had been laid there the previous day. There were still hordes of fans there too, all wanting to see the house Ali was raised in and say hello to his brother, who had been by his side throughout all the good and bad times.

Since 2011, the world had lost Joe Frazier, Ken Norton and Muhammad Ali.

Six months after returning home, in December 2016, another shock and another loss, this time Ali's best and most loyal pal, Howard Bingham, passed away aged 77. It was said Howard had taken over a million photos of Ali during his life and he was one of the people behind the creation of the Ali center and orchestrating Ali's surprise appearance at the 1996 Atlanta Olympics.

'Enjoy life – it's later than you think' – that was one of Ali's favourite sayings. He actually wrote it on his shorts and gave them to a lucky fan in Birmingham, England, in June 1979 at a boxing exhibition with Jimmy Ellis. Ali followed that motto through all the dramas of his life. In my own life, Muhammad Ali is part of that select group of people that I think of every day. Just thinking about him is a pleasure in itself, not just for me but for millions. People will still be thinking about him 100 years after we have all passed.

Muhammad Ali and Jerry Quarry – thanks for the wonderful memories.

BIBLIOGRAPHY

Black Crusoe, White Friday: Paddy Monaghan, Satellite Books, Middlesex, 1979.

Everything is Pickrick. The Life of Lester Maddox: Bob Short. Mercer University Press. Georgia. 1999.

Empire of Deceit: Dean B. Allison & Bruce B. Henderson, Columbus Books, Kent, 1986

Hard Luck (The Triumph & Tragedy of "Irish" Jerry Quarry: Steve Springer & Blake Chavez. Lyons Press. Connecticut. 2011.

Joe Bugner: Joe Bugner with Stuart Mullins, New Holland Publishers, London 2013.

Kamp Olympik: Don Bragg with Theresa Bragg and Patricia Doherty. AHLP Books, New Jersey, 2008.

Loser & Still Champion: Budd Schulberg: New English Library. 1973.

Muhammad Ali's Greatest Fight: Howard L. Bingham & Max Wallace: M. Evans and Company Inc, New York 2000.

Muhammad Ali, His Life & Times: Thomas Hauser with Muhammad Ali. Robson Books, London, 1991.

Muhammad Ali: Tyneside 1977: Russell Routledge. Amberley Publishing, Gloucestershire. 2014

Original Gangster: Frank Lucas with Aliya. S. King, Ebury Press, 2010

Papa Jack: Randy Roberts: Robson Books, London, 1986.

Race & the Shaping of Twentieth-Century Atlanta: Ronald H. Bayor. The University of North Carolina Press. 1996.

Shadow Box: George Plimpton: Lyons & Burford, New York, 1977.

Sting Like a Bee: Jose Torres: Abelard-Schuman Ltd. New York 1971.

The Greatest: My Own Story: Muhammad Ali with Richard Durham. MacGibbon Ltd, London 1976.

The Holy Warrior (Muhammad Ali): Don Atyeo & Felix Dennis. Bunch Books, London, 1975

Magazines
Atlanta Magazine
Boxing News
Boxing Illustrated
Boxing Monthly
Ebony Magazine
Jet Magazine
Newsweek
The Ring Magazine
Sports Illustrated
The Atlanta Journal and Constitution Magazine
TV Times Magazine

Newspapers
Daily Mirror – UK
Sunday Mirror – UK
Daily Express – UK
The Times – UK
Daily Star – UK
Evening Chronicle (Tyneside UK)
The Sun – UK

Anderson Daily Bulletin – Anderson, Indiana.
Aiken Standard – Aiken, South Carolina.
Argus-Leader – Sioux Falls, South Dakota.
Arizona Daily Star – Tucson, Arizona.
Arizona Republic – Phoenix, Arizona.
Asbury Park Press – Asbury Park, New Jersey.
Asheville Citizen-Times – Asheville, North Carolina.
Battle Creek Enquirer – Battle Creek, Michigan
Beckley Post-Herald. Beckley, West Virginia.
Bennington Banner – Bennington, Vermont.
Chicago Tribune – Chicago, Illinois.
Courier Post – Camden, New Jersey
Daily Press – Newport, Virginia.
Delaware County Daily Times – Chester, Pennsylvania.
Democrat and Chronicle – Rochester, New York.
Detroit Free Press – Detroit, Michigan.
Fairbanks Daily News-Miner – Fairbanks, Alaska.
Fort Lauderdale News – Florida.
Great Falls Tribune – Great Falls, Montana.
Hartford Courant – Hartford, Connecticut.
Independent Press – Telegram – Long Beach, California.
Journal and Courier – Lafayette, Indiana.

Kingsport News – Kingsport, Tennessee.
Lubbock Avalanche-Journal – Lubbock, Texas.
New York Daily News – New York.
Pensacola News Journal – Pensacola, Florida.
Philadelphia Daily News – Philadelphia, Pennsylvania.
Playground Daily News – Fort Walton Beach, Florida.
Port Angeles Evening News – Port Angeles, Washington.
Reno Gazette-Journal – Reno Nevada.
San Antonio Express – San Antonio, Texas.
Star-Gazette – Elmira, New York.
Standard-Speaker – Hazleton, Pennsylvania.
St Louis Post Dispatch – St Louis, Missouri.
Tallahassee Democrat – Tallahassee, Florida.
Tucson Daily Citizen – Tucson, Arizona.
Warren Times Mirror – Warren, Pennsylvania.
The Akron Beacon Journal – Akron, Ohio.
The Age – Melbourne, Australia.
The Argus – Fremont, California.
The Atlanta Journal – Atlanta, Georgia
The Atlanta Constitution – Atlanta, Georgia.
The Baltimore Sun – Baltimore, Maryland
The Bee – Danville, Virginia.
The Bridgeport Post – Bridgeport, Connecticut.
The Capital: Annapolis – Maryland.
The Clarion-Ledger – Jackson, Mississippi
The Courier-Journal – Louisville, Kentucky.
The Courier-News – Bridgewater, New Jersey.
The Corpus Christi Caller-Times – Corpus Christi, Texas.
The Cumberland News – Cumberland, Maryland.
The Daily Messenger – Canandaigua, New York.
The Daily Record – Raleigh, North Carolina.
The Daily Report – Ontario, California.
The Daily Republican – Monongahela, Pennsylvania.
The Daily Times – Salisbury, Maryland.
The Daily Tribune – Wisconsin Rapids, Wisconsin.
The Delta Democrat-Times – Greenville, Mississippi.
The Des Moines Register – Des Moines, Iowa.
The Dixon Evening Telegraph – Dixon, Illinois.
The Evening Standard – Uniontown, Pennsylvania.
The Fresno Bee. The Republican – Fresno, California.
The Greenville News – Greenville, South Carolina.
The Herald – Jasper, Indiana.
The Indianapolis Star – Indianapolis, Indiana.
The Jacksonville Daily Journal – Jacksonville, Illinois.
The Kingston Daily Freeman – Kingston, New York.

The La Crosse Tribune – La Crosse, Wisconsin.
The Louisville Courier – Louisville, Kentucky.
The Los Angeles Times – Los Angeles, California.
The Manhattan Mercury – Manhattan, Kansas.
The Miami News – Miami, Florida.
The Morning Call – Allentown, Pennsylvania.
The Morning News – Wilmington, Delaware.
The New York Times – New York.
The News-Item – Shamokin, Pennsylvania.
The News Journal – Wilmington, Delaware.
The Odessa American – Odessa, Texas.
The Ogden Standard-Examiner – Ogden, Utah.
The Oneonta Star – Oneota, New York.
The Palm Beach Post – West Palm Beach, Florida.
The Philadelphia Inquirer – Philadelphia, Pennsylvania.
The Pittsburg Press – Pittsburg, Pennsylvania.
The Piqua Daily Call – Piqua, Ohio.
The Portsmouth Herald – Portsmouth, New Hampshire.
The Post-Standard – Syracuse, New York.
The Press and Sun-Bulletin – Binghamton, New York.
The Raleigh Register – Beckley, West Virginia.
The San Bernardino County Sun – San Bernardino, California.
The Sheboygan press – Sheyboygan, Wisconsin.
The Sydney Morning Herald – Sydney, New South Wales, Australia.
The Times – Munster, Indiana.
The Times Record – Troy, New York.
The Times Standard – Eureka, California.
The Town Talk – Alexandria, Louisiana.

Programme

Muhammad Ali v Jerry Quarry 1970: House of Sports Inc. Sports Action Inc

Websites

BoxRec.com
Georgia.Gov
Georgiaencyclopedia.org
Newspaper.com
ProQuest Archiver

INDEX